Endorsements

Fullness of Christ is the result of struggling with hardships while living with integrity and faith throughout the ups and downs of life.

My husband, Valy, is truly a man of God who always encouraged me to seek God's face in the darkest of valleys, knowing that there is a loving Father who has our best interest at heart.

Valy is a very loving, compassionate, deep thinker, and a healthy role model for his family and everyone else who knows him. He truly lives for Jesus with a contagious passion.

I hope and pray that this book will help you get closer to God. May He grant you both revelation and understanding as you read it and may it produce a deep transformation of your heart.

—Elena Vaduva, MA, LPC, NCC New Life Directions Counseling, Livonia, MI, USA

From the first day of meeting and coming to know Valy Vaduva I've known someone with a passionate desire to not only know about Jesus but to LIVE Jesus.

Grace-based, hope-filled, love-motived, this book is filled with encouragement to grow up into the fullness of Christ which is the birthright of every born-again child of God. The living truth of our new creation realities and capabilities through our death, burial, and resurrection with Christ come through loud and clear.

This insightful proclamation is not just for the individual, but also for the church, the whole body of Christ learning to share His life in common as our source and supply for living to God's glory.

If trying hard to be like Jesus is wearing you out, you may want to read about trusting Jesus to live His life through you by His indwelling Spirit. The words and ideas in this book are not just for learning but for living!

—Steve Pettit, Pastor, CenterPoint Christian Fellowship, Gainesville, FL, USA

Fullness of Christ is born out of Valy's passion for seeing Christians grow into spiritual maturity. I commend him for bringing to our attention such an important topic. Throughout this book you will be challenged, encouraged, and assisted in the process of becoming more like Christ and expressing God's nature—agape love.

I encourage you to read it carefully and apply the biblical principles emphasized in this book. I pray that you'll be blessed and experience the fullness of Christ!

—Simion Timbuc, Senior Pastor, Bethesda Romanian Pentecostal Church, Troy, MI, USA

Valy is a man whose passion is to see others attain the fullness of Christ. His journey has been difficult, and yet magnificent, as he continues to surrender all to Christ. He is on fire for others to experience the same. In his books he breaks down the components of that fullness, using Sola Scriptura as his structure. This isn't a book of his thoughts, with a little Scripture thrown in. Rather, it is a book of Scripture that uses his words to connect and shed light on God's Words.

—Margaret L. Michael, MA, LPC, BCPCC, Director of Restore Ministries, Oak Pointe Church, Novi, MI, USA

Valy Vaduva's book, *Fullness of Christ,* is a much-needed volume on the importance of Great Commission discipleship and spiritual growth. He makes a strong biblical case that evangelism without discipleship leaves the church immature. Biblical teaching that overlooks union with Christ and the deeper meaning of the Cross ends up being merely academic, legalistic or both. This book gives clear teaching on grace-oriented, Christ-centered discipleship with helpful explanations of related terminology, doctrines, and disciplines. I commend this book with Valy and Elena Vaduva's life coaching and discipleship training ministry.

—Dr. John Woodward, Director of Counseling and Training Grace Fellowship International, Pigeon Forge, TN, USA

Thank you! It's always encouraging for me to read and hear the true message of the cross and of our death, burial, resurrection, and ascension with the Lord Jesus Christ. Please continue spreading this Good News. I'm so tired of the '*easy believeism*' that shares only half of the gospel. For me, it has taken years to 'get it,' but the Holy Spirit has been persistent in being My Teacher and Guide into this Truth.

Complete In Christ,

—Phil and Darlene Leistner, Administrative Pastor Fountain of Grace, Prattville, AL, USA

Fullness of Christ

Expressing God's Nature and Character In and Through You

Valy Vaduva

Upper Room Fellowship Ministry
Livonia, Michigan, USA

Fullness of Christ: *Expressing God's Nature and Character in and through you*

This title is also available as an eBook.

Published by Upper Room Fellowship Ministry (URFM), Livonia, MI 48150
www.urfm.org

ISBN: 978-1-930529-34-2 (sc)
ISBN: 978-1-930529-35-9 (e)

Library of Congress Control Number: 2018909441

This book is a work of non-fiction. Unless otherwise noted, the author and the publisher make no explicit guarantees as to the accuracy of the information contained in this book and in some cases, names of people and places have been altered to protect their privacy. The views expressed in this work are solely those of the author and do not necessarily reflect the views of the publisher.

Because of the dynamic nature of the Internet, any web addresses or links contained in this book may have changed since publication and may no longer be valid.

Dedication

To my Lord and Savior Jesus Christ, Who looked for me, found me and, when I was an adolescent, saved me; Who called me into the disciples-making ministry.

My heart overflows with a good theme; I address my verses to the King; My tongue is the pen of a ready writer.
—Psalm 45:1

To my wife, Elena, who is an integral part of this ministry, who fully supports me. Without her this book would not have been published.

To my children, Evelina, Timotei, Dorian, Cristina, and their spouses, who also support me and encourage me to keep on keeping on.

Thank you all!

Contents

Preface

For we write nothing else to you than what you read and understand, and I hope you will understand until the end.
—2 Corinthians 1:13

Therefore, I will always be ready to remind you of these things, even though you already know them, and have been established in the truth which is present with you.
—2 Peter 1:12

The New Testament fascinates me because it is full of statements that lead the reader to the conclusion that God Himself is interested in the spiritual growth and maturity of His beloved children. In the Sermon on the Mount, Jesus says: "Therefore you are to be perfect, as your heavenly Father is perfect" (Matthew 5:48). Peter takes this concept and writes: "You shall be holy, for I am holy" (1 Peter 1:16). Sadly, the Church at large is plagued by spiritual immaturity; as Chuck Colson once observed, "The American church is 3000 miles wide and half an inch deep."[1]

I became intrigued by the lack of spiritual growth in my own life and in the lives of Christians around me. Perhaps many of you have also been thinking about this topic. Well, welcome to the club of "Concerned Christians." I was bombarded by this question repeatedly: Why do Christians lack interest in attaining the fullness of Christ? The great apostle Paul agonizes for the believers in Galatia in order to see Christ formed in them. Do you sense the depth of Paul's cry? "My children, with whom I am again in labor until Christ is formed in you" (Galatians 4:19).

In Ephesians, Paul spells out God's desire for the church leadership and for every living member of the Body of Christ to "attain ... to the stature which belongs to the fullness of Christ" (Ephesians 4:13). When Paul uses the term attain, he is not implying achieving the fullness of Christ through self-effort. Paul shares with individual members of the Church to continue receiving the ministry of the gifts He has placed in His Body. These include: apostles, prophets, evangelists, pastors, and teachers—*God's hand at work in this world.* By receiving God's gift of ministry, all parts of the spiritual body attain, "the unity of the faith, and of the knowledge of the Son." This grace- oriented, Holy Spirit driven process results in spiritual growth and maturity, thereby leading to the fullness of Christ. Now, the whole spiritual body, "being fitted and held together" may freely express the life and love of God.

In Colossians, Paul considers that the very essence of all he does as a minister of the Gospel for the Body of Christ is to "present every man complete in Christ" (Colossians 1:28).

Peter is admonishing those who have tasted the goodness of God to an ardent desire for the "pure milk of the word" (1 Peter 2:2), to grow spiritually and thus understand the full meaning of salvation. Then, in his second epistle, he urges believers to apply "all diligence" in order to "grow in the grace and knowledge of our Lord and Savior Jesus Christ" (2 Peter 3:18).

By God's grace, now I am more convicted than ever that pressing diligently towards spiritual maturity is the only way to be spotless and blameless, to continue in steadfastness of faith, and to be on guard against unprincipled men who distort the Truth. Steadfastness, being able to guard and defend the faith, being spotless in conduct, and blameless in character, are some important characteristics of spiritually mature people. The desire is to be properly prepared for the second coming of the Lord Jesus. James teaches us that even trials and tribulations are orchestrated by God for producing in us the stature of a "perfect" man and to be a "complete" believer. He writes so convincingly:

> Consider it all joy, my brethren, when you encounter various trials, knowing that the testing of your faith produces endurance. And let endurance have its perfect result, so that you may be perfect and complete, lacking in nothing. (James 1:2–4)

My interest in knowing why believers do not mature spiritually grew to the point that I made this field a priority in my life and ministry. As a result, in 2004, I decided not to pursue my engineering career anymore, and instead dedicated my entire heart, soul, time and energy to this endeavor.

I pray and believe that the pages of this book will address the question: Why are Christians spiritually immature? After searching the Scriptures and Christian literature, I think that Christians do not mature because they are not mindful of how the cross (i.e., the call to deny himself, take up the cross, and follow Christ) is central to their identity as followers of Jesus. Believers often fail to appropriate the life of the cross as genuine disciples on a day-to-day basis.

Why is this?

First, there is the problem of knowledge. I think many lack a clear understanding about biblical teaching regarding the way of the cross.

Second, there is a problem of the will. Even born-again believers or indwelled Christians still have their free will intact. So many of them can and do exercise their free will by refusing to take up the cross and follow Jesus on daily basis. They incorrectly assume that the cost of discipleship outweighs the benefits of being a genuine disciple of Jesus.

Third, many Christians are stuck due to unresolved wounds and trauma of the past. Because of these aspects, many believers often fail to appropriate the crucified lifestyle.

Over time, all these factors have led to the state which the

Church is in today. Prayerfully and carefully, in the content of this book, we will try to explore these matters and look for a Bible-founded, faith-based, grace-oriented solution.

I can tell you from the very beginning that many findings in this book apply to me as well. I am not an expert in this field by any stretch of the imagination. Therefore, please pray for this author who is in the same boat as many of you. If Paul said that he had not arrived yet, I can subscribe to his statement even more, but I have decided to press on. He writes: "Not that I have already obtained it or have already become perfect, but I press on so that I may lay hold of that for which also I was laid hold of by Christ Jesus" (Philippians 3:12).

I refuse to think that Jesus is coming for a Bride who is a little girl playing in the sandbox every day, crying, "Poor me, what is going to happen in the world now?" To the contrary, I believe with all my heart that Christ is coming for a beautiful Bride, a mature and perfect lady (Ephesians 5:26–27) who diligently seeks the healing from past wounds (Matthew 8:17; Isaiah 53:4–5), freedom from past lies and traumas (John 8:31–36), and in the name of Jesus conquers demonic forces (Ephesians 6:13) advancing the Kingdom of God (Mark 16:20).

I know many of you have multitudes of questions. I cannot promise that I have all the answers. Only God knows it all. I am sure that in my limited research, I have not turned over all the stones. However, I can assure you of one thing—I have a passionate desire for every believer's spiritual growth and maturity. I pray and believe that the radical discipleship practiced by our spiritual forefathers can become the number one priority of the Church today.

Join me in prayer that prior to Christ's return, the Church will be "in all her glory, having no spot or wrinkle or any such thing; but that she would be holy and blameless" (Ephesians

5:27), ready to be presented to the Father and to be revealed to the entire creation. Paul writes that even the created universe is looking forward to this glorious event. He writes: "For the anxious longing of the creation waits eagerly for the revealing of the sons of God" (Romans 8:19).

My ardent desire is to glorify God and lift Christ. Under the guidance of the Holy Spirit, through these chapters, I offer my contribution to the spiritual edification of the Body of Christ. So, help me God!

With Love in Christ's Service,

Valy Vaduva

Ordained Minister/Life Coach/Spiritual Mentor

---

[1] Diane Singer, *A Vision for the American Church, Christian Worldview Journal.* Published on April 14, 2014. www.colsoncenter.org. Accessed on August 18, 2018. http://www.colsoncenter.org/the-center/columns/changepoint/21576-a-vision-for-the- american-church-1.

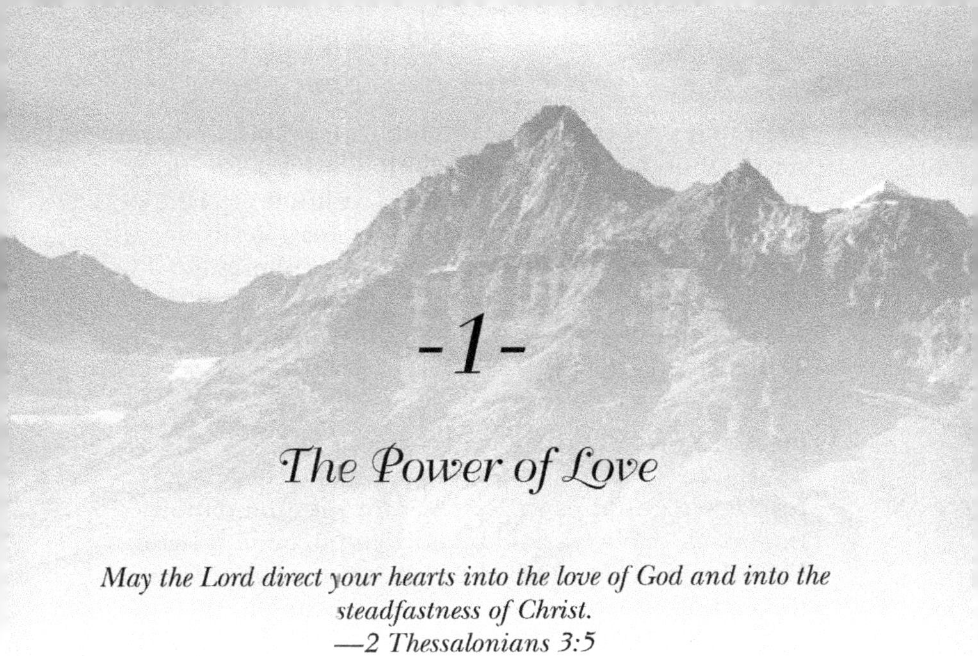

-1-

The Power of Love

May the Lord direct your hearts into the love of God and into the steadfastness of Christ.
—2 Thessalonians 3:5

A few years ago, I was on a mission trip to India. The last night there, the Holy Spirit impressed upon my heart and mind Paul's prayer from Ephesians 3:14–21. Immediately in my mind and my heart were formed some special links and connections regarding the concept of agape love and its ramifications in all aspects of our lives. I woke up and jotted down the main ideas. I shared this message with the congregation that organized the mission trip there. I am also using this opportunity to share with you the impressions that I received during that special night in India.
Here is Paul's prayer:

> For this reason I bow my knees before the Father, from whom every family in heaven and on earth derives its name, that He would grant you, according to the riches of His glory, to be strengthened with power through His Spirit in the inner man, so that Christ may dwell in your hearts through faith; and that you, being rooted and grounded in love, may be able to comprehend with all the saints what is the breadth and length and height and depth, and to know the love of Christ which surpasses knowledge, that you may be filled up to all

> the fullness of God. Now to Him who is able to do far more abundantly beyond all that we ask or think, according to the power that works within us, to Him be the glory in the church and in Christ Jesus to all generations forever and ever. Amen. (Ephesians 3:14–21)

1. We Are Created (Predestined) in Love

Furthermore, in Ephesians 1:4–6 we read:

> Just as He chose us in Him before the foundation of the world, that we would be holy and blameless before Him. In love He predestined us to adoption as sons through Jesus Christ to Himself, according to the kind intention of His will, to the praise of the glory of His grace, which He freely bestowed on us in the Beloved.

Wow! The revelation that is compressed in these verses is so strong! In order to be absolutely overwhelmed by this revelation, we must place all the emphasis on the phrase in love. Everything that God does flows from the depth of His nature—agape love. "God is love," says the apostle of love in 1 John 4:8(b). So, if you and I are part of God's family and we enjoy these special privileges to be called sons and daughters of God Almighty, it is because of the love of God. What a wonderful privilege!

John also writes:

> See how great a love the Father has bestowed on us, that we would be called children of God; and such we are. For this reason, the world does not know us, because it did not know Him. Beloved, now we are children of God, and it has not appeared as yet what we will be. We know that when He appears, we will be like Him, because we will see Him just as He is. (1 John 3:1–2)

These are powerful verses that complement the passage from Ephesians. You may never have felt such love from your biological parents. Maybe you had a strict father who hit the table with his fist all the time, demanding obedience without any explanation. Maybe your mother, who gave you earthly life, was sensitive and emotional and everybody had to walk on eggshells not to upset her. Maybe you were the "oops!" child, born at the wrong time and considered an accident that should not have happened. Or you may have been a child conceived out of wedlock, so your mother was ashamed of you and your father disappeared from your life before you were born. For these reasons, almost your whole life you grew up, emotionally speaking, with major deficiencies.

You did not feel accepted, appreciated, and approved for most of your childhood. So, how in the world can you relate to the heavenly Father's love? It is difficult to believe that despite your negative circumstances, you were indeed created in love. Let me assure you with all sensitivity and compassion: you are not an accident! In God's family you are no stranger or intruder; you are more than welcome—you are beloved.

Everything that God does flows from the depth of His nature—*agape love.*

You are created in love, and despite a lack of unconditional love from your biological parents, now God tells you, "I love you before the foundation of the world!" Our heavenly Father had you in mind before the sun, the moon, and the stars. You are a beloved child of God. He has created you in the agape love. Believe and trust in God's Word. If you truly do this, it will offer emotional healing for your broken heart and your soul after being beaten up by the many rejections you experienced.

2. We Are Saved by Love

O, what a beautiful message! "But God, being rich in mercy, because of His great love with which He loved us, even when we were dead in our transgressions, made us alive together with Christ (by grace you have been saved)" (Ephesians 2:5). Again, the emphasis should be placed on "because of His great love." The bottom line is this: we are saved by love. We are not in God's family because we deserved it, because we are better than others, because we have sinned less than others, because we go to church gatherings more often than others, because we belong to a Christian denomination that is closer to the truth than others, because we understand biblical doctrines more correctly than others, because we practice church sacraments more accurately than others, and the list could go on.

When it comes to the topic of salvation, God's grace is the only answer. The Word of God is clear: "For by grace you have been saved through faith; and that not of yourselves, it is the gift of God; not as a result of works, so that no one may boast" (Ephesians 2:8–9). After such a statement, the only thing we may add is the period at the end of the sentence.

In God's family you are no stranger or intruder; you are more than welcome— you are beloved.

Of course, it is a great danger to think that since God's grace is free for us, it is something cheap—meaning that it cost God nothing. Not at all! God forbids us of such thought. God's grace is free but is not cheap. Grace is free for humankind but extremely costly for God—costing the life of the only begotten Son of God. "For God so loved the world, that He gave His only begotten Son, that whoever believes in Him shall not perish, but have eternal life" (John 3:16).

Keep in mind this acronym: GRACE means **G**od's **R**iches at **C**hrist's **E**xpense.

3. We Are Destined for Love

I find the passage from Ephesians 3:17–19 magnificent:

> So that Christ may dwell in your hearts through faith; and that you, being rooted and grounded in love, may be able to comprehend with all the saints what is the breadth and length and height and depth, and to know the love of Christ which surpasses knowledge, that you may be filled up to all the fullness of God.

Wow! We are destined for love. Do you realize what kind of destiny God has placed in front of us? Again, the focus must be on the terms "being rooted and grounded in love," "to know the love of Christ," and "be filled up to all the fullness of God" (emphasis mine).

Rooted and Grounded in Love

Being grounded has to do with building structures. Being rooted has to do with the life of the tree. The destiny that God put before us involves both being rooted and grounded in the agape love of God. In order to reach the head, who is Christ (Ephesians 4:15), it is necessary that in the process of spiritual growth and maturity, we are both rooted and grounded in love. Oh, how important is this concept!

Knowing Christ's Love

The destiny that God has set in front of us cannot be achieved by theoretical knowledge alone. Knowing Christ's love requires a concrete experiential knowledge of God's affection, something that touches the deepest fiber of our inner beings. Paul writes so that "[you] may be able to comprehend with all the saints what is the breadth and length and height and depth, and to know the love of Christ" (Ephesians 3:18–19). This is not a strictly theological, intellectual understanding about agape love (i.e., what is the Greek language etymology of the word agape, various definitions, illustrations, theological concepts, etc.). This implies an experiential knowledge of all sizes and dimensions of Christ's love: it's breadth and length, it's height and depth.

This work is the most profoundly deep work that God has called us to participate in. Such work requires the agony of saints in prayer: *"O, dear God strengthen us with power through the Holy Spirit in the inner man, so we know by experience the dimensions of your love."*

No wonder Paul was inspired to pray the second time:

> For this reason, I bow my knees before the Father … that He would grant you, according to the riches of His glory, to be strengthened with power through His Spirit in the inner man. (Ephesians 3:14, 16)

He understood that this kind of revelation-knowledge requires an exquisite kind of prayer.

So, let's pray insistently.

O, heavenly Father, open the eyes of our hearts, as you did for Peter, James, and John at the Mount of Transfiguration (Matthew 17:2; Mark 9:2; Luke 9:29), to see Jesus for who He really is. We want and we fully understand "what is the hope of His calling, what are the riches of the glory of His inheritance in the saints (Ephesians 1:18). Amen.

Reaching the fullness of God

We are destined for love. Paul is praying for the saints to *be "filled up to all the fullness of God."* Let's think for a while. If the destiny our heavenly Father calls us to is agape love; if agape love is the nature of God, the very essence of our great creator and Father God; then, by agape love, we are destined to reach the fullness of God. We have no words to express or to describe this.

What does it mean for a man, a finite creature (even if he or she is a saved person) to reach the fullness of God? Who can describe it? Only the Lord Jesus, and those to whom God wishes to reveal it. As Paul says: "Things which eye has not seen and ear has not heard, and which have not entered the heart of man, all that God has prepared for those who love Him" (1 Corinthians 2:9).

Knowing Christ's love requires a concrete experiential knowledge of God's affection, something that touches the deepest fiber of our inner beings.

So, we can clearly see that being filled with the fullness of God requires knowledge (through experience) of Christ's love. John, the apostle of love, puts the dot on the "i" when he writes: "We have come to know and have believed the love which God has for us. God is love, and the one who abides in love abides in God, and God abides in him" (1 John 4:16).

The only prayer we can utter is this: "Father God, we too,

wholeheartedly desire to know and believe Your love, and finally, to remain in You. Amen."

4. We Are built in Love

The Church is not an organization. God's Church is a Body—a spiritual Body. Each living member in the Body of Christ, as it grows, as it develops and matures, is called to contribute to the spiritual edification of the entire spiritual organism.

The Bible says:

> But speaking the truth in love, we are to grow up in all aspects into Him who is the head, even Christ, from whom the whole body, being fitted and held together by what every joint supplies, according to the proper working of each individual part, causes the growth of the body for the building up of itself in love. (Ephesians 4:15–16)

Magnificent, isn't it?

Paul, in Ephesians 2, presents the Church as a spiritual temple in the Lord. This spiritual temple does not appear out of the blue. As a living temple, it takes shape and progressively grows toward the ultimate goal: *a holy temple in the Lord.* Paul writes: "In whom the whole building, being fitted together, is growing into a holy temple in the Lord" (Ephesians 2:21). Through this process of "being fitted together" and growing (present continuous), the Church is perpetually becoming a habitation of God through the Holy Spirit. Paul explains, "In whom you also are being built together into a dwelling of God in the Spirit" (Ephesians 2:22). Oh, what a lovely view! **A spiritual sanctuary where God Himself dwells!**

This is such a beautiful and glorious Church that is built on the proper and solid foundation: "The foundation of the apostles and prophets" (Ephesians 2:20). Only on such a magnificent spiritual structure will God install the glorious corner stone: Christ. Paul finishes the verse, "Christ Jesus Himself being the corner stone" (Ephesians 2:20). Imagine that for a moment! That is a splendid view, isn't it? The spiritual Body of Christ with all its members (being deeply rooted in agape love) building itself up in love.

We can only pray to God like this: "Lord, awaken all of us to the call: the glorious church that is 'building up of itself in love.'"

5. We Are called to Love

In Ephesians 5:1-2, we read:

> Therefore, be imitators of God, as beloved children; and walk in love, just as Christ also loved you and gave Himself up for us, an offering and a sacrifice to God as a fragrant aroma.

There is no higher calling in the life of a Christian, than the call to walk in love. In fact, John tells us, "The one who does not love does not know God" (1 John 4:8a). The objective of spiritual growth and maturity is not that believers gain more intellectual knowledge. As Paul explains: "the goal of our instruction is love" (1 Timothy 1:5).

Accumulation of mere theological knowledge without inner transformation makes us proud and arrogant (cf. 1 Corinthians 8:1). We are called to pursue love that edifies others. Our mission is to pursue love within the global church; to have love for all the saints; to practice love among believers of the local church. More importantly, we are called to practice love in our own families.

Practicing love for all the saints

Paul writes:

> For this reason, I too, having heard of the faith in the Lord Jesus which exists among you and your love for all the saints, do not cease giving thanks for you, while making mention of you in my prayers. (Ephesians 1:15–16)

Displaying genuine love in the local church

In Ephesians 4:1–2 we read:

> Therefore I, the prisoner of the Lord, implore you to walk in a manner worthy of the calling with which you have been called, with all humility and gentleness, with patience, showing tolerance for one another in love.

Showing Christ's love within the family unit

The Bible says: "Husbands, love your wives, just as Christ also loved the church and gave Himself up for her" (Ephesians 5:25).

For each of these subpoints we could write volumes. May the Holy Spirit guide, inspire, persuade, and empower us to "walk in love, just as Christ also loved [us]" (Ephesians 5:1–2). There is no greater calling than the calling to love. And there is no greater fulfillment than reaching God's destiny for us: agape love.

Let us never forget these:

- We are created (predestined) in love
- We are saved by love
- We are destined for love
- We are built in love
- We are called to love

Praise God for all His wonderful works that He has done and continues to do in the lives of His people! And all of these because His nature is agape love.

Reflection Questions

Please reflect upon the following questions, briefly elaborate, and then share your thoughts with a friend or your small group.

1. What did the Holy Spirit whisper to your heart through this chapter? What did you like the most in this chapter?

2. What new concepts and ideas did you learn from this chapter? Which concept are you committed to implementing in your life?

3. Please ponder upon the concepts below then list your thoughts and feelings. Use additional space if necessary:
3.1. "We Are Created (Predestined) in Love"?

3.2. "We Are Saved by Love"?

3.3. "We Are Destined for Love"?

3.4. "We are built in Love"?

3.5. "We are called to Love"?

4. What idea or concept captured your attention the most during reading this chapter?

5. List the best aha moments you had while reading this chapter.

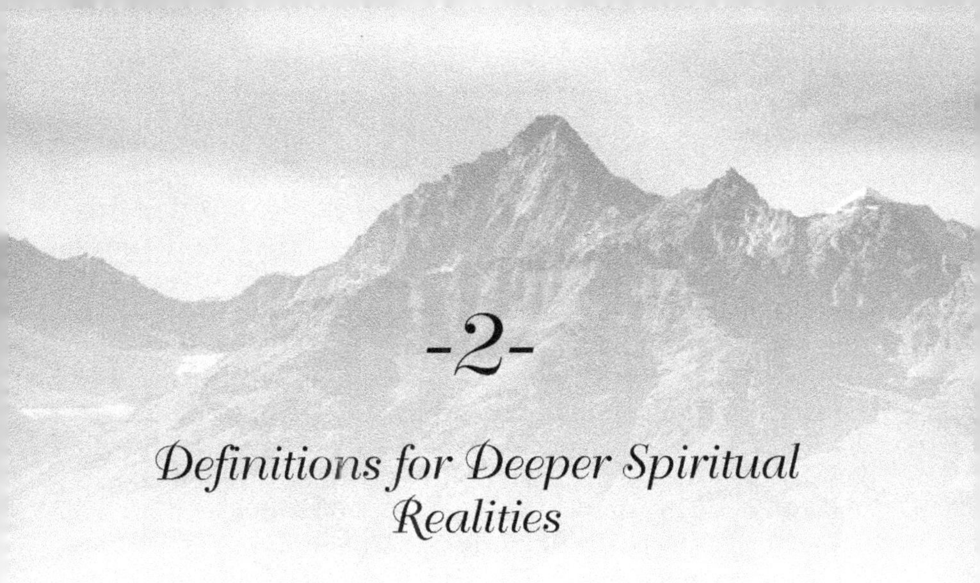

-2-

Definitions for Deeper Spiritual Realities

I have been crucified with Christ; and it is no longer I who live, but Christ lives in me; and the life which I now live in the flesh I live by faith in the Son of God, who loved me and gave Himself up for me.
— Galatians 2:20

My deepest desire for my readers is to understand the full counsel of God for their lives. I don't necessarily want to introduce new terms. But sometimes, to communicate deeper spiritual realities, having the right terminology is important.

Understanding Terminology

First Adam

The first human being created by God. "So also, it is written, 'The first man, Adam, became a living soul'" (1 Corinthians 15:45a).

Last Adam

Jesus Christ, the Son of God who, by incarnation, become also the Son of Man. "The last Adam became a life-giving spirit" (1 Corinthians 15:45b).

The Exchanged Life

The exchanged life is the great exchange that took place at the cross. During the crucifixion of the Son of God, the entire Adamic race was crucified. Whoever accepts Jesus Christ as life, experiences the exchanged life of their self-centeredness for Christ's sufficiency. Paul gets to the heart of what the exchanged life is all about when he writes: "I have been crucified with Christ; and it is no longer I who live, but Christ lives in me; and the life which I now live in the flesh I live by faith in the Son of God, who loved me and gave Himself up for me" (Galatians 2:20). This statement is phenomenal! Paul is conveying that we have been united with Christ on the cross in all aspects: death, burial, resurrection, and ascension. This is not a metaphor, but instead, it is a deep spiritual reality. I like the way Richard F. Hall explains it: "The exchanged life is the exchange (with Christ at the cross) of self-centered life lived out of the Christian's own resources as if he were still in Adam, for a Christ-centered life lived out of Christ's resources because he (the Christian) is in Christ."[2] In a nutshell, this is the exchanged life.[3]

The Cross

The term cross has different meanings for different people. For some people, the cross means just the wooden instrument the Romans used to crucify the criminals of the empire, including Jesus. For others, the cross means only the substitutionary death of Jesus, but nothing more beyond that. This is the view of the vast majority of Christians today.

When I use the term the cross, I am referring to the complete work of Christ in His death, burial, resurrection, and ascension. The cross is the single point in the universe where, in God's spiritual economy, we are identified with Christ in all the facets of His work. The crucifixion of Christ is, and is going to remain, the most unique event in history's entirety. It has been done once and for all, as Peter writes: "For Christ also died for sins once

The cross is the single point in the universe where, in God's spiritual economy, we are identified with Christ in all the facets of His work.

for all" (1 Peter 3:18). Therefore, it will never be repeated. On that cross, almost two thousand years ago, God united us with Jesus and made us partakers of the death, burial, resurrection, and exaltation of Christ. Paul writes: "Or do you not know that all of us who have been baptized into Christ Jesus have been baptized into His death?" (Romans 6:3). This is a mystery! From the cross there are rays which, if we let them, will shine with much brightness into our hearts.

Following are some of its rays:

United with Christ in His death

We were placed in Christ through God's infinite wisdom and the unlimited power of the Holy Spirit. And when Christ died on that cross, we also died with Him. This mystery has been in the heart of God, before the foundation of the world, to save us and to bring us, as sons and daughters, into glory with His only begotten Son. The Bible teaches us:

> We speak God's wisdom in a mystery, the hidden wisdom which God predestined before the ages to our glory; the wisdom which none of the rulers of this age has understood; for if they had understood it they would not have crucified the Lord of glory. (1 Corinthians 2:7–8)

All this unspeakable wisdom has been hidden in the cross. And up until today, "The word of the cross is foolishness to those who are perishing, but to us who are being saved it is the power of God" (1 Corinthians 1:18).

United with Christ in His burial

After Christ died, He was buried. Paul writes:

> For I delivered to you as of first importance what I also received, that Christ died for our sins according to the Scriptures, and that He was buried. (1 Corinthians 15:3–4)

The Nicene Creed[4] states: "And was crucified also for us under Pontius Pilate; He suffered and was buried." Since we were united with Christ in His death, when He was buried, we were also buried with Him. The Scripture tells us, "Therefore we have been buried with Him through baptism into death" (Romans 6:4). This is so important for our assurance that our "old man" definitely died. As far as I know, people don't bury people who are still alive. Thus, the "old man" does not exist anymore. This is why water baptism, in my opinion, has such a deep spiritual significance: **our old man is gone.** Too bad this aspect is scarcely explained to new believers, a cause of the much damage to the church.

United with Christ in His resurrection

Paul writes: "And that He was raised on the third day according to the Scriptures" (1 Corinthians 15:4). Regarding this spiritual reality, the Nicene Creed states: "And the third day He rose again, according to the Scriptures." Christ is alive now and forevermore! This is a powerful reality! If people take this away from Christianity, we have just another dead religion. The death of Christ is only half of the truth. The other half is the resurrection. But not only did Jesus rise; we also have risen with Him. If we were in Christ when He died, then we were in Christ when He was resurrected.

Paul writes: "For if we have become united with Him in the likeness of His death, certainly we shall also be in the likeness of His resurrection" (Romans 6:5).

Furthermore, in Ephesians, we read: "even when we were dead in our transgressions, [He] made us alive together with Christ (by grace you have been saved) and raised us up with Him" (Ephesians 2:5-6). Wow! Isn't this really good news? Yes, it is!

United with Christ in His ascension

We have not only been united with Christ in His death, been buried with Him, and been raised up with Him, but we also have ascended with Him in the heavenlies. Regarding Christ's ascension, the Nicene Creed states: "And ascended into heaven, and sits on the right hand of the Father." Paul goes deeper than this when he writes: "and seated us with Him in the heavenly places in Christ Jesus" (Ephesians 2:6). Do you see this? The Word of God emphasizes the truth of our being in Christ Jesus. And because we are in Christ, whatever happened to Him is also true of us. This is breathtaking! I am awestruck! It is such a deep mystery!

No wonder Paul prayed:

> I pray that the eyes of your heart may be enlightened, so that you will know what is the hope of His calling, what are the riches of the glory of His inheritance in the saints, and what is the surpassing greatness of His power toward us who believe. These are in accordance with the working of the strength of His might which He brought about in Christ, when He raised Him from the dead and seated Him at His right hand in the heavenly places, far above all rule and authority and power and dominion, and every name that is named, not only in this age but also in the one to come. And He put all things in subjection under His feet, and gave Him as head over all things to the church, which is His body, the fullness of Him who fills all in all. (Ephesians 1:18–23)

Other important terms that require explanations are *in Christ, Christ in us, Christ our life, and indwelled by Christ.*

Let ask ourselves: What does it mean to be in Christ and have Christ in us? What does the Bible teach when it talks about Christ, our life?

Understanding these terms helps us understand the fullness of what the Scriptures are teaching us concerning the Christian life.

In Christ

Based on the Bible, I believe with all my heart that Jesus Christ is within all genuine born-again believers, regardless of their church denomination. Paul declares categorically: "There is one body and one Spirit … one God and Father of all who is over all and through all and in all" (Ephesians 4:4, 6). Genuine believers are led to know by revelation that Christ is their life. John writes: "He who has the Son has the life" (1 John 5:12a). Paul describes this spiritual reality with these words: "For to me, to live is Christ" (Philippians 1:21). In other words, Paul identifies himself with Christ.

Christ in us

Moreover, Christ is within every genuine believer. This is true even though a particular believer does not know this by experience. The entire work of redemption hinges on the finished work of Christ. Paul writes: "And in Him you have been made complete, and He is the head over all rule and authority" (Colossians 2:10). Then Paul makes the connection between Christ being our life and the spiritual reality, the fact, that we are in Him. "When Christ, who is our life, is revealed, then you also will be revealed with Him in glory" (Colossians 3:4).

Christ—our life

Each genuine born-again believer is a partaker of eternal life, or Christ's life. John writes: "These things I have written to you who believe in the name of the Son of God, so that you may know that you have eternal life" (1 John 5:13).

I like the way Peter explains this divine truth: "For by these He has granted to us His precious and magnificent promises, so that by them you may become partakers of the divine nature, having escaped the corruption that is in the world by lust" (2 Peter 1:4).

If we combine what Peter wrote with the passage written by John, we understand that we are partakers of Christ's life. Halleluiah! Glory to God!

Indwelt by Christ

The term indwelt Christian conveys the true and deep meaning of a genuine disciple of Christ—one who is born from above and actually has the Holy Spirit indwelling him or her. We know it was in Antioch, during the first century, when the outside world called the followers of Jesus "Christians."

Luke writes: "And the disciples were first called Christians in Antioch" (Acts 11:26). I am sure that the world called them Christians because, through the transforming power of the Holy Spirit, they were displaying the love and the character of Christ. This does not mean that everyone who calls himself or herself a Christian in the twenty-first century, is actually a disciple of Christ. True Christians are those who have been born from above by the Spirit of God (John 3:3–6) and in whom the Spirit of God lives (Romans 8:9). That is God's definition of a Christian.

Eternal life

Eternal life is not something that God fastens onto our life after we die. Eternal life is God's life; "it" is the very person of Christ. Listen to Jesus' words: "I am the way, and the truth, and the life; no one comes to the Father but through Me" (John 14:6).

As believers, we are partakers of eternal life; thus, we have been spiritually united with Christ in His death, burial, resurrection, and ascension. Scripturally speaking, we are seated in heaven with Christ at the right hand of the Father. However, though these are immutable truths, not every believer experiences all of these in their lives.

These are not simple truths that we just brush over without mediating their deep meanings. Let's look at some Bible verses to firmly establish these realities in our hearts. "It is a trustworthy statement: For if we died with Him, we will also live with Him" (2 Timothy 2:11). This verse should cause us to stop and meditate in awe of its deep meaning. When did Christ die? Everybody knows this. Christ died almost two thousand years ago." If that is true, then two thousand years ago, when Christ died, you and I died with Him. Is the apostle speaking about our physical death or the death of our soul? No. He is talking about the spiritual side of our being.

True Christians are those who have been born from above by the Spirit of God, and in whom the Spirit of God lives.

The Bible talks about our spiritual union with Christ in His death. This, says the apostle, is a trustworthy statement. Similarly: "For the love of Christ controls us, having concluded this, that one died for all, therefore all died" (2 Corinthians 5:14). Christ's death is fundamental for our salvation. Knowing through experience that we also died with Him is fundamental for our sanctification.

Paul writes:

> Therefore, we have been buried with Him through

> baptism into death, so that as Christ was raised from the dead through the glory of the Father, so we too might walk in newness of life" (Romans 6:4; see also Colossians 2:12)

Many people have heard and eventually understood the part of the Gospel about the death of Christ for the salvation of world. But only a few have gazed longer at these Scriptures and pondered over the fact that when Jesus died, the entire human race died with Him. This includes you and me.

Following are some other terms that must be brought also to our attention: *the old man, the new man, flesh, in the flesh, according to the flesh, in the Spirit, according to the Spirit, sin or indwelling sin, and sins.* Without going into too many details, these terms can be defined as follows:

The old man

It refers to the unregenerate human spirit that all human beings inherited from Adam. Like the old saying, "What is born of the cat eats mice." The Scripture teaches us that all human beings are born dead to God and alive to sin and the devil. Paul writes:

> And you were dead in your trespasses and sins, in which you formerly walked according to the course of this world, according to the prince of the power of the air, of the spirit that is now working in the sons of disobedience" (Ephesians 2:1–2).

The new man

This term refers to the regenerate human spirit. The new man comes into being at the moment of salvation, when by faith in the name of Christ, through the renewing power of the Holy Spirit, the believing person is born again. Paul explains this spiritual reality: "He saved us, not on the basis of deeds which we have done in righteousness, but according to His mercy, by the washing of regeneration and renewing by the Holy Spirit" (Titus 3:5; see also John 3:3, 5).

The Flesh

The flesh refers to living independently of God. This includes self-effort, self-sufficiency, and coping mechanisms developed over time by human beings trying to meet their physical, psychological, and even spiritual needs independent from God.

The Greek word for flesh (sarx) has been erroneously translated in the NIV and NLT versions of the Bible as sinful nature. The Bible never uses the term sinful nature. (Note: Depending on the context, the word flesh can also simply mean body. It is my personal belief that flesh is not identical with old man.

In the flesh

This refers to the position of any unbeliever or unregenerate person who, by physical birth, is "in Adam."

Jesus explains this reality to Nicodemus:

> That which is born of the flesh is flesh, and that which is born of the Spirit is spirit. Do not be amazed that I said to you, "You must be born again." (John 3:6–7)

The person who has not yet been born again by the Spirit is in the flesh. Therefore, he or she has no choice but to live independently from God. The Bible is very specific about this. Paul writes: "Among them we too all formerly lived in the lusts of our flesh, indulging the desires of the flesh and of the mind, and were by nature children of wrath, even as the rest" (Ephesians 2:3). A genuine born-again believer cannot be in the flesh. He has been transferred out of that state. However, he or she may walk according to the flesh.

According to the flesh

This is the behavior, attitude, or mindset of a person functioning independently of God. All unregenerate people (all unbelievers) have no choice but to live according to the flesh. Paul writes: "Those who are in the flesh cannot please God" (Romans 8:8). The born-again believer can choose to walk according to the flesh or walk according to the Spirit. "For those who are according to the flesh set their minds on the things of the flesh, but those who are according to the Spirit, the things of the Spirit" (Romans 8:5; see also Galatians 5:25).

In the Spirit

This is the position of the born-again believer, someone born from the Spirit and indwelled by Christ. Thus, he or she has the zoe life—God's life, or Christ's life—residing inside their heart. This is explained the best by John:

> And the testimony is this, that God has given us eternal life, and this life is in His Son. He who has the Son has the life; he who does not have the Son of God does not have the life. (1 John 5:11–12)

According to the Spirit

This describes the behavior, mind-set, or attitude of a believer who is living in dependence upon the Holy Spirit. Thus, he or she expresses their new identity—Jesus' life. It is my personal belief that as believers mature in the grace and knowledge of Christ (cf. 2 Peter 3:18), they are displaying more visibly the life and character of Christ through them. This is what the indwelt Christian is all about. Paul writes: "For all who are being led by the Spirit of God, these are sons of God" (Romans 8:14). This is the true meaning of abiding in Christ.

Sin or indwelling sin

This simply means the power of sin. It is an unholy force or power which holds all people who are in Adam (unregenerate people, unbelievers) captive and, therefore, separated from God.

The Scripture teaches us:

> And you were dead in your trespasses and sins, in which you formerly walked according to the course of this world, according to the prince of the power of the air, of the spirit that is now working in the sons of disobedience. (Ephesians 2:1–3)

Furthermore, Paul writes: "For we know that the Law is

spiritual, but I am of flesh, sold into bondage to sin" (Romans 7:14).

Sins

This refers to acts, attitudes, and behaviors inconsistent with God's nature (agape love, His character) God's holiness, and God's perfect Law.

May God continue to deepen our understanding of these truths through the power and illumination of the Holy Spirit, according to His will.

Reflection Questions

Please reflect upon the following questions, briefly elaborate, and then share your thoughts with a friend or your small group.

1. What did the Holy Spirit whisper to your heart through this chapter? What did you like most from this chapter?

2. What new concepts and ideas did you learn from this chapter? Which concept are you committed to implementing in your life?

3. In your own words, please elaborate on the following theological concepts:
3.1 The Exchanged Life

3.2. The Cross

3.3. The believer union with Christ in His death, burial, resurrection, and ascension
3.4. The old man

3.5. The new man

3.6. The flesh

4. Are there any concepts or terms that you still have difficulties in getting biblical answers. Please elaborate.

5. List the best aha moments you had while reading this chapter.

Endnotes:

[2] Richard F. Hall, *Foundations of Exchanged Life Counseling,* (Aurora, CO: Cross-Life Expressions, 1993), 57.
[3] For more on this topic please refer to the chapter with the same title: "The Exchanged Life."
[4] Nicene Creed. *Christian Classics Ethereal Library* (CCEL)., www.ccel.org. Accessed on July 23, 2018, https://www.ccel.org/creeds/nicene.creed.html.

-3-

Spiritual Growth in Christ

For the equipping of the saints for the work of service, to the building up of the body of Christ; until we all attain to the unity of the faith, and of the knowledge of the Son of God, to a mature man, to the measure of the stature which belongs to the fullness of Christ.
— Ephesians 4:12–13

Spiritual growth is an imperative in our lives as Christians. In my humble opinion it should be the main focus, without exception, in all churches and denominations. What is spiritual growth? Let me attempt to address this question by providing you with some background information. God awakened me to the imperative of spiritual growth and maturity decades ago.

During that time the Holy Spirit guided me to put together this simple definition:

> Spiritual growth is the work of God through His grace by which God's children are transformed according to the image of Christ in the inner self and are empowered to die to the false self and live in righteousness and holiness.

Later, I found out that there is an entire field within Christianity called spiritual formation. During the Master of Arts in Spiritual Formation and Leadership program at Spring Arbor University, I learned that Christian spiritual formation is "the process of being conformed to the image of Christ for the sake of others."[5]

Dallas Willard writes that "spiritual formation for the Christian basically refers to the Spirit-driven process of forming the inner world of the human self in such a way that it becomes like the inner being of Christ Himself."[6] According to John Wesley's teaching, to be sanctified means "To be renewed in the image of God, in righteousness and true holiness."[7]

The Bible verse that best describe the concept of spiritual transformation is found in 2 Corinthians 3:18: "But we all, with unveiled face, beholding as in a mirror the glory of the Lord, are being transformed into the same image from glory to glory, just as from the Lord, the Spirit." As we grow in Christ, our moral condition is brought by the Spirit of God into conformity with our legal status before God. John writes: "But as many as received Him, to them He gave the right to become children [Gr. *teknion*][8] of God, even to those who believe in His name" (John 1:12).

Spiritual growth is a normal continuation of what was done at the point of salvation. Every willing child of God may experience spiritual growth. The desire of the Father God did not send His only begotten Son to save us and then have us continue to live as the rest of the world. Sadly, many Christians have a narrow and dull understating of salvation: accept Christ in order to go to heaven when we die. But the Bible teaches us more than that. When a new life is conferred upon the repentant believer, it contains the entire DNA of the (zoe) life of God.

Peter writes:

> Grace and peace be multiplied to you in the knowledge of God and of Jesus our Lord; seeing that His divine power has granted to us everything pertaining to life and godliness, through the true knowledge of Him who called us by His own glory and excellence. (2 Peter 1:2–3)

As we continue in our journey as Christ's disciples (cf. Luke 9:23–24), as we surrender to God's will (cf. Romans

12:1), as we feast on the Word of God (1 Peter 2:1–3) and continue to renew our minds (Romans 12:2), the Holy Spirit continues to transform us in the image and likeness of Jesus (cf. 2 Corinthians 3:18). Of course, this does not happen on some sort of automatic pilot, nor does it take place overnight. Nevertheless, it is a grace-based process. It is done, by faith, in Christ, and by the Sprit.

Spiritual growth is an integral part of salvation. It does not matter too much what you call it: spiritual growth and maturity, discipleship, spiritual formation, or sanctification. I believe with all my heart that it should be the normal Christian life for all believers, regardless of the type of Church or denomination they belong to.

The author of Hebrews explains it so beautifully:

> For it was fitting for Him, for whom are all things, and through whom are all things, in bringing many sons to glory, to perfect the author of their salvation through sufferings. For both He who sanctifies and those who are sanctified are all from one Father; for which reason He is not ashamed to call them brethren. (Hebrews 2:10–11)

God desires all His children to reflect the character of Jesus Christ. Period.

Often, in the spiritual growth seminars I teach in various churches across the world, I tell the audience that the Christian's spirituality is like a journey between two major milestones marked by two Bible verses: first is the *spiritual birth* (cf. John 1:12), and second is *spiritual maturity* (cf. Romans 8:14).

John writes: "But as many as received Him, to them He gave the right to become children [Gr. *teknion*] of God, even to those who believe in His name" (John 1:12).

Paul writes: "For all who are being led by the Spirit of God, these are sons [Gr. *huios*][9] of God" (Romans 8:14). Interestingly enough those two verses mention the words children and sons, which in Greek have very specific meanings. The word child [*teknion*] (used in John 1:12) represents just a newborn baby; an heir who does not yet reflect the Father's likeness and nature. The word used by Paul in Romans 8:14 is sons [*huios*]. This word emphasizes the likeness of the believer to the heavenly Father, i.e., resembling His character. You see that the likeness of the Father is what defines a mature son of God. In other words, the child of God—*teknion* (the infant child John talks about in the first chapter)—is not necessarily a mature son [*huios*]. Jesus used the word *huios* to clearly show the difference between immature children and mature sons of God.

Matthew writes:

> But I say to you, love your enemies and pray for those who persecute you, so that you may be sons [*huios*] of your Father who is in heaven; for He causes His sun to rise on the evil and the good, and sends rain on the righteous and the unrighteous. (Matthew 5:44–45)

Commenting on the passage above, W.E. Vine writes:

> The disciples were to do these things, not in order that they might become children of God, but that, being children (note "your Father" throughout), they might make the fact manifest in their character, might "become sons."[10]

Regarding Christian perfection, John Wesley writes: "Q: What is implied in being a perfect Christian? A: Loving God with all our heart, and mind, and soul. (Deuteronomy 6:5.)" [11]

Spiritual growth expressed in the Gospels

The Lord Jesus in His Sermon on the Mount says: "Therefore you are to be perfect, as your heavenly Father is perfect" (Matthew 5:48).

According to an older version of *Webster's Dictionary*, perfect means:

> 1. Finished; complete; consummate; not defective; having all that is requisite to its nature and kind; as a perfect statue; a perfect likeness; a perfect work; a perfect system.

2. Fully informed; completely skilled; as men perfect in the use of arms; perfect in discipline.
3. Complete in moral excellencies.[12]

According to *Scofield Reference Notes*:

> Perfect—implies full development, growth into maturity of godliness, not sinless perfection. (See Ephesians 4:12, 13). In this passage the Father's kindness, not His sinlessness is the point in question. (See also, Luke 6:35, 36).[13]

Regarding Christian perfection John Wesley does not imply sinlessness, but gradual victory over sin and gradual growth in grace.

He writes:

> Q: When does inward sanctification begin? A: In the moment a man is justified. (Yet sin remains in him, yea, the seed of all sin, till he is sanctified throughout.) From that time a believer gradually dies to sin and grows in grace.[14]

Spiritual growth expressed in the book of Acts

O, how much I like what the beloved physician, Luke, writes: "They were continually devoting themselves to the apostles' teaching and to fellowship, to the breaking of bread and to prayer" (Acts 2:42). This verse sums up the basic elements of spiritual growth. The word continually suggests the process of spiritual maturity. We don't grow into Christlikeness overnight; it is a day-by-day process.

The word devoting suggests the practice of spiritual disciplines. Christians are invited to intentionally create space for God so the Holy Spirit transforms them into the image of Christ. Paul captures this idea very well in 2 Corinthians 3:18: "But we all, with unveiled face, beholding as in a mirror the glory of the Lord, are being transformed into the same image from glory to glory, just as from the Lord, the Spirit." God gave us the grace to do the "beholding as in the mirror."

The expression: "with unveiled face" indicates that it is our responsibility to be transparent with God and with others.

Commenting on 2 Corinthians 3:18, Oswald Chambers, writes:

> The greatest characteristic a Christian can exhibit is this completely unveiled openness before God, which allows that person's life to become a mirror for others. When the Spirit fills us, we are transformed, and by beholding God we become mirrors. You can always tell when someone has been beholding the glory of the Lord, because your inner spirit senses that he mirrors the Lord's own character. Beware of anything that would spot or tarnish that mirror in you. It is almost always something good that will stain it—something good, but not what is best.[15]

Amazingly enough, Acts 2:42 includes the most important spiritual disciplines which are part of the process of spiritual growth and maturity.

These are:

- *Apostles' teaching.* It is the discipline of Bible study.
- This is one of the most important disciplines in the process of discipleship.
- *Fellowship.* It represents community. I believe that this is another spiritual discipline. Community is as important as the discipline of Bible study. Without community we cannot experience spiritual growth. Spiritual formation does not happen in a vacuum, just as individuals. This could lead to egoism and individualism. We are called to build each other up in Christ's Body, the Church.
- *Breaking of bread.* This indicates the practice of the Lord's Supper, Eucharist, or Holy Communion. It is clear that the Lord's Supper is another important holy habit for discipleship.
- *Prayer.* It is the discipline of talking with God. This means that communicating with God in the assembly of like- minded believers is of tremendous importance

for spiritual growth.

What strikes me is that the newly formed Church in Jerusalem started the spiritual formation process immediately after Pentecost. Isn't it amazing? This tells me loud and clear that spiritual growth should be the normal Christian life and faith for the 21st century Church as well.

Spiritual growth expressed in the Epistles

If one does a careful expository study of the epistles, he or she can be assured of at least one major reality: spiritual growth is assumed and expected in the lives of Christians. In other words, in light of the epistles, Christians are supposed to grow and mature spiritually. Let's examine a few passages.

Romans 8:3–14

This is one of my all-time favorite passages when I preach and teach about spiritual growth and maturity. Spiritual growth and maturity has to do with the mindset of the Spirit. "For those who are according to the flesh set their minds on the things of the flesh, but those who are according to the Spirit, the things of the Spirit" (Romans 8:5). That's why it is so important to be renewed "in the spirit of your mind" (cf. Ephesians 4:23).

John Piper once said: "This is how the mind is renewed by steadfastly gazing at the glories of Christ for what they really are."[16] Spiritual growth implies transformation (metamorphosis), "by the renewing of your mind" (cf. Romans 12:2).

Webster Merriman Dictionary defines metamorphosis this way: "1: (a) Change of physical form, structure, or substance, especially by supernatural means. (b) A striking alteration in appearance, character, or circumstances."[17]

Spiritual growth and maturity is not about information but transformation.

Therefore, spiritual growth and maturity is not about information but transformation. Paul makes this aspect very clear in his writings (see especially 2 Corinthians 3:18 and Romans 12:2).

The supreme goal of spiritual maturity is to be free to rule with Christ (see Romans 5:17, Galatians 5:1). The love of God, as spiritual fruit in us, is evidenced by self-control (Galatians 5:23). When we are led by the Spirit we are mature sons [*huios*] of God freely displaying Christ's character in us.

1 Corinthians 3:1–3

First Corinthians 3:1–3 is another great passage. In this letter Paul explains that God is in the business of spiritual growth: "So then neither the one who plants nor the one who waters is anything, but God who causes the growth" (1 Corinthians 3:7).

Church planting is a wonderful and rewarding thing, but God is not in the business of planting only. Church service and good outreach programs are beautiful things, but God is not for watering only. God expects spiritual growth in all His churches. If Christians don't grow spiritually, they are no different from the "mere men" (v. 3) from the world. When the atmosphere in the church is filled with "jealousy and strife," it is because its members are fleshly Christians.

To be a Christian and fleshy at the same time is an oxymoron. Christian spirituality and carnality are incompatible.

1 Corinthians 13:1–13

First Corinthians 13, the "love chapter," is called by some people the *hinge chapter*. On one side, we have 1 Corinthians 12, where Paul teaches about spiritual gifts. On the other side, we have 1 Corinthians 14, where Paul teaches how to exercise these gifts. In between, at the hinge, is chapter 13—the love chapter. Agape love is God's very essence. "God is love" (cf. 1 John 4:8).

Growing in Christ's love enables Christians to exercise the spiritual gifts in such a way that edifies others. Paul admonishes believers in Corinth to grow in God's love, giving them his own example: "When I was a child, I used to speak like a child, think like a child, reason like a child; when I became a man, I did away with childish things" (1 Corinthians 13:11). The process is clear: we move from the child-like state to the adult-like state. Our speech, reason, and values are transformed by God's love into Christ-like character.

Galatians 5:16–26

This passage is a masterpiece when it comes to spiritual growth and maturity. In this letter Paul contrasts the "deeds of the flesh" and the "fruit of the Spirit." Paul makes his point very clear: "Now those who belong to Christ Jesus have crucified the flesh with its passions and desires" (Galatians 5:24).

In other words, those who are saved by the cross of Christ are expected to live in the Spirit. Salvation implies growing in the character of Christ.

Dallas Willard writes:

> The fruit of the Spirit simply is the inner character of Jesus Himself that is brought about in us through the process of Christian spiritual formation. It is the outcome of spiritual formation. It is Christ formed in us."[18]

Paul writes straight to the point: "If we live by the Spirit, let us also walk by the Spirit" (Galatians 5:25).

Ephesians 4:11–16

Another favorite passage of mine is in the letter to the Ephesians. I find myself running to this text of the New Testament over and over again, especially when I have to explain to others that spiritual maturity is not optional.

Spiritual growth and maturity do not happen on automatic pilot. It requires our willful participation in the process. Later in this chapter, Paul states very clearly that it is our responsibility to "lay aside the old self" (v. 22).

In Ephesians 4:11–16, Paul emphasizes that all offices of the Church—*apostles, prophets, evangelists, pastors, and teachers*—are called for the sole purpose of "equipping of the saints," and "building up of the body of Christ" (v. 12). The goal set before them is attaining the state of a "mature man," even the "fullness of Christ" (v. 13).

The ultimate intention of God is to have a Body—the body of Christ, in which all members are "fitted and held together" and the entire body, in perfect health, is "building up of itself in love" (v. 16).

Ephesians 6:10–20

At the end of his letter to the Ephesians, Paul teaches believers about spiritual warfare. In one of my monthly teaching letters I shared the following thoughts:

> Once we accepted Christ in our lives, many of us expected life would go smoothly. Not so. Why is that? As soon as we were rescued from the domain of darkness, and God transferred us to the kingdom of His beloved Son, we made Satan our personal enemy. Yes, he is a defeated foe (Colossians 2:15), but don't be fooled into believing that Satan cannot deceive you just because you are a Christian. On the contrary, because we are Christians, Satan works the hardest to:
>
> - Lie to us (John 8:44)
> - Steal, kill, and destroy (John 10:10)
> - Devour us (1 Peter 5:7)
> - Tempt us (1 Corinthians 7:5)
> - Deceive us (2 Corinthians 2:13)
> - Place various snares on our path (2 Timothy 2:24–16)
> - Design various schemes against us (Ephesians 6:11)
> - Continually accuse us (Revelation 12:9).[19]

In the context of spiritual war, it is important for believers to understand what it means to overcome the evil one. **As in any combat, it requires fighting.** Spiritual warfare implies a real fight too. And, in order to stand against the devil the Christian must "take up the full armor of God" (v. 11). To be able to take up the full armor one must grow spiritually. Infants, little children, or toddlers don't dress up in military armor for a real war. But grown-up individuals, who are properly trained for the battle,

As soon as we were rescued from the domain of darkness, and God transferred us to the kingdom of His beloved Son, we made Satan our personal enemy.

are required to dress up and arm themselves with all necessary weaponry for the real war.

It is interesting that, if we look carefully at the verb tenses used in this passage, the protective elements of the armor (the belt of truth, the breastplate of righteousness, the sandals of the gospel of peace) are given by God when we are born again. But the offensive pieces of the armor: the shield of faith, the helmet of salvation, the sword of the Spirit, are given to us when we are "strong in the Lord" (v. 10), in other words, when we are mature in Christ.

Colossians 3:8–10

In this passage, Paul explains that after people are born again, they must lay aside all evil practices and "put on the new self" (v. 10). This is a process of renewal of the inner person according to the image of Christ. If you are creative, you will see that Colossians 3:8–10 contains a beautiful definition of spiritual growth. If I were you, I would come up with an expanded definition of spiritual growth. I assure you it would be a good exercise!

Here is the definition that I came up with:

> Spiritual growth is the work of the divine Vinedresser (John 15:1–2) through His grace by which Christ's disciples are enabled through the Holy Spirit (Romans 8:13) to "put to death the deeds of the body" (i.e.: anger, wrath, malice, slander, abusive speech, lying, etc.), and putting on the new self "who is being renewed to a true knowledge according" to Christ's image (Colossians 3:8–10) in order to edify others (Ephesians 4:16) and glorify God (John 15:8).

Hebrews 2:9–18

The author of this letter makes it clear that spiritual growth—"bringing many sons to glory"—is what God intended before the foundation of the world in Christ. In Ephesians 1:4, Paul writes: "Just as He chose us in Him before the foundation of the world, that we would be holy and blameless before Him. In love ..." I find this verse remarkable! Why? Because before any star was ever created, God made this plan to include us in love, fully knowing that Adam was going to fail in the Garden.

Peter also writes: "For He was foreknown before the foundation of the world but has appeared in these last times for the sake of you" (1 Peter 1:20). This is another verse that makes my jaw drop wide open in awe of God's mystery! Why? This tells us that before any human being was born on this planet, Christ already knew about the cross. He accepted the Father's cup in the Garden of Gethsemane. Christ went to the cross for our sake. What a mystery!

In a deeper sense this communicates that spiritual growth and maturity is springing from the very heart of the Father: "For both He who sanctifies and those who are sanctified are all from one Father; for which reason He is not ashamed to call them brethren" (Hebrews 2:11). Spiritual growth also requires suffering. That is why the cross of Christ, the cruciform love, are key concepts to spiritual growth and maturity. Paul understood this very well. The cross is the only avenue to identify ourselves with Christ and find our true identity.

Many times, preachers explain only 2 Corinthians 5:17: "Therefore if anyone is in Christ, he is a new creature; the old things passed away; behold, new things have come." This is an awesome truth! But seldom is it connected with Galatians 2:20: "I have been crucified with Christ; and it is no longer I who live, but Christ lives in me; and the life which I now live in the flesh I live by faith in the Son of God, who loved me and gave Himself up for me." This verse is the bridge to understanding what it really means to be in Christ and reveals what "but Christ lives in me" really means.

Hebrews 5:11–14, 6:1–3

These passages are among my favorite texts in the area of spiritual growth. The author of Hebrews makes it clear that, in this process, God expects Christians to change their spiritual diet. In other words, as we grow up in the grace of Christ, we should move from milk to solid food. These Scriptures convey with clarity that the Holy Spirit expects us to grow. Christians are expected to progressively leave the "elementary teaching" and "press on to maturity" (Hebrews 6:1). The tragedy is that in the 21st century too many Christians are wearing diapers and crying for the same old milk bottle. Too many have become "dull of hearing" (Hebrews 5:11). Tragic, isn't it?

James 1:2–4

James also writes about the importance of becoming perfect in God. He writes that in the process of perfecting us God uses various trials. But after passing through all these special furnaces we come out at the other end "perfect and complete, lacking in nothing" (James 1:4b).

1 Peter 2:1–3

Peter addresses spiritual growth as well. He admonishes newborn babies to drink the pure milk of the Word (v. 2a) in order to grow in respect to salvation (v. 2b). Peter makes it clear that salvation is not just a one-time deal. Genuine salvation implies spiritual growth. To avoid any misunderstandings, I have to underline that spiritual growth is part of salvation, not an addition to it. Nor should readers interpret what I am writing outside of context. I am not saying, nor implying, that born again believers should grow to prove that they are saved. No way. May it never be.

What I am saying is that genuine Christians grow spiritually because they are born in God's family. But this is not an automatic thing. Many Christians are in danger of remaining spiritual babies until the second coming of the Lord. When Paul writes about our responsibilities as believers to "work out your salvation" (Philippians 2:12), he is not preaching legalism. Please pay attention to the context. He is not teaching that salvation is by works. Paul writes to believers, people who experienced spiritual birth. Paul continues: "For it is God who is at work in you, both to will and to work for His good pleasure" (Philippians 2:13). The paradox is that spiritual growth is still God's grace working on our lives. We just have to continue to receive it by faith in Christ and "grow in the grace and knowledge of our Lord and Savior Jesus Christ" (2 Peter 3:18a).

2 Peter 1:2–12

I like the thoughts that the Holy Spirit inspired Peter to write about! It is clear that Peter teaches about spiritual growth and maturity. I call this passage the ladder of spiritual growth and maturity. It clearly states that God "granted to us everything pertaining to life and godliness." Now, since we have all that, it takes to fully grow in Christ, it is our responsibility to apply "all diligence" so our faith is displayed with "moral excellence." Towards the end of the ladder, we are called to apply all diligence to "brotherly kindness," LOVE.

Paul explains that "Love does no wrong to a neighbor; therefore, love is the fulfillment of the law" (Romans 13:10).

Peter concludes his thought on the ladder of spiritual growth and maturity with these thoughts:

- First: "For as long as you practice these things, you will never stumble" (2 Peter 1:10b).
- And second: "In this way the entrance into the eternal kingdom" (2 Peter 1:11a).

The Way to the kingdom of God is grace. Period. There is no doubt about it. However, practicing spiritual disciplines with all diligence keeps us on the center of this Way. (See Matthew 7:13–14, and Luke 13:24.) It is just a matter of obedience after we are saved and not in order to be saved.

Jesus Himself communicates the concept of obedience very well: "Why do you call Me, 'Lord, Lord,' and do not do what I say?" (Luke 6:46).

Matthew is even bolder than Luke when he writes: "Not everyone who says to Me, 'Lord, Lord,' will enter the kingdom of heaven, but he who does the will of My Father who is in heaven will enter" (Matthew 7:21).

1 John 2:12–14

In this passage John writes confidently to the three categories of spiritual growth in the church:

- *Little children.* "I am writing to you, little children, because your sins have been forgiven you for His name's sake" (1 John 2:12).
- *Young men.* "I am writing to you, young men, because you have overcome the evil one" (1 John 2:1b).
- *Fathers.* "I have written to you, fathers, because you

> know Him who has been from the beginning" (1 John 2:14).

In these verses, the idea of spiritual growth from stage to stage is obvious.

To the topic of babyhood and the necessity for Christians to grow up, Chuck Swindoll writes:

> I love babies. I think others ought to have as many as they wish. I think it's a delightful, enjoyable experience to watch babies grow up and to become little people, little men and women, adolescents, and functioning persons But ... they are dependent and demanding. They are unable to feed themselves. They are unable to stay out of messes. They love to be the center of attention. They are driven by impulses, such as hunger, pain, sleep. They're irritated when they're dirty, even though they made the mess, and you've gotta clean it up. They have no manners, no control. They have little attention span, no concern for others, no abilities or skills. Spiritual babies must grow up. Some of the most difficult people to live with, in the church of Jesus Christ, are those who have grown old in the Lord but haven't grown up in Him.[20]

Yeah! Too bad, but this is a reality in many churches today, which proves *a visible lack of spiritual growth.* But does the unfaithfulness of people nullify the faithfulness of God? I don't think so. Paul writes: "If we are faithless, He remains faithful, for He cannot deny Himself" (2 Timothy 2:13). God is still faithful to His initial plan, and I don't think His standard of bringing "many sons to glory" is going to be lowered. Otherwise, this would mean that the image of Christ during the 21st century could be lowered, in comparison with His image during the first century, just to accommodate our own superficiality, immaturity, lack of interest in spiritual growth, rejection of the Cross, and unwillingness to accept the lifestyle of discipleship. I think this can never be the case, because: "Jesus Christ is the same yesterday and today and forever" (Hebrews 13:8).

Reflection Questions

Please reflect upon the following questions, briefly elaborate, and then share your thoughts with a friend or your small group.

1. What did the Holy Spirit whisper to your heart through this chapter? What did you like the most from this chapter?

2. What new concepts and ideas did you learn from this chapter? Which concept are you committed to implementing in your life?

3. Please elaborate on the following concepts. Use additional space if necessary:
3.1. Spiritual growth expressed in the Gospels. Share your favorite verses from the four Gospels which talk about this topic.

3.2. Spiritual growth expressed in the Epistles. What is your all-time favorite passage?

3.3 Carefully read 1 Corinthians 3:1–9. Please give a brief explanation of this passage.

3.4. Carefully read Hebrews 5:11–14, 6:1–3. Please give a brief explanation of this passage.

3.5. Carefully read 2 Peter 1:2–12. Please give a brief explanation of this passage.

4. What idea or concept captured your attention the most during reading this chapter?

5. List the best aha moments you had while reading this chapter?

Endnotes:

[5] M. Robert Mulholland Jr., *Invitation to a Journey*, (Downers Grove, IL: Inter Varsity Press, Downers Grove, IL, 1993), 12.
[6] Dallas Willard, *Renovation of the Heart: Putting on the Character of Christ*, (Colorado Springs: Navpress, 2002), 22.
[7] Thomas Jackson (editor), The Works of John Wesley, A Plain Account of Christian Perfection, [First Conference, June 25, 1744], (Vol. 11, pp. 366-446, 1872), article 17. Accessed on April 20, 2011. http://gbgm-umc.org.
[8] Teknion, (Strong # 5040) = little child, diminutive of teknon; an infant, i.e. (plural figuratively) darlings (Christian converts), little children. (James Strong, LL.D., S.T.D., The New Strong's Exhaustive Concordance of the Bible, (Nashville, Thomas Nelson Publishers, 1996), 89.
[9] Hyiós, (Strong # 5207) properly, a son (by birth or adoption); (figuratively) anyone sharing the same nature as their Father. For the believer, becoming a son of God begins with being reborn (adopted) by the heavenly Father— through Christ (the work of the eternal Son). Hyiós (son) emphasizes likeness of the believer to the heavenly Father, i.e. resembling His character more and more by living in faith (God's inwrought persuasons), Hyiós (son) highlights the (legal) right to the Father's inheritance, i.e., as the believer lives in conformity with the Father's nature (purpose). (HELPS Word- Studies, copyright © 1987, 2011 by Helps Ministries, Inc).
[10] W.E. Vine, *Vine's Complete Expository Dictionary of Old and New Testaments Words*, (Grand Rapids, MI: Thomas Nelson, 1996), 585.
[11] Thomas Jackson, "A Plain Account of Christian Perfection," (1872), article 17. Accessed on April 20, 2011.
https://www.ccel.org/w/wesley/perfection/perfection.html.
[12] Perfect. Accessed on May 17, 2011. http://webstersdictionary1828.com/Dictionary/Perfect.
[13] Perfect. *Scofield Reference Notes* (1917 edition). Accessed on May 17, 2011. https://www.biblestudytools.com/commentaries/scofield-reference-notes/matthew/matthew-5.html.
[14] *A Plain Account of Christian Perfection*, [Second Conference, August 1, 1745], 1872, article 17.
[15] Oswald Chambers, "Transformed by Beholding," Accessed on June 3, 2014. http://utmost.org/transformed-by-beholding/.
[16] John Piper, "The Renewed Mind and How to Have It." Accessed on March 2011. http://www.desiringgod.org/.
[17] Metamorphosis. Accessed in December 2010. http://www.merriam-webster.com/ dictionary/metamorphosis.
[18] Dallas Willard, "Idaho Springs Inquiries Concerning Spiritual Formation." Accessed on March 24, 2011. http://www.dwillard.org.
[19] Valy Vaduva, "Put On, May Teaching Letter," (URFM, Livonia, MI:

May 2018), 1, 2.
[20] Charles R. Swindoll, *The Tale of The Tardy Oxcart,* (Nashville, TN: Word Publishing, 1988), 80.

-4-

The Main Ingredients for Spiritual Growth

But solid food is for the mature, who because of practice have their senses trained to discern good and evil.
— Hebrews 5:14

In any process there are ingredients, steps, or phases. The same is true in our case. Without going into too much detail I am going to list some important ingredients for spiritual growth and discuss a few key aspects of each of them.

Ingredients for spiritual growth

1. God's uncreated life

Jesus told His disciples that He is the Good Shepherd. He came to give life to His sheep. Christ was not talking about the ordinary life here on earth. The Lord was talking about zoe life.

Thayer's and Smith's Bible Dictionary defines life:

> The state of one who is possessed of vitality or is animate; the vital spirit, the breath of life. Zoe Life of the absolute fullness of life, both essential and ethical, which belongs to God, and through Him both to the

hypostatic "logos" and to Christ in whom the "logos" put on human nature.[21]

This is the real and genuine life, active and vigorous, devoted to God, blessed, in the portion even in this world of those who put their trust in Christ, but after the resurrection to be consummated by new accessions, among them a more perfect body, and to last forever.

We can't even begin to discuss about spiritual growth and maturity without comprehending the concept of zoe life.

If we are to replace the English word life with the original word zoe, John 10:10(a) reads like this: "I have come that they may have *zoe* and may have *zoe* abundantly."

No one, who is separated from Christ, can have this type of life. Jesus is "the way, and the truth, and the life; no one comes to the Father but through Me" (John 14:6). The same truth is expressed by His beloved apostle John close to the end of the first century: "He who has the Son has the life; he who does not have the Son of God does not have the life" (1 John 5:12).

These are not arguments which I am using to convince the reader that there is a higher life, a zoe life out there. What I am trying to say is that without the zoe life we cannot even begin to talk about the process of spiritual growth. These are biblical facts which must be incorporated by faith in one's life if she or he truly desires to be transformed inside out into the likeness of Christ.

2. The Spirit of God

Spiritual growth requires the presence of God's Spirit at spiritual birth. During His earthly ministry Jesus has a theological conversation with Nicodemus. This man was a ruler of the Jews, a Pharisee, who was very educated in the Old Testament Scriptures. Jesus told him point blank: "Truly, truly, I say to you, unless one is born again, he cannot see the kingdom of God" (John 3:3). In other words, religion or theology cannot enlighten someone to see the kingdom of God. Of course, as many of us were when we first read the Gospel of John, Nicodemus was perplexed and, maybe, even confused by Jesus' radicality and directness. The poor old scholar of the Jewish Law asked: "How can a man be born when he is old?"

Christ did not tell him: "Go back and study the Old Testament Survey, re-take all the exams and you will find out the answer." Instead, Jesus explained: "Truly, truly, I say to you, unless one is born of water and the Spirit he cannot enter into the kingdom of God" (John 3:5). To be sure that professor Nic gets it, Jesus continues: "That which is born of the flesh is flesh, and that which is born of the Spirit is spirit" (John 3:6).

Spiritual birth is a supernatural act produced only by the Holy Spirit through the living and incorruptible Word of God in His unthinkable grace.

You see that spiritual birth is not produced by the right theology or the right doctrine. Spiritual birth is a supernatural act produced only by the Holy Spirit through the living and incorruptible Word of God in His unthinkable grace. Paul explains: "He saved us, not on the basis of deeds which we have done in righteousness, but according to His mercy, by the washing of regeneration and renewing by the Holy Spirit" (Titus 3:5).

Similarly, Peter writes: "For you have been born again not of seed which is perishable but imperishable, that is, through the living and enduring word of God" (1 Peter 1:23).

Paul underlines this truth very well. He writes: "Therefore, if anyone is in Christ, he is a new creature; the old things passed away; behold, new things have come" (2 Corinthians 5:17).

Let us be very clear. Spiritual growth requires the presence of the Holy Spirit and His revelation (cf. John 6:63, 16:13). In fact, the third Person of the Trinity is the Author and the Agent of spiritual transformation.

In 2 Corinthians 3:18, Paul teaches us: "But we all, with unveiled face, beholding as in a mirror the glory of the Lord, are being transformed into the same image from glory to glory, just as from the Lord, the Spirit."

3. The Word of God

Spiritual growth and maturity require daily encounters with the Word of God. The first disciples from the church in Jerusalem were devoting themselves to the apostles' teaching (see Acts 2:42). This was a practice not only for the church in Jerusalem but for the churches planted by Paul among the Gentiles. The disciples among some of these churches were "examining the Scriptures daily." Luke writes: "Now these were more noble-minded than those in Thessalonica, for they received the word with great eagerness, examining the Scriptures daily to see whether these things were so" (Acts 17:11).

A Christian cannot grow and truly get to a state of spiritual maturity without having a personal relationship with the Word of God.

A Christian cannot grow and truly get to a state of spiritual maturity without having a personal relationship with the Word of God. Peter, in his sincerity and without any sophistication, writes: "Like newborn babies, long for the pure milk of the word, so that by it you may grow in respect to salvation" (1 Peter 2:2).

4. Spiritual Parents

Jesus gave the first disciples the model for spiritual growth—discipleship. He gave us the Great Commission with a very specific mission statement: *make disciples* (see Matthew 28:19–20). Today, Jesus continues to issue the same call of "*Follow Me*" (Matthews 16:24, Luke 9:23). Spiritual growth implies character modeling. Jesus tells us: "A pupil is not above his teacher, but everyone, after he has been fully trained, will be like his teacher" (Luke 6:40). Spiritual growth and maturity, many times, implies a teacher-disciple dynamic or a mentor-mentee type of relationship. This is a deep spiritual relationship. Paul writes about this: "For if you were to have countless tutors in Christ, yet you would not have many fathers, for in Christ Jesus I became your father through the gospel" (1 Corinthians 4:15).

In one of my spiritual growth seminars I define spiritual fathers like this:

> A spiritual Abba is a spiritually mature individual (cf. Hebrews 5:14) who is preoccupied with (and for) the well-being of the spiritual children (cf. 2 Corinthians 11:29 and Galatians 4:19). A spiritual father not only gives birth to spiritual children through the gospel (cf. 1 Corinthians 4:15), but spends and expands himself for the wellbeing of the spiritual children (cf. 2 Corinthians 12:15) until Christ is formed in them.[22]

Paul writes: "My children, with whom I am again in labor until Christ is formed in you" (Galatians 4:19). Spiritual parents know this godly truth about character modeling. More specifically, they know that spiritual growth is about the Spirit of God modeling and transforming us into the likeness of Christ when we are engaging in a correct spiritual relationship with Christ and with each other. Paul understood and modeled this principle. He writes: "You are witnesses, and so is God, how devoutly and uprightly and blamelessly we behaved toward you believers; just as you know how we were exhorting and encouraging and imploring each one of you as a father would his own children" (1 Thessalonians 2:10–11, emphasis mine). (See also 1 Corinthians 4:16; 11:1).

Spiritual growth and maturity, many times, implies a teacher- disciple dynamic or a mentor-mentee type of relationship.

If there is a crisis in the world today it is not the energy crisis or the financial crisis; the crisis it is a lack of spiritual fathers. In a complex essay titled, "Issues of Laity and Clergy Spiritual Growth," Dick Rausher writes:

> Almost without exception, the institutional church's focus is on intellectual formation for ministry, and it virtually ignores the spiritual formation of its members. We have too many pastors preaching about spirituality who have not had the support or institutional encouragement to develop their own spirituality. They have not done their spiritual growth work. They are reading about spirituality from a map and have not been supported and encouraged to make the journey.

Rausher continues:

> We need these spiritually mature teachers in the Church who have actually made the journey, so they can lead others into the deserts of their own souls.[23]

I am not the only one who thinks that we are badly missing spiritually mature teachers in our churches.

5. Community

As I mentioned already, spiritual formation is done in a community context, as Luke writes in Acts 2:42: "They were continually devoting themselves." Jesus told His disciples that "upon this rock"—Christ Himself—"I will build My church" (Matthew 16:18). It is obvious that Christ builds a church formed by individuals and these individuals go to church. In other words, the Church is Christ's Body built by many members, not many individual members trying, somehow, to become the Body of Christ.

Spiritual formation requires a genuine community, an ekklesia type of Church.

Spiritual formation requires a genuine community, an ekklesia[24] type of Church. Paul understood this very well, which is why he writes: "For the body is not one member, but many" (1 Corinthians 12:14) and: "You also are being built together into a dwelling of God in the Spirit" (Ephesians 2:22).

6. Spiritual Disciplines

The practice of spiritual disciplines, (i.e., prayer, silence and solitude, study, fasting, meditation, submission, service, guidance, confession, worship, and celebration) is inseparable from spiritual formation. Richard Foster writes:

> The spiritual disciplines, then, are the God-ordained means by which each of us is enabled to bring the individualized power–pack we all possess–the human body–and place it before God as 'a living sacrifice' (Romans 12:1).[25]

This is not a modern form of legalism. In other words, we are not called to try harder. ***We are called to a process of intentionally training in godliness*** (Timothy 4:7).

In summary, spiritual formation is a must. Our brief journey into the New Testament clearly demonstrates this general conclusion: God desires all His children to reflect the character of Jesus Christ (cf. 2 Corinthians 3:18). Period.

The goal set before the church is attaining the state of a *"mature man,"* even the *"fullness of Christ"* (Ephesians 4:13).

The following statements support the general conclusion:

- *Spiritual formation is a process.* The idea of spiritual growth from stage to stage is extremely obvious in the New Testament (2 Peter 1:5–7).
- *Genuine salvation implies spiritual growth* (1 Peter 2:2). Spiritual formation is part of salvation, not an addition to it. Genuine children of God are expected to grow up (Hebrews 5:12–14).

- *Spiritual formation is not for elite Christians.* God is not into elitism or favoritism. God expects all of His children to grow up in all of His churches (Ephesians 2:21).
- *To remain immature, to be a Christian and fleshy at the same time, is an oxymoron.* Christian spirituality and carnality are incompatible (1 Corinthians 3:1). If we are saved by the cross of Christ we are expected to live in the Spirit (Galatians 5:24).
- *Salvation implies growing up in the character of Christ* (Ephesians 4:15). Spiritual growth implies transformation (metamorphosis) "by the renewing of your mind" (Romans 12:2). Therefore, spiritual growth and maturity or spiritual formation is not about information but transformation (Ephesians 4:23).
- *Spiritual growth requires suffering* (1 Peter 2:21). The cross of Christ, the cruciform love, is the key concept to spiritual formation (Galatians 2:20, 6:14). In the process of perfecting us God uses various trials (James 1:2–4). But in the end, we are made perfect in Him who is perfect (Hebrews 12:2;1 Thessalonians 5:23–24; Philippians 1:6).

The tragedy is that many believers don't see that spiritual growth and maturity (or spiritual formation) is springing from the heart of the Father. Let's sum it up. The main ingredients of Spiritual Growth are:

1. *God's uncreated life* (John 10:10, 1 John 5:12).
2. *The Spirit of God* (John 3:3, 5, Titus 3:5).
3. *The Word of God* (John 8:31–32).
4. *Spiritual Parents* (Galatians 4:19, 1 Corinthians 4:15),
5. *Community* (Acts 2:42, Matthew 16:18).
6. *Spiritual disciplines* (1 Corinthians 9:25–27, 2 Timothy 1:7).

I pray and I hope that the 21st century Church would wake up to Christ's Great Commission—making disciples and start investing in people and their spiritual development rather than in buildings, programs and marketing strategies. My sincere amen goes after Paul's prayer for the church in Ephesus:

> For this reason I too, having heard of the faith in the Lord Jesus which exists among you and your love for all the saints, do not cease giving thanks for you, while making mention of you in my prayers; that the God of our Lord Jesus Christ, the Father of glory, may give to you a spirit of wisdom and of revelation in the knowledge of Him. I pray that the eyes of your heart may be enlightened, so that you will know what is the hope of His calling, what are the riches of the glory of His inheritance in the saints, and what is the surpassing greatness of His power toward us who believe. These are in accordance with the working of the strength of His might which He brought about in Christ, when He raised Him from the dead and seated Him at His right hand in the heavenly places, far above all rule and authority and power and dominion, and every name that is named, not only in this age but also in the one to come. And He put all things in subjection under His feet, and gave Him as head over all things to the church, which is His body, the fullness of Him who fills all in all. (Ephesians 1:15–23)

This is my prayer for the 21st century church. Amen.

Reflection Questions

Please reflect upon the following questions, briefly elaborate, and then share your thoughts with a friend or your small group.

1. What did you like the most from this chapter?

2. What new concepts did you learn from this chapter?

3. In your own words, please elaborate on the following theological concepts:
3.1. God's uncreated life. Read the definition of life by Thayer's and Smith's Bible Dictionary.

3.2. Spiritual parents. Read Dick Rausher's quote (p. 51,52) carefully from his essay titled "Issues of Laity and Clergy Spiritual Growth."

4. Carefully read Ephesians 4:11–16. Please give a brief explanation of this passage.

5. What was your most significant aha moment after reading this chapter?

Endnotes:

[21] Strong's Number: 2222. Thayer and Smith, *Greek Lexicon entry for Zoe,* 1999.
[22] Valy Vaduva, "Spiritual Mentors" – Audio, (Ypsilanti, MI: Upper Room Fellowship Ministry, 2008), CD #9.
[23] Dick Rausher, "Issues of Laity and Clergy Spiritual Growth," accessed on April 19, 2011, http://www.stonyhill.com/article.
[24] Strong's Greek Lexicon Number, G1577, (Gr. ἐκκλησία), ekklesia, a calling out, i.e., (concretely) a popular meeting especially a religious congregation Jewish synagogue, or Christian community of members on earth or saints in heaven or both). Accessed on April 25, 2011, http://studybible.info.
[25] Richard Foster, *Life with God: Reading the Bible for Spiritual Transformation,* (New York, NY: Harper One, 2008), 13.

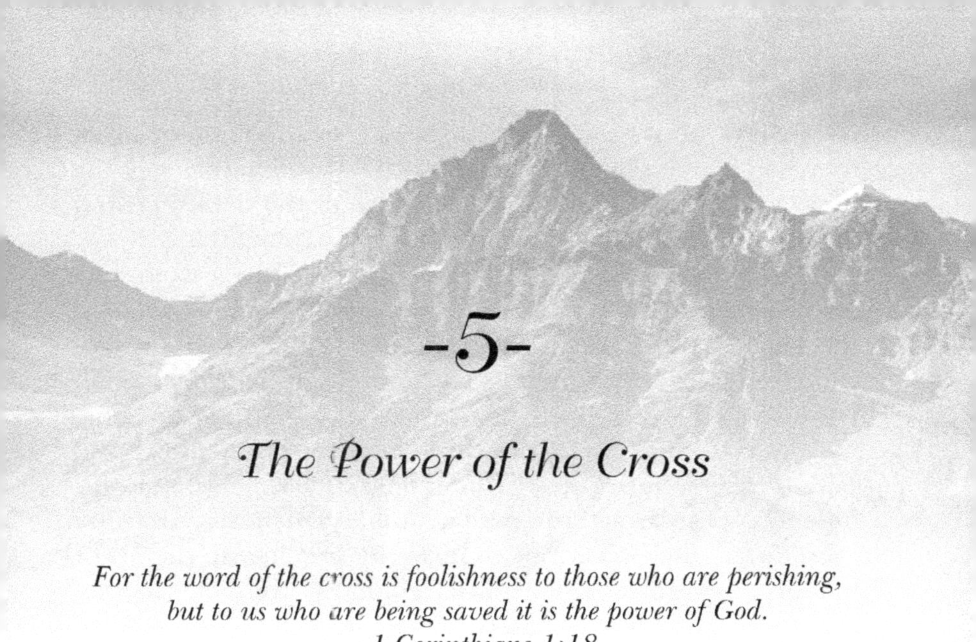

-5-

The Power of the Cross

For the word of the cross is foolishness to those who are perishing,
but to us who are being saved it is the power of God.
— 1 Corinthians 1:18.

For I determined to know nothing among you except Jesus Christ,
and Him crucified.
— 1 Corinthians 2:2

Two thousand years ago, Pontius Pilate, (AD 26–36), the fifth prefect of the Roman province of Judaea, told the multitudes who eagerly waited for his decision: "Behold, the Man!" (John 19:5). The Man was none other than the Son of God. On that special day He was crucified on a Roman cross. But on the first day of the week "the surpassing greatness" (cf. Ephesians 1:19) of God's power raised Christ from the dead. The Risen Jesus came where the disciples were assembled, a room with the doors locked "for fear of the Jews," and said to them: "Peace be with you" (John 20:19). The disciples rejoiced! Jesus "showed them both His hands and His side" (John 20:20).

Thomas, one of Jesus' disciples, had not been there when the Lord appeared to the rest of the disciples. Full of joy and assurance, the other disciples told him that they saw the Lord. But Thomas could not believe them. He wanted some personal proof. He told them with conviction that he would not believe until he saw with his own eyes the same proof as they had. "Unless I shall see in His hands the imprint of the nails, and put my finger into the place of the nails, and put my hand into His side, I will not believe" (John 20:25).

To be honest, I am glad that Thomas had the guts to state his position. If I had been there, I would probably have had the same reaction as he. But I am happy that Jesus did not condemn him. Scripture tells us: "And after eight days again His disciples were inside, and Thomas with them. Jesus came, the doors having been shut, and stood in their midst, and said, 'Peace be with you.'" (John 20:26). Please note that this time Thomas was with them. The omniscient Jesus, knowing everything, including the motives of the heart, the most hidden thoughts, fears, and emotions of all people, approached Thomas directly, saying to him: "Reach here your finger, and see My hands; and reach here your hand, and put it into My side; and be not unbelieving, but believing" (John 20:27). Upon assessing the evidence, Thomas's response was an amazing one: "My Lord and my God!" (John 20:28). This is a powerful statement which means that Thomas believed and accepted Jesus' Lordship and His Divinity. Jesus explains how important it is for people to believe in God even without such evidence. "Because you have seen Me, have you believed? Blessed are they who did not see, and yet believed" (John 20:29).

You see? You and I, today, are more blessed if we accept and believe the Lordship of Jesus and His divinity. As Paul exhorts us: "that if you confess with your mouth Jesus as Lord, and believe in your heart that God raised Him from the dead, you shall be saved" (Romans 10:9). Let me briefly explain it.

To be saved it requires two aspects:

- First, confess with your mouth the Lordship of Jesus
- Second, believe in your heart Christ's Divinity—that God raised Him from the dead.

Paul continues: "for with the heart man believes, resulting in righteousness, and with the mouth he confesses, resulting in salvation" (Romans 10:10). I like this Scripture! This is so simple, clear and straightforward. The *righteousness* of Christ is imputed to the believing heart and the verbal declaration results in *salvation*. This is how people are born again. This is how a sinner enters into an amazing relationship with God.

Let us return to the passage from John 20. There, the Scripture clearly tells us: "Many other signs therefore Jesus also performed in the presence of the disciples, which are not written in this book; but these have been written that you may believe that Jesus is the Christ, the Son of God; and that believing you may have life in His name." (John 20:30–31). We understand why it was very important for the early disciples to experience all these things before and after the Resurrection of Jesus, because they were then able to communicate, both orally and in writing, the Gospel of Jesus.

It is no wonder that John, the Apostle of Love, at the end of the first century, between 85–95 AD, writes with such confidence the following:

> What was from the beginning, what we have heard, what we have seen with our eyes, what we beheld and our hands handled, concerning the Word of Life—and the life was manifested, and we have seen and bear witness and proclaim to you the eternal life, which was with the Father and was manifested to us—what we have seen and heard we proclaim to you also, that you also may have fellowship with us; and indeed our fellowship is with the Father, and with His Son Jesus Christ. And these things we write, so that our joy may be made complete. (1 John 1:1–4)

Do you hear John? He is writing about all sorts of mystic experiences with the Word of Life. Can you imagine it? Everything that they had *heard*, *seen*, and *touched* with their hands, was concerning the Word of Life. Then, being empowered by the Holy Spirit, they went on and *"proclaimed the eternal life."* I love it, I love it, I love it!

What was the purpose? And what is the purpose? The

purpose was and is: "that you also may have fellowship with … the Father, and with His Son Jesus Christ" as the apostles did. Let me underline it: this is so crucial. This is part of our spiritual inheritance. And how do we accomplish this? Very simple—*by faith*.

Faith

Before we can go further let's spend a few minutes on this fundamental subject. Faith is the spiritual principle which governs salvation for all human beings, past, present and future. Faith is organically linked to God—the object of faith. Faith is directly linked to the Word of God. Paul states: "So faith comes from hearing, and hearing by the word of Christ" (Romans 10:17).

Jesus said to Thomas: "Because you have seen Me, have you believed?" And to us Christ is saying: "Blessed are those who have not seen and yet have believed." Scripture is very clear regarding saving faith: "And without faith it is impossible to please Him, for he who comes to God must believe that He is, and that He is a rewarder of those who seek Him" (Hebrew 11:6).

Therefore, we must know what the center of the Christian faith is. Paul writes to the Corinthians: "For indeed Jews ask for signs, and Greeks search for wisdom; but we preach Christ crucified, to Jews a stumbling block, and to Gentiles foolishness, but to those who are the called, both Jews and Greeks, Christ the power of God and the wisdom of God" (1 Corinthians 1:22–24).

Faith is the spiritual principle which governs salvation for all human beings, past, present, and future.

There is nothing wrong with signs and wonders, nor is it wrong to be wise and seek more wisdom. But signs, wonders and human wisdom are not supposed to be the foundation of our faith. Paul writes with great confidence: "we preach Christ crucified." This preaching was, and still is, a stumbling block for many people. More than this, Paul makes the following statement: "And when I came to you, brethren, I did not come with superiority of speech or of wisdom, proclaiming to you the testimony of God. For I determined to know nothing among you except Jesus Christ, and Him crucified" (1 Corinthians 2:1–2). Did you hear that? If that was extremely important to Paul it should be vitally important to us too. I hope everybody agrees with it. We should declare also: "We are determined to know nothing among the church except Jesus Christ, and Him crucified." Powerful statement, isn't it?

We can declare with all confidence that, according to the Word of God, the crucifixion of Jesus is at the heart of the Christian faith. We shall be on guard regarding any form of cheap grace. Dietrich Bonhoeffer, (1906–1945), author of *The Cost of Discipleship*, warned us regarding cheap grace.

He wrote:

> The preaching of forgiveness without requiring repentance, baptism without church discipline, communion without confession, absolution without personal confession. Cheap grace is grace without discipleship, grace without the cross, grace without Jesus Christ, living and incarnate.[26]

Let us not forget that cheap grace is grace without the cross. In other words, we can say that in fact the cross of Christ is the central message of the whole Bible. John the Evangelist tells us: "For God so loved the world, that He gave His only begotten Son, that whoever believes in Him should not perish, but have eternal life" (John 3:16). Believers across all Christian denominations agree that this is the premier verse of the entire Bible. Why? Because it states that because God loves us He gave. In the verb ***g-a-v-e*** is hidden the cross of Christ. Jesus truly is God's Supreme Sacrifice for all human beings, as John the Baptist introduced Christ almost two thousand years ago: "Behold, the Lamb of God!" (John 1:36).

What is the context of John 3:16? Let's find out. Just a couple of verses earlier, in John 3:14–15, we have the image of a bronze serpent lifted onto a pole in order to save the Israelites who were bitten by poisonous snakes. "And Moses made a bronze serpent and set it on the standard; and it came about, that if a serpent bit any man, when he looked to the bronze serpent, he lived" (Numbers 21:9). What a story! What a statement! What a wonderful prophecy! John quotes Jesus' words: "And as Moses lifted up the serpent in the wilderness, even so must the Son of Man be lifted up; that whoever believes may in Him have eternal life" (John 3:14–15).

Salvation is by faith alone, in Christ alone, God's gift alone, for His glory alone.

Later, in John's Gospel, Christ declares: "And I, if I be lifted up from the earth, will draw all men to Myself" (John 12:32). Do you see this? Christ is talking in one sense about His crucifixion and in a deeper sense about His Resurrection and Ascension. The cross of Jesus is the magnet—I will draw all men to Myself. This is the context that makes John 3:16 a very powerful verse!

If we put all these great concepts together, the conclusion is simple: Salvation is by faith alone, in Christ alone, God's gift alone, for His glory alone. O, what a grace! What a gift! This is what I call Good News!

Paul writes:

> For by grace, you have been saved through faith; and that not of yourselves, it is the gift of God. (Ephesians 2:8–9)

It means that the entire Old Testament, with the symbols which, in one way or another, points to Christ, is an integral part of the redemptive story. It is part of the Gospel—the Good News for humanity.

In the Old Testament we find various Scriptures which, in a direct statement or in a hidden manner, are considered by many as types[27] [28] of Christ.

Some of the types of Christ are:

- *Adam,* believe it or not, is a powerful type of Christ. See Romans 5:15 and 1 Corinthians 15:45.
- *The Tree of Life,* we read about it in Genesis, in the Garden of Eden, before the Fall.
- *The Seed of the woman* (cf. Genesis 3:15), still in the Garden of Eden but after the Fall.
- *Melchizedek* (cf. Genesis 14), is a type of the Son of God. The author of Hebrews explains, "Without father, without mother, without genealogy, having neither beginning of days nor end of life, but made like the Son of God, he abides a priest perpetually" (Hebrews 7:3).

Other symbols or types of Christ are:

- *Isaac* (cf. Genesis 22)
- *Jacob's Ladder* (cf. Genesis 28)
- *Joseph* (cf. Genesis 37-48)
- *The Scepter of Judah* (Genesis 49)
- *Moses* is also a type of Christ
- *The Passover Lamb* (cf. Exodus 12:13) is considered by most Christians as a clear type of Christ.

More types of Christ:

- *The First fruits* (cf. Exodus 22)
- *The Veil* from the Tabernacle (cf. Exodus 40:21)
- *The Veil* from the Temple (cf. 2 Chronicles 3:14)
- *Sacrifices from Leviticus,* most of them are considered types of Christ.
- *The Scapegoat* (cf. Leviticus 16:20–22) is a beautiful type of Christ, who became the scapegoat for all of us.
- *The Rock* which Moses struck twice (cf. Numbers 20),
- *The Bronze serpent* (cf. Numbers 21) that we talked about earlier are also types of Christ.

The list continues with:

- *The Star of Jacob* (cf. Number 24)
- *The Great Prophet* proclaimed in Deuteronomy 18
- *Joshua* (cf. Joshua 1:5)
- *The Stone* of Nebuchadnezzar's dream (cf. Daniel 2:35, 45)
- *The Man of Sorrows*, acquainted with grief (cf. Isaiah 53), is probably the most powerful type of Christ and prophesy about Christ's suffering and death.
- The Sun of Righteousness is one more type that I would like to include here is the (cf. Malachi 4:2).

All of these symbols are types of Christ, prophesying about the One who one day would come to fulfill everything that the Scripture foretold.

Therefore, the salvation of those who lived in the Old Testament times depended on their faith in the same Christ who was to come. The New Testament speaks of salvation through the Christ, who has already come. John tells us: "but these have been written that you may believe that Jesus is the Christ, the Son of God; and that believing you may have life in His name" (John 20:31).

So, we can firmly declare that the justification of man was, is, and will be only through faith. In the past (BC)—by faith looking into the future at the cross; in the present (AD)—by faith looking into the past at the same cross. (See diagram 1).

Do you see this? If we remove the cross from the Gospel, we compromise the whole salvation message of God for the world. This is exactly the aspect that Paul argues so directly in his epistle to the Galatians. He writes: "Grace to you and peace from God our Father, and the Lord Jesus Christ, *who gave Himself for our sins*, that He might deliver us out of this present evil age, according to the will of our God and Father" (Galatians 1:3–4). Then he writes: "I am amazed that you are so quickly deserting Him who called you by the grace of Christ, for *a different gospel*; which is really not another; only there are some who are disturbing you and want to distort the gospel of Christ" (Galatians 1:6–7).

Diagram 1

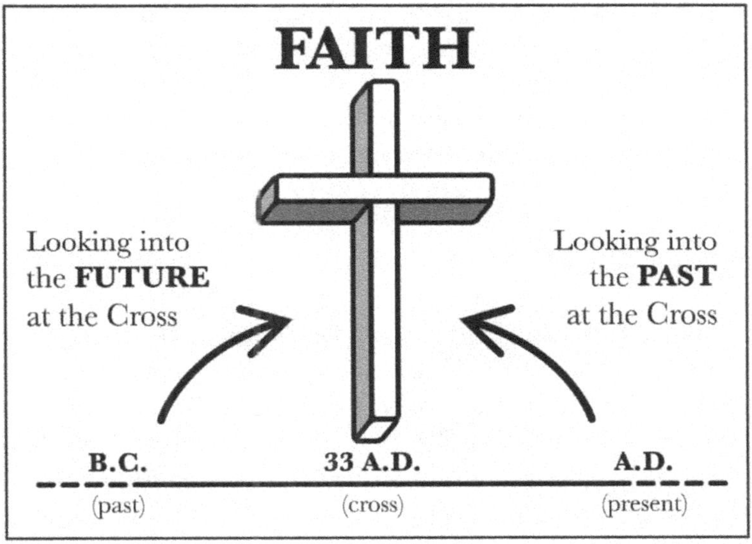

The Centrality of the Cross

The cross of Christ is the central message of the Bible. The cross of Christ was very important in Paul's preaching and writings. So, if the cross of Christ is so important, we should ask ourselves: What is the significance of the cross? I am glad you asked! This is a very good question. Let's start with the definition of the cross

The Definition of the Cross

The cross is an instrument of death. It was very well known in the time of Jesus.[29] Personally, I like very much the definition given by one of my favorite Christian writers, A.W. Tozer. He writes:

> The CROSS is a symbol of death. It stands for the

abrupt, violent death of a human being. The man in Roman times who took up his cross and started down the road had already said good-by to his friends. He was not coming back. He was going out to have it ended. The cross made no compromise, modified nothing, spared nothing; it slew all of the man, completely and for good. It did not try to keep on good terms with its victim. It struck cruel and hard, and when it had finished its work, the man was no more."[30]

The Significance of the Cross

Almost two thousand years, *the Son of God* (John 1:34, 1:49, 3:18, 5:25, 11: 4, 11:27, 19: 7, 8:31), considered also, *the Son of Man* (John 1:51, 6:27, 8:28, 10:36, 12:23, 1:31), *the Perfect Man*—Jesus, as *the Representative of the entire Adamic Race* (Luke 3:38, John 19:5, Romans 5:13–15; 1 Corinthians 15:22 3:45) *died on the cross* during the time of Pontius Pilate (1 Timothy 6:13).

It is extremely important to know that almost every time we see the word cross in the New Testament it refers to Jesus Christ, who sacrificed Himself for the entire world through the horrible death, cruel and grotesque on the cross (see Philippians 2:8). The cross communicates the theological significance of the finished, full and complete work of Christ at Calvary.

The cross communicates the theological significance of the finished, full and complete work of Christ at Calvary.

The Apostle John writes: "When Jesus therefore had received the sour wine, He said, *"It is finished!"* And He bowed His head, and gave up His spirit" (John 19:30). The expression: *"It is finished"* used by Jesus before He gave His spirt into the hands of the Father in Greek is *tetelestai.* The verb *tetelestai* indicates an action that happened in the past and its benefits and effects continuing in the present. It is good to know that the same inscription *tetelestai* was imprinted on the Loan Certificates when the debt was paid in full.

We can say with confidence that, before He gave His spirit, Jesus declared: *Everything that humanity owes to my Father God has been paid in full.*

Paul captures this theological significance of the cross the best when he writes: "When you were dead in your transgressions and the uncircumcision of your flesh, He made you alive together with Him, having forgiven us all our transgressions, having canceled out the Certificate of Debt consisting of decrees against us, which was hostile to us; and He has taken it out of the way, having nailed it to the cross" (Colossian 2:13–14). Glory to God! Praise Jesus! ***Tetelestai***—*It is finished! It has been paid in full!*

The verb *tetelestai* indicates an action that happened in the past and its benefits and effects continue in the present.

It is clear that because of the first Adam, all men, without exception, were sentenced to death. They all became slaves to sin, have become sons of disobedience, belonging to the devil. Why? "For all have sinned and fall short of the glory of God" (Romans 3:23). We all, therefore, were born dead in sin and sons of disobedience.

Paul writes:

> And you were dead in your trespasses and sins, in which you formerly walked according to the course of this world, according to the prince of the power of the air, of the spirit that is now working in the sons of disobedience. Among them we too all formerly lived in the lusts of our flesh, indulging the desires of the flesh and of the mind, and were by nature children of wrath, even as the rest" (Ephesians 2:1–3).

We were, are and will be, ***s-a-v-e-d***. How?

- By the finished work of Christ (Acts 4:12).

- By His Sacrificial Atonement (1 John 2:2).
- By Jesus' Death (Romans 5:10, 6:10, Philippians 2:8,
- Colossians 1:22, Hebrew 2:9, 14–15, 1 Peter 3:18, Hebrew 5).
- By the precious blood of a lamb, through Christ's Resurrection from the dead (Romans 1:4, 6:5; 1 Corinthians 3:21; 2 Timothy 1:10; 1 Peter 1:3, 3:21).
- By His Ascension to the right hand of God (Ephesians 2:6).
- By the Holy Spirit (Romans 5:5; 1 Corinthians 2:12, 6:11; Ephesians 1:13).

As Paul writes:

> But God, being rich in mercy, because of His great love with which He loved us, even when we were dead in our transgressions, made us alive together with Christ (by grace you have been saved), and raised us up with Him, and seated us with Him in the heavenly places in Christ Jesus, so that in the ages to come He might show the surpassing riches of His grace in kindness toward us in Christ Jesus" (Ephesians 2:4–7).

So far, we can conclude that the cross of Christ means:

- First, the entire redemptive work accomplished historically (legally, theologically, and spiritually) in the death, burial, resurrection, and ascension of the Lord Jesus Himself (see Philippians 2:8, 9).
- Second, in a wider sense, the union of believers with Christ by grace (see Romans 6:4; Ephesians 2:5, 6).

This is the theological position stated by Watchman Nee in *The Normal Christian Life*. With this position agree many great men and women of God such as: Andrew Murray, Amy Carmichael, Oswald Chambers, Paul E. Billheimer, F.J. Huegel, L.E. Maxwell, A.W. Tozer, and others.

Paul writes so clearly:

> For it was the Father's good pleasure for all the fullness to dwell in Him, and through Him to reconcile all things to Himself, having made peace through the blood of His cross; through Him, I say, whether things on earth or things in heaven. (Colossians 1:19–22)

Effects and Benefits of the Cross in the life of Christ's disciples

1. Through the cross we have access to Christ's Resurrected Supernatural Life

Paul writes:

> Much more then, having now been justified by His blood, we shall be saved from the wrath of God through Him. For if while we were enemies we were reconciled to God through the death of His Son, much more, having been reconciled, we shall be saved by His LIFE. (Romans 5:9–10)

These two verses, at least for me, have a great legal significance. They describe two crucial stages in the process of salvation in the life of the individual.

Side A of the Cross represents the reconciliation aspect God made through the blood of Christ, through His death on the cross. The blood of Christ realized our justification. The Bible says: "having now been justified by His blood" and, "when we were enemies, we were reconciled to God through the death of His Son."

Let us imagine two chairs positioned on each side of the cross. While we were sinners we sat on the seat of God's enemies (see Colossians 1:21). If Christ would not have shed His blood for us we all would have been worthy of hell—the second death, sent to that horrible location without any questions or comments. The Word actually says: "and without shedding of blood there is no forgiveness" (Hebrews 9:22b).

Diagram 2

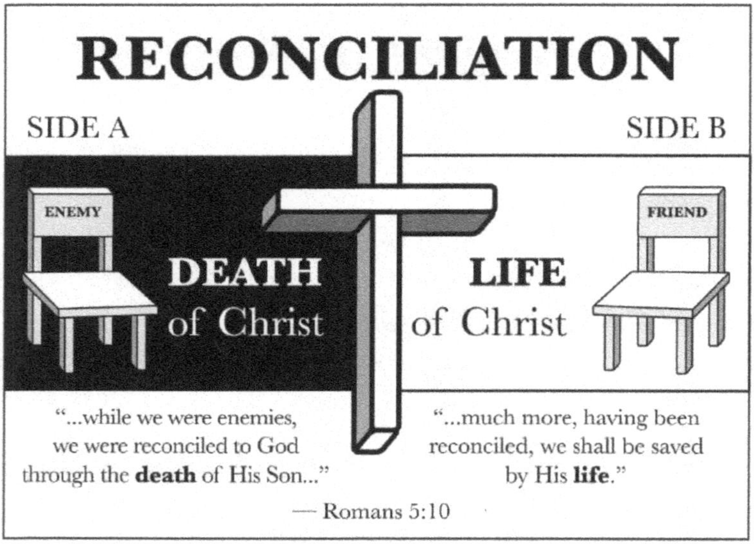
RECONCILIATION
SIDE A
SIDE B
ENEMY
FRIEND
DEATH of Christ
LIFE of Christ
"...while we were enemies, we were reconciled to God through the death of His Son..."
"...much more, having been reconciled, we shall be saved by His life."
— Romans 5:10

Side B of the Cross speaks about the salvation through Christ's Resurrected Life. ***The work of salvation is not over when we are born again.*** This is just the beginning. It is so true—we have been justified. It was very important that we have been reconciled to God by the blood of Christ. Go back to the illustration of the two chairs. In this phase, during side B of the cross, we are no longer enemies of God—we are seated as friends of God. From now on the salvation continues with the process of sanctification produced by the Resurrected life of Jesus working in our lives. Scripture tells us: "Much more, having been reconciled, we shall be saved by His life" (Romans 5:10). I call these concepts *the two sides of the Cross*. (See diagram 2).

2. The cross of Christ has transferred us from Adam into Christ

Jesus came down to earth as the Son of God—one

hundred percent God. Christ also became one hundred percent man—the Son of Man. I know it is difficult to wrap our limited human minds around these deep theological concepts, but please bear with me. With wisdom from the Holy Spirit, I hope to shed some light on this.

The Death of Jesus, as the representative of the whole human race, is crucial. The Resurrection of Christ, by the Holy Spirit, has an extraordinary significance. Please think about it. When a person expresses sincere faith in the Lord Jesus Christ, declaring that God raised Him from the dead, that person enters salvation.

Paul writes:

> That if you confess with your mouth Jesus as Lord, and believe in your heart that God raised Him from the dead, you will be saved; for with the heart a person believes, resulting in righteousness, and with the mouth he confesses, resulting in salvation. (Romans 10:9–10)

This moment is considered (John 3:3, 5) the new birth. At that moment the Holy Spirit places the person, spiritually speaking, in Christ. Now, through faith in the death and resurrection of the Lord Jesus Christ the solidarity and the union—the spiritual identification with Jesus—becomes effective.

Paul explains very nicely:

> Or do you not know that all of us who have been baptized into Christ Jesus have been baptized into His death? Therefore, we have been buried with Him through baptism into death, so that as Christ was raised from the dead through the glory of the Father, so we too might walk in newness of life. For if we have become united with Him in the likeness of His death, certainly we shall also be in the likeness of His resurrection. (Romans 6:3–5)

It makes perfect sense. To experience resurrection, one must experience death first. The body of Christ on that cross is our eternal link to the new life as beings of a new race, as citizens of Kingdom of God. We could spend more than a chapter just to unpack these verses.

Diagram 3

"The cross is thus the power of God which translates us from Adam to Christ."
– W. Nee, The Normal Christian Life, 47

The point is simple: To live a victorious life, the believer, as a disciple of Christ, must know these aspects and, by faith, experience them from the inside out. That is why I love how brother Nee explains this concept: "The cross is thus the power of God which translates us from Adam to Christ."[31] (See diagram 3).

3. Through the cross of Christ we have Victory over sin

We stated earlier that we are saved by grace alone. Paul asks a rhetorical question: "What shall we say then? Are we to continue in sin so that grace may increase?" (Romans 6:1). Then he provides the answer to it: "May it never be! How shall we who died to sin still live in it?" (Romans 6:2). Do you hear what Paul is saying? Wow! This is incredible!

Diagram 4

DEAD TO SIN
SIN
FREEDOM
"For he who has died is **freed** from sin."
– Romans 6:7

The immediate effect of the cross of Christ is the victory over the sin principle in the life of the believer. Praise the Lord! Sin itself is not dead. Instead, we—believers—through the body of Christ have died to sin. (See diagram 4). John Wesley explained it as being "[f]reed both from the guilt and from the power of it [sin]."[32]

To be sure that his audience understood it very well, Paul explains:

> Or do you not know that all of us who have been baptized into Christ Jesus have been baptized into His death? Therefore, we have been buried with Him through baptism into death, so that as Christ was raised from the dead through the glory of the Father, so we too might walk in newness of life. For if we have become united with Him in the likeness of His death, certainly we shall also be in the likeness of His resurrection. (Romans 6:3–5)

This is a very powerful statement! It cannot be more straightforward and more precise than that.

I touched on this earlier, but it is worth repeating. This is precisely the place where the devil comes and offers all sorts of religious interpretations. Some of them sound very pious; nevertheless, Satan confuses Christians causing to forget who they are in Christ and trick them into acting independently of Christ, trying to overcome sin while operating in the power of the flesh. The tragedy is that at this junction, the enemy fooled many believers.

Sin itself is not dead. Instead, we — believers — through the body of Christ have died to sin.

Every disciple of Christ should know that there are only two possibilities: (1) either humans are in Adam *and dead in sin,* (2) or in Christ and *dead to sin.*

Paul writes of believers: "Knowing this, that our old self was crucified with Him, in order that our body of sin might be done away with, so that we would no longer be slaves to sin" (Romans 6:6).

4. The cross of Christ assures us Victory over the flesh

Perhaps one of the most annoying battle Christians are facing is the battle between the flesh and Spirit. Paul writes: "For the flesh sets its desire against the Spirit, and the Spirit against the flesh; for these are in opposition to one another, so that you may not do the things that you please" (Galatians 5:17). We should understand this and not confuse the *flesh*[33] with the *human body* or the *old man*. As I said earlier, "our old self was crucified with Him" (Romans 6:6a). In fact, Paul emphasizes it: "knowing this." Knowing what? He explains it: "knowing this, that our old self was crucified with Him, in order that our body of sin might be done away with" (Romans 6:6).

Christians have flesh too. We all tried to live life based on our own resources, rather than Christ's. When Christians are not abiding in Christ and not walking according to the Spirit, they too, are living independently of God, thus operating by the flesh. Therefore, as believers, we must pay close attention to the mindset we are in and at the source of life for meeting our needs for love, acceptance, worth, and security: the flesh or Christ. If we let it, the flesh desires to dominate, control, impose its views, and lead our lives.

The bottom line is that the flesh wants to fulfill bodily desires. Paul writes: "because the mind set on the flesh is hostile toward God; for it does not subject itself to the law of God, for it is not even able to do so" (Romans 8:7).

L. E. Maxwell, in his book *Born Crucified*, writes:

> We shall discover: In our service for Christ, self-confidence and self-esteem; in the slightest suffering, self-saving and self-pity; in the least misunderstanding, self-defense and self- vindication; in our station in life, self-seeking and self-centeredness; in the smallest trials, self-inspection and self-accusation; in the daily routine, self-pleasing and self-choosing; in our relationships, self-assertiveness and self- respect; in our education, self-boasting and self-expression; in our desires, self-indulgence and self-satisfaction; in our successes, self- admiration and self-congratulation; in our failures, self-excusing and self-justification; in our spiritual attainments, self-righteousness and self-complacency; in our public ministry, self-reflection and self-glory; in life as a whole, self-love and selfishness. The flesh is an "I" specialist.[34]

I agree that this quote is difficult to understand, but it is worth reading it several times to get the point of what the author wants to convey.

The flesh has the tendency to worship its own "trinity"– "Me," "Myself," and "I." The danger of letting the flesh down from its proper location—the cross—is great. In his letter to the Galatians, after describing the deeds of the flesh, Paul concludes that: "I forewarn you, just as I have forewarned you, that those who practice such things will not inherit the kingdom of God" (Galatians 5 21b).

Diagram 5

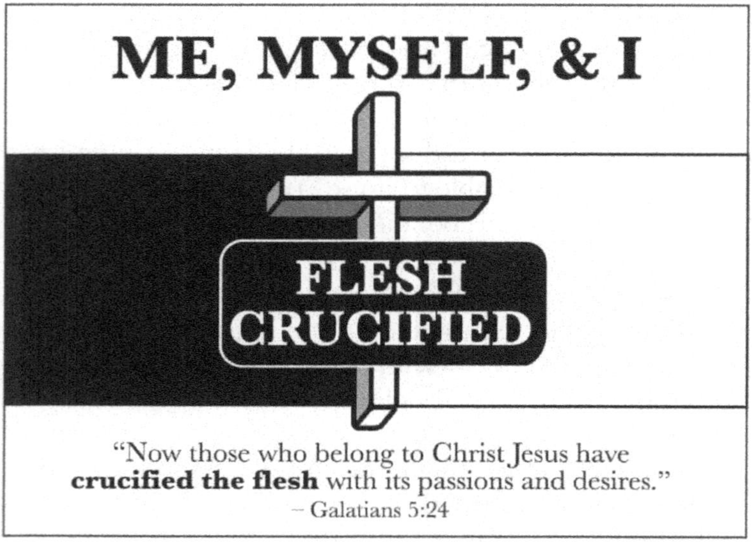
ME, MYSELF, & I
FLESH
CRUCIFIED
"Now those who belong to Christ Jesus have **crucified the flesh** with its passions and desires."
– Galatians 5:24

The flesh is like an octopus with multiple tentacles; it does not die tentacle-by-tentacle, it only dies if its head is crushed. Paul continues: "Now those who belong to Christ Jesus have crucified the flesh with its passions and desires" (Galatians 5:24). Note that the solution to the flesh is not religion, or a 12-step program, or even more theological education. The solution to the flesh is the cross—death by crucifixion with Christ.

The flesh has the tendency to worship its own "trinity"- "Me," "Myself," and "I."

When Jesus spoke, "It is finished," Christ provided the solution to the flesh as well. Paul writes: "so then, brethren, we are under obligation, not to the flesh, to live according to the flesh, for if you are living according to the flesh, you must die" (Romans 8:12). What is a Christian supposed to do? Paul gives the solution in Galatians 5:24: "Now those who belong to Christ Jesus have crucified the flesh with its passions and desires."

Based on the complete and definitive work performed by the Lord Jesus Christ at Calvary, through His body, we can have victory over the flesh. (See diagram 5). I say we can because this victory will not happen automatically. It is up to us to voluntarily surrender our body on God's altar, as Paul writes: "Therefore I urge you, brethren, by the mercies of God, to present your bodies a living and holy sacrifice, acceptable to God, which is your spiritual service of worship" (Romans 12:1). Therefore, by the Spirit, we must mortify the deeds of the body. This appears to be such a cruel statement, but nevertheless it is in the Bible.

After the Fall, the world became a system led by Satan himself.

Please let me ask you: How were the lambs sacrificed to God in the Old Testament? Of course, by putting them to death. Similarly, we have, by the Spirit, to mortify the deeds of the body. Paul explains, "but if by the Spirit you are putting to death the deeds of the body, you will live" (Romans 8:13). Only the cross offers such a Victory.

5. Through the cross of Christ we have Victory over the world

We need victory over the world. That is clear. But how? I am trying to explain how a Christian is supposed to relate to the world to ensure he or she has victory over the world. Jesus tells us: "These things I have spoken to you, so that in Me you may have peace. In the world you have tribulation, but take courage; I have overcome the world" (John 16:33). The truth is that by the cross of Christ we too have overcome the world. Why? Because we are in Christ and Christ is in us. So, whatever is true of Him is also true of us.

We must understand that, after the Fall, when Adam and Eve violated God's command, the world became a system led by Satan himself. John writes: "Now judgment is upon this world; now the ruler of this world will be cast out" (John 12:31). The world, as a system, according to the Bible, is called the domain of darkness. In Ephesians, Paul explains: "in which you formerly walked according to the course of this world, according to the prince of the power of the air, of the spirit that is now working in the sons of disobedience" (Ephesians 2:2). Both passages refer to the fact that this world is ruled by Satan, called "the ruler of this world" and "the prince of the power of the air."

The Bible urges us: "Do not love the world nor the things in the world. If anyone loves the world, the love of the Father is not in him" (1 John 2:15). Our entire loyalty must be directed towards God and His kingdom. We must not compromise or sympathize with the world. Let us not be fooled. The whole world lies in the power of the evil one, as John writes 1 John 5:19. ***Please do not confuse human beings, who need salvation, with the world as a corrupt, evil, deceiving system.*** God loves people. He has already sacrificed His Son for all mankind. The premier verse of the whole Bible confirms this fact: "For God so loved the world, that He gave His only begotten Son, that whoever believes in Him shall not perish, but have eternal life" (John 3:16).

Jesus came to destroy the works of the devil. John writes: "The Son of God appeared for this purpose, to destroy the works of the devil" (1 John 3:8). As we know, Jesus was tempted in all points, yet without sin. Therefore, Satan did not have any real claims of accusation against Him. The Bible tells us: "the ruler of the world is coming, and he has nothing in Me" (John 14:30). When Jesus gave His life on the cross, He defeated the devil himself and thus overcame the entire world system.

Jesus Himself explains this:

> How can Satan cast out Satan? If a kingdom is divided against itself, that kingdom cannot stand. If a house is divided against itself, that house will not be able to stand. If Satan has risen up against himself and is divided, he cannot stand, but he is finished! But no

> one can enter the strong man's house and plunder his property unless he first binds the strong man, and then he will plunder his house. (Mark 3:23–27)

Diagram 6

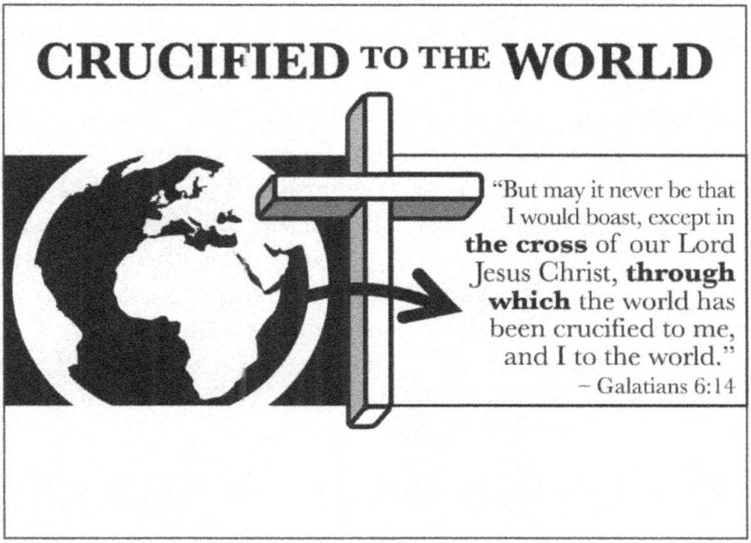

CRUCIFIED TO THE WORLD
"But may it never be that I would boast, except in the cross of our Lord Jesus Christ, through which the world has been crucified to me, and I to the world."
– Galatians 6:14

The Pharisees accused Jesus of casting out demons by the ruler of demons (see Matthew 12:24). What a stupid and unfounded accusation. I admire how clearly, and down to earth Jesus responded to those people (see Matthew 12:29 and Mark 3:23–27 quoted above). The Lord is the One who bound "the strong man," meaning Satan, plundered his house, and saved us from his dominion. Jesus defeated the devil in his own backyard. Paul explains it very well: "When He had disarmed the rulers and authorities, He made a public display of them, having triumphed over them through Him" (Colossians 2:15).

The world, as a world system, is totally in opposition to God's kingdom.

I love the way the author of Hebrews explains this:

> Therefore, since the children share in flesh and blood, He Himself likewise also partook of the same, that through death He might render powerless him who had the power of death, that is, the devil, and might free those who through fear of death were subject to slavery all their lives. (Hebrews 2:14–15)

The world, as a world system, is totally in opposition to God's kingdom. The good news is that by the cross, Jesus overcame the world. Moreover, we are separated from the world through the cross. (See diagram 6). Paul writes with great confidence: "But may it never be that I would boast, except in the cross of our Lord Jesus Christ, through which the world has been crucified to me, and I to the world" (Galatians 6:14). Therefore, as disciples of Christ, even if we are facing strong opposition from the surrounding culture, by living a crucified life, we can walk in the victory given by God through the cross of Jesus. Wow! Praise the Lord! This is very good news!

6. Through the Body of Christ on the cross we have died to the Law to live for God

Many Christians, indeed, believe salvation is by grace through faith in Jesus Christ. But when it comes to living the Christian life, they consider that it must be by works, complying to the Old Testament Law, or at least to portions of it, like the Ten Commandments.

Paul had long suffered from the so-called Judaizes—believers who lived according to Jewish customs. They did not understand the message of the Gospel and always had misinterpreted both Paul's ministry and his writings.

Moreover, having zeal without much understanding, went through the churches freshly planted by Paul and pressured Gentile believers to be circumcised and urged them to keep the Law. Luke writes about this: "Some men came down from Judea and began teaching the brethren, 'Unless you are circumcised according to the custom of Moses, you cannot be saved'" (Acts 15:1).

Because of this teaching, which spread quickly through the churches of Galatia, Paul wrote his epistle to the Galatians. To better understand Paul's argument, one should carefully read and study, through and through, the entire epistle to the Galatians.

Paul emphasizes: "But I, brethren, if I still preach circumcision, why am I still persecuted? Then the stumbling block of the cross has been abolished" (Galatians 5:11). Toward the end of this epistle Paul writes: "Those who desire to make a good showing in the flesh try to compel you to be circumcised, simply so that they will not be persecuted for the cross of Christ" (Galatians 6:12).

What cannot save us cannot sanctify us either.

Diagram 7

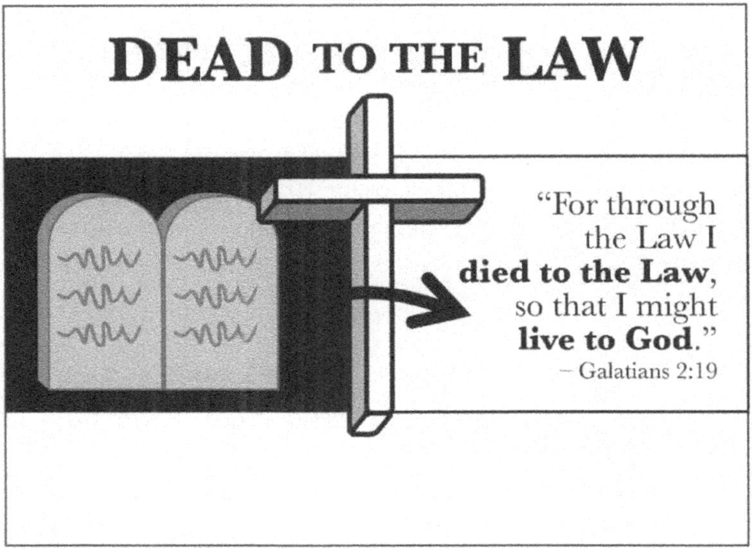
DEAD TO THE LAW
"For through the Law I **died to the Law**, so that I might **live to God**."
– Galatians 2:19

Listen carefully to what Paul says: "For those who are circumcised do not even keep the Law themselves, but they desire to have you circumcised so that they may boast in your flesh" (Galatians 6:13). Do you get now what their real motivation was?

The question Paul posed to the believers in Galatia is straightforward: "This is the only thing I want to find out from you: ***did you receive the Spirit by the works of the Law, or by hearing with faith?*** " (Galatians 3:2). I am sure that after this question, which, to the original audience, was like a cold shower, the next statement was like a deep cut to the flesh. "Are you so foolish? Having begun by the Spirit, are you now being perfected by the flesh?" (Galatians 3:3). Do you understand what kind of danger the believers in Galatia faced?

Many believers in our days as well focus on their efforts to living the Christian life rather than cultivating a real intimacy with the Holy Spirit. Please remember: *What cannot save us cannot sanctify us either.* If only Jesus can save, then only He can sanctify us.

I like the way Paul explains this concept: "Therefore, my brethren, you also were made to die to the Law through the body of Christ, so that you might be joined to another, to Him who was raised from the dead, in order that we might bear fruit for God" (Romans 7:4). He explains it so clearly to the Galatians: "For through the Law I died to the Law, so that I might live to God" (Galatians 2:19). I urge you to pay attention to this verse, especially as part of the context of Galatians 2:20, one of the most famous verses in the letter to the Galatians.

7. Through the cross of Christ we are transferred from the Domain of Darkness into the Kingdom of Light

Through the cross of Christ, we were transferred from the domain of darkness into the Kingdom of Light. (See diagram 8). The domain of darkness is led by the prince of darkness—*Satan.* The Kingdom of Light is led by the Prince of Light—*Jesus* Christ. These are the words of Jesus: "I am the Light of the world; he who follows Me will not walk in the darkness, but will have the Light of life" (John 8:12). Paul proclaims this truth with passion: "For He rescued us from the domain of darkness, and transferred us to the kingdom of His beloved Son" (Colossians 1:13).

Before the spiritual rebirth we lived in darkness, but now the situation is totally different. Paul explains: "for you were formerly darkness" (Ephesians 5:8a). Now we are part of the light, as it is written: "but now you are Light" (Ephesians 5:8b). Therefore, we are exhorted to walk and live as such, namely, "walk as children of Light" (Ephesians 5:8c). This walk is evidenced by various fruits of the Light, such as: all goodness and righteousness and truth.

Diagram 8

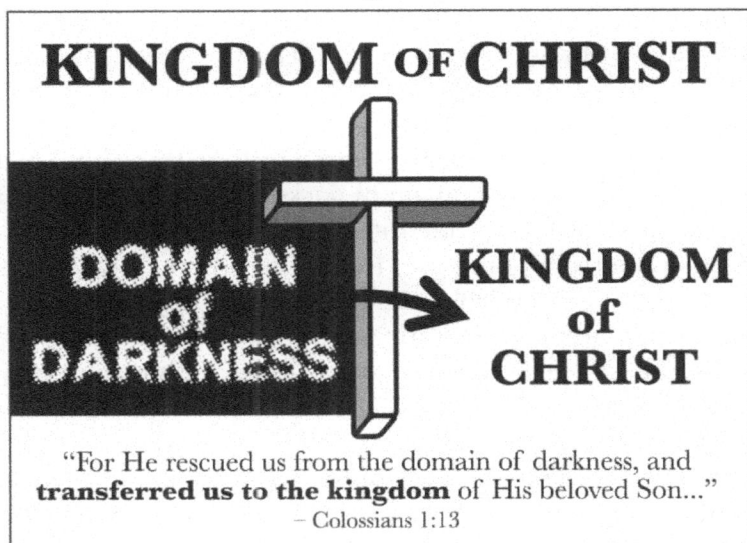

"For He rescued us from the domain of darkness, and **transferred us to the kingdom** of His beloved Son..."
– Colossians 1:13

Due to the wonderful work carried out by Christ on the cross of Calvary, our eyes, once blinded by the enemy of our souls, have been enlightened by the Word, through the Spirit. So, we came back "from darkness to light and from the dominion of Satan to God" (Acts 26:18).

Praise God! Because of the finished work of Christ at the cross, now "you are all sons of light and sons of day" (1 Thessalonians 5: 5). I am urging all readers to pay attention to the tense of the verb Paul uses "are" (*present tense*), not "will be" (*future tense*). What a privilege! Now we belong to God. We are a chosen race, a royal priesthood, a holy nation, a people for God, chosen by Him to be His own possession (cf. 1 Peter 2:9). What an honor! Now we are called to proclaim: "the excellencies of Him who has called [us] out of darkness into His marvelous light" (1 Peter 2:9b). Wow! What a Gospel!

As children of light, we are in the process of laying aside "the old self with its evil practices" (Colossians 3:9) "inherited from [y]our forefathers" (1 Peter 1:18) while living in the domain of darkness, and putting on "the new self who is being renewed according to the image of Christ" (Colossians 3:10).

Moreover, we are called to "put on the armor of light" (Romans 13:12). Ultimately, we are exhorted to "put on the Lord Jesus Christ" (Romans 13:14). Therefore, we are instructed to have nothing to do with "the unfruitful deeds of darkness, but instead even expose them" (Ephesians 5:11).

Of course, throughout the Church history, there has been a struggle between the domain of darkness and the Kingdom of light, and it will continue to be until the return of Christ. But let's understand once and for all that the real struggle is not against "flesh and blood;" but it is "against the rulers, against the powers, against the world forces of this darkness, against the spiritual forces of wickedness in the heavenly places" (Ephesians 6:12).

The good news is Christ has defeated all these spiritual forces. Through Him, because of the cross, we are victorious. I mentioned this before, but it is worth repeating: "When He had disarmed the rulers and authorities, He made a public display of them, having triumphed over them through Him" (Colossians 2:15).

In conclusion, we can state with confidence, in Christ, despite all opposition, we are more than conquerors.

I suggest reading the following passage out loud:

> But in all these things we overwhelmingly conquer through Him who loved us. For I am convinced that neither death, nor life, nor angels, nor principalities, nor things present, nor things to come, nor powers,

nor height, nor depth, nor any other created thing, will be able to separate us from the love of God, which is in Christ Jesus our Lord. (Romans 8:37–39)

Reflection Questions

Please reflect upon the following questions, briefly elaborate, and then share your thoughts with a friend or your small group.

1. What did the Holy Spirit whisper to your heart through this chapter? What did you like the most from this chapter?

2. What new concepts and ideas did you learn from this chapter? Which concept are you committed to implementing in your life?

3. What do you think about the relationship between faith and the cross of Christ? What about the centrality and significance of the cross?

4. Please elaborate on the effects and the benefits of the cross. Use additional space if necessary:
Effect 1:

Effect 2:

Effect 3:

Effect 4:

Effect 5:

Effect 6:

Effect 7:

5. List the biggest aha moments you had while reading this chapter.

Endnotes:

[26] Dietrich Bonhoeffer, *The Cost of Discipleship,* trans. R.H. Fuller, rev. ed. (Macmillan, New York: 1959), 45.
[27] Type: a simple definition could be: A type is a shadow cast on the pages of the Old Testament history by a truth whose full embodiment or antitype is found in the New Testament revelation. Simple explanation: Types are prophetic in nature. Types are designed as an integral part of redemptive history. Types, in one way or another, point to Christ.
[28] For a longer list of the types of Christ, feel free to consult Torrey's book, *The New Topical Text Book,* 1897.
[29] Valy Vaduva, "Three Kinds of Disciples," Audio, (Ypsilanti, MI: Upper Room Fellowship Ministry, 2007).
[30] A.W. Tozer, *Man—The Dwelling Place of God,* accessed on May 20, 2017, https://www.worldinvisible.com/library/ tozer/5j00.0010/5j00.0010.10.htm.
[31] Watchman Nee, *The Normal Christian Life,* (Wheaton, IL: Tyndale House, 1977), 47.
[32] Brandon O'Brien, "What does it mean to be dead to sin?" www.christianitytoday.com. Accessed on April 21, 2015. http://www.christianitytoday.com/biblestudies/ bible-answers/theology/dead-to-sin.html.
[33] For more explanations about the flesh please read Chapter 6 "Sarx Blocks Spiritual Metamorphosis," from my *The Journey of Transformation: Becoming Like Christ Through Spiritual Metamorphosis. Click on https://bit.ly/41HPFfp to buy it on Amazon.*
[34] L.E. Maxwell, *Born Crucified,* (Moody Press, Chicago, IL: 1973), 86, 87.

-6-

A New Heart

Moreover, I will give you a new heart and put a new spirit within you; and I will remove the heart of stone from your flesh and give you a heart of flesh.
—Ezekiel 36:26

"But this is the covenant which I will make with the house of Israel after those days," declares the LORD, "I will put My law within them and on their heart I will write it; and I will be their God, and they shall be My people."
—Jeremiah 31:33— James 1:2

A while back the Holy Spirit prompted me to look carefully into the subject of the heart. It was a wonderful experience studying and reflecting on God's Word. The Lord spoke to me deeply and clearly through His Word! Glory to Him!

A Person's Heart

I was amazed with the fact that the word "heart," (Hebrew lebab/leb, Greek kardia), appears more than 750 times in the Bible, making it the most common anthropological term in the Scripture. This should make us all think that God is very interested in a person's heart and the real status of their spiritual being. I need to make a distinction that, with very few exceptions, when the Bible talks about heart, it does not refer to the internal organ of the circulatory system that ensures blood circulation.

When the Word of God talks about the heart it refers to a person's center for both physical and emotional-intellectual-moral activities. In essence, the heart is the most vital and innermost part of a human being; what a person is in his or her essence; the center of all emotions, dispositions, and inclinations; the innermost character, personality, and human attributes. The heart treasures the most profound sentiments (affectionate love, generosity, compassion, courage, and enthusiasm), thoughts, and devotions of a person.[35] Sometimes it is used figuratively for any inaccessible thing hidden deep in the inner part of a human being. Keep in mind this crucial distinction when you read the Bible. The Holy Spirit dwells in the new heart when we are born again. Through this kind of heart, God's children can communicate with their heavenly Father.

The heart is the most vital and innermost part of a human being, the center of all emotions, dispositions, and inclinations.

Let's journey together through various Bible passages and see what God wants to reveal about our hearts.

Before we start this journey, I would like to share with you what the Holy Spirit impressed upon my heart. He drew my attention to three passages from the Old Testament:

- Joshua 15:13–20
- 1 Chronicles 4:9-10
- 1 Chronicles 12:32

After reading these passages fifty times, I prayed for wisdom and understanding so I can live from the center of my heart as a true disciple. I also prayed for knowledge and discernment to understand how the Church can prepare for Christ's return while advancing the Kingdom of God.

A Clean Heart

The passage from Joshua 14:6–14 expressly spoke to me. Please open your Bible and read the verses right now so as to familiarize yourself with the story.

In verse 7 Caleb declared: "I was forty years old when Moses the servant of the LORD sent me from Kadesh-Barnea to spy out the land, and I brought word back to him as it was in my heart." This verse pierced deeply in my heart, especially the second part of the verse. The NIV renders the last part of the verse this way: "According to my convictions." The Contemporary English Version (CEV) reads: "Everything I said was true." Good News Translation (GNT) communicates it this way: "an honest report." God's Word Translation (GW) states: "I reported to him exactly what I thought." The Message writes: "An honest and accurate report." Lastly, the Romanian Bible renders it like this" "According to my clean heart." These little details are extremely important!

Caleb's honest (and clean) heart saved him from death and gave him favor in God's eyes. This made a huge difference in the course of history. Think about it: from a group of more than one million people, only Caleb and Joshua entered the Promised Land. This fact made me determined to study the subject of a Person's Heart, especially:

1. What makes the Heart Unclean and Hard and
2. How we can have a Clean and Pliable Heart.

If an honest and clean heart set Caleb apart so drastic--ally from the rest of the Israeli leaders, it means that God is extremely interested in the condition of our hearts. So, I went on an exploration journey. What the Bible revealed to me is phenomenal!

God desires to develop leaders: disciples who are capable to change the course of history. Numbers 13:1–2 tells us about the men who were sent to explore the land of Canaan. Note that these people were not ordinary men, they were leaders among their tribes.

When God sends us into the mission field to do His work, He wishes for us to look at the *fruit*, not at the *obstacles*. According to Numbers 13:17–20, the exploration of the land took place during "the time of the first ripe grapes." The Holy Spirit helped me understand that God could have sent them to that land during any season but the Lord of time and eternity, who knows the end from the beginning, intentionally selected this season—*of the first ripe grapes*.

Every time we want or expect success in ministry, we should also expect great opposition or obstacles.

The fruits are directly proportional to the obstacles (in this case, giants). The Bible tells us that the spies followed Moses' commands, which were coming directly from God. Please carefully read Numbers 13:21–27. We can clearly understand that all the Israeli leaders saw the same things:

(a) *Giants* (verse 22),
(b) *Very large fruits* (verse 23).

This impressed me very much. The Spirit of God opened my eyes to understand that every time we want or expect success in ministry (i.e., large fruits), we should also expect great opposition or obstacles (i.e., giants). When leaders have fearful and unclean hearts, they can only see the obstacles rather than victory in God's name. What especially surprised me was the report given by these ten leaders to Moses and the people. Hewrites:

> But the people who live there are powerful, and the cities are fortified and very large. We even saw descendants of Anak there." But the men who had gone up with him said, "We are not able to go up against the people, for they are too strong for us. (Numbers 13:28–29, 31).

However, what is even more impressive is the *minority report*. The two leaders with honest (and clean) hearts saw God's victory greater than any obstacle. Let us read: "Then Caleb silenced the people before Moses, and said, "We should go up and take possession of the land, for we can certainly do it"" (Numbers 13:30).

Leaders with fearful (and unclean) hearts deform, twist, and exaggerate reality and frighten the already weak hearts of the people.

The Word of God tells us:

> So, they gave out to the sons of Israel a bad report of the land which they had spied out, saying, "The land through which we have gone, in spying it out, is a land that devours its inhabitants; and all the people whom we saw in it are men of great size. There also we saw the Nephilim (the sons of Anak are part of the Nephilim); and we became like grasshoppers in our own sight, and so we were in their sight." (Numbers 13:32–33)

Based on the negative report given by the majority, the Israelites wished to *die* rather than *live*. Hard to believe, isn't it? Moses writes:

> Then all the congregation lifted up their voices and cried, and the people wept that night. All the sons of Israel grumbled against Moses and Aaron; and the whole congregation said to them, "Would that we had died in the land of Egypt! Or would that we had died in this wilderness!" (Numbers 14:1–2).

Wow! What a sad story! People with a fearful and unclean heart, prophesy with their own mouths about their own fate—*death in the wilderness*. Beware: Spoken words, reports, and declarations have power over our lives and could influence our future.

Here are their own words: "Why is the LORD bringing us

into this land, to fall by the sword? Our wives and our little ones will become plunder" (Numbers 14:3a).

Moreover, people with a fearful heart prefer to return to Egypt rather than trusting in God and fighting for His promises: "Is it not good for us to return to Egypt?" (Numbers 14:3b).

Let's keep in mind the application for us today—Egypt symbolizes the World. If we are not careful with what is going on in our hearts we can be paralyzed by fear of people or the unknown. We too may get overwhelmed by the "giants" and start making compromises with the world.

The good news is that the leaders with an honest and hopeful heart take a radical position of obedience towards God to avoid compromise, despite opposition from the multitudes. The Scripture teaches us: "Joshua the son of Nun and Caleb the son of Jephunneh, of those who had spied out the land, tore their clothes" (Numbers 14:6).

Moreover, in critical situations, visionary leaders do their best to direct the hearts of people toward obedience and radical trust in God. Listen to these words: "Only do not rebel against the LORD; and do not fear the people of the land, for they will be our prey. Their protection has been removed from them, and the LORD is with us; do not fear them" (Numbers 14:9). By doing this, people of good intent are always in danger from the multitudes. Let us read: "And all the congregation said to stone them with stones" (Numbers 14:10a). However, the leaders with an honest heart are saved by the glory of God. The Bible testifies: "And the glory of Jehovah appeared in the tabernacle of the congregation, to all the sons of Israel" (Numbers 14:10b).

I found it very interesting and at the same time even scary that the people with an unclean heart self-prophesied destruction. Indeed, that is exactly what happened. People who followed the leaders with unclean hearts did not see the victory of the Lord and died in the desert.

The Bible tells us:

> Say to them, As I live says the LORD: just as you have

> spoken in My hearing, so I will surely do to you; your corpses will fall in this wilderness, even all your numbered men, according to your complete number from twenty years old and upward, who have grumbled against Me. Surely you shall not come into the land in which I swore to settle you, except Caleb the son of Jephunneh and Joshua the son of Nun. (Numbers 14:28–30)

Additionally, the leaders who brought the negative report to the multitudes, a report that was against God's promises, died a terrible death.

Joshua tells us:

> As for the men whom Moses sent to spy out the land and who returned and made all the congregation grumble against him by bringing out a bad report concerning the land, even those men who brought out the very bad report of the land died by a plague before the LORD. (Numbers 14:36–37)

All over the Bible we find record upon record that testifies God's faithfulness and goodness. He knows men from inside out. God rewards those with a clean heart. In Numbers it is written: "But Joshua the son of Nun and Caleb the son of Jephunneh remained alive out of those men who went to spy out the land" (Numbers 14:38).

We can conclude that purity of heart is a guarantee for God's blessing. Jesus tells us: "Blessed are the pure in heart! For they shall see God" (Matthew 5:8).

Sickness of the Heart

Based on Numbers chapters 14 and 15, we see how the heart can be problematic; actually, the heart is quite sick. If we are not yet convinced, let's look at other passages. The book of Genesis records that after Adam and Eve fell into sin, the mind of man was driven towards evil. Moses writes: "Then the LORD saw that the wickedness of man was great on the earth, and that every intent of the thoughts of his heart was only evil continually" (Genesis 6:5). Wow!

God Himself testifies that people are inclined towards evil even from their youth. This signifies that the sickness of the heart is hereditary. The Bible tells us:

> The LORD smelled the soothing aroma; and the LORD said to Himself, "I will never again curse the ground on account of man, for the intent of man's heart is evil from his youth; and I will never again destroy every living thing, as I have done." (Genesis 8:21)

We have many other Bible verses which indicate that people suffer from a hereditary "sickness of the heart." For example: Proverbs 6:14, 11:20, Jeremiah 17:9; Ezekiel 11:21; Hosea 5:4, 7:2; Matthew 12:34, 15:18–19; Mark 7:6, 21; Romans 2:5, Ephesians 4:18; and Hebrews 3:10, among other passages.

Fatal Sickness

After mankind fell into sin, all began to suffer from sickness of the heart until the present day. Something inside mankind rotted beyond their ability to repair with their own resources or efforts. The psalmist writes: "For the redemption of his soul is costly, and he should cease trying forever" (Psalm 49:8). Even though this is repeated somewhere else, it is important to state it here too: Theologians call this state of being spiritual death.

This "sickness of the heart" affects millions upon millions of people, and if not dealt with properly it will be fatal!

The apostle Paul explains this concept very clearly in the book of Ephesians:

> And you being dead in deviations and sins, in which

> you formerly walked according to the course of this world, according to the ruler of the authority of the air, the spirit now working in the sons of disobedience, among whom we also all conducted ourselves in times past in the lusts of our flesh, doing the things willed of the flesh and of the understanding, and were by nature the children of wrath, even as the rest. (Ephesians 2:1–3)

The Old Testament Law could not offer any solution to this kind of heartsickness. Therefore, humanity is totally lost. Paul explains: "Nevertheless knowing that a man is not justified by the works of the Law … since by the works of the Law no flesh will be justified" (Galatians 2:16). Another New Testament writer tells us: "Not like the Covenant which I made with their fathers on the day when I took them by the hand to lead them out of the land of Egypt, for they did not continue in My Covenant, and I did not care for them, says the Lord" (Hebrews 8:9).

As you may have observed, the problem was and still is extremely serious. This "sickness of the heart" affects millions upon millions of people, and if not dealt with properly it will be fatal!

The Big Solution

After the fall, the Creator took a close look at the condition of mankind and declared that this kind of spiritual battle cannot continue forever. In the book of Genesis, we are told the following: "Then the LORD said, "My Spirit shall not strive with man forever, because he also is flesh" (Genesis 6:3).

I could imagine that the Great Physician, Jesus Christ, also took a look at mankind's condition, and full of an infinite love declared: "There is a solution!"

All the angels asked: "What solution, what solution?"

The Great Physician answered: "A heart transplant! We just must find a donor to save mankind."

I could imagine that when the conversation came to this

moment there was a great silence in heaven. No one offered to be a donor! I could imagine that the heart of the Father God agonized: "Whom shall I send, and who will go for Us?" At this point the Great Physician said the monumental words: "Father, "Here am I. Send me!" (Isaiah 6:8).

The solution for "healing" mankind cost the Creator the very life of His only beloved Son. Here is the heart of God and the spiritual center of the entire Bible: "For God so loved the world that He gave His only begotten Son, that whoever believes in Him shall not perish, but have eternal life" (John 3:16).

The solution for "healing mankind cost the Creator the very life of His only beloved Son.

The Heart Transplant

The Old Testament prophets of God foretold this phenomenal heart transplant God had in mind. Probably one of the clearest prophesies is in Ezekiel 36:26–27:

> Moreover, I will give you a new heart and put a new spirit within you; <u>and I will remove the heart of stone from your flesh and give you a heart of flesh</u>. I will put My Spirit within you and cause you to walk in My statutes, and you will be careful to observe My ordinances.

I underlined the phrase that the prophet used to describe God's extraordinary act to emphasize the spiritual concept of heart transplant. Ezekiel is not the only prophet who prophesied about this phenomenon.

Jeremiah spoke regarding this as well in chapter 31:31–34:

> "Behold, days are coming," declares the LORD, "when I will make a new covenant with the house of Israel and with the house of Judah, not like the

> covenant which I made with their fathers in the day I took them by the hand to bring them out of the land of Egypt, My covenant which they broke, although I was a husband to them," declares the LORD. "But this is the covenant which I will make with the house of Israel after those days," declares the LORD, "I will put My law within them and on their heart I will write it; and I will be their God, and they shall be My people. They will not teach again, each man his neighbor and each man his brother, saying, "Know the LORD," for they will all know Me, from the least of them to the greatest of them," declares the LORD, "for I will forgive their iniquity, and their sin I will remember no more."

These truths are re-affirmed in the New Testament by the author of the book of Hebrews:

> This is the covenant that I will make with them after those days, says the Lord: "I will put my laws upon their heart and on their mind, I will write them." He then says, "and their sins and their lawless deeds I will remember no more." (Hebrews 10:16–17)

Wow! Isn't this extraordinary? Of course, it is! Praise the Lord! Only God can do something like this.

A New Creation

The person who encounters God by faith and enters in a Covenant relationship with Him, through Jesus Christ, becomes a completely new creature.

- The Old Testament Law was not able to do that.
- Religion, whichever that may be, cannot do this.
- Evolution, no matter how many billions of years we allocate to it, cannot accomplish this.
- No human effort, no matter how brilliant it may be,

can perfect the human condition.

Only God can! And He did it already. It is His marvelous Gift in the Person of His Son—Jesus Christ.
We cannot work for this Gift. All we can do is receive it through faith, agreeing with God's Word that Jesus finished it all at Calvary two thousand years ago. This is done on the basis of true repentance, admitting that we are at fault, agreeing that by birth we were deep in sin. This is clearly stated by the apostle Paul.

He writes:

> For by grace, you have been saved through faith; and that not of yourselves, it is the gift of God; not as a result of works, so that no one may boast. (Ephesians 2:8–9)

In other words, because of our relationship with Jesus Christ, we experience this phenomenal transformation. He is the only One who completely renews our being. Let us read: "Therefore, if anyone is in Christ, he is a new creature; the old things passed away; behold, new things have come." (2 Corinthians 5:17). Actually, in light of this verse, God re-created us.

The person who encounters God by faith and enters in a Covenant relationship with Him, through Jesus Christ, becomes a completely new creature.

Conclusions

1. Being a new creation in Christ is more than having all sins forgiven

Forgiveness of our sins is important. Receiving the promise of heaven when we die is a good thing, but being a new creation is something wonderful that we cannot dare water down.

I like the way David Needham writes:

> Contrary to much popular teaching, becoming a Christian is more than having something taken away (sins forgiven), or having something added to you (a new nature plus the assistance of the Holy Spirit); it is becoming someone you had never been before. It is justification + reconciliation and regeneration.[36]

2. The new heart determines what we do

The Gospel of Christ is not about behavior modification. Jesus did not come to reinforce the Law of Moses; He came to give us new life, new direction, and new destiny. God, through the Holy Spirit, is in the business of total transformation from the inside out.

Neil T. Anderson writes:

> Understanding your identity in Christ is essential for living the Christian life. People cannot consistently behave in ways that are inconsistent with the way they perceive themselves. You don't change yourself by your perception. You change your perception of yourself by believing the truth. If you perceive yourself wrongly, you will live wrongly because what you are believing is not true. If you think you are a no-good bum, you will probably live like a no-good bum. If, however, you see yourself as a child of God who is spiritually alive in Christ, you will begin to live accordingly. Next to knowledge of God, a knowledge of who you are is by far the most important truth you can possess.[37]

Reflection Questions

Please reflect upon the following questions, briefly elaborate, and then share your thoughts with a friend or your small group.

1. What did the Holy Spirit whisper to your heart through this chapter? What did you like the most from this chapter?

2. What new concepts and ideas did you learn from this chapter? Which concept are you committed to implementing in your life?

3. What does it mean to be born with a "sick heart"? What is the main reason for this "fatal sickness"?

4. In your own words, please elaborate and share the following theological concepts:
4.1. What does it mean to receive a spiritual heart transplant? Please describe it and briefly elaborate.

4.2. What does it mean to be a new creation? Please briefly elaborate.

5. List the best aha moments you had while reading this chapter.

Endnotes:

[35] Heart. www.merriam-webster.com. https://www.merriam-webster.com/dictionary/heart (Accessed on February 27, 2018). Note: Author's adaptation of the Webster's definition.
[36] David Needham, *Alive for the First Time*, (Sisters, OR: Questar Publishers, 1995), pp. 72, 73.
[37] Neil T. Anderson, *Victory over the Darkness*, (Ventura, CA: Regal Books, 2000), p. 47.

-7-

The Greatest Exchange Ever

Yet those who wait for the LORD Will gain new strength;
They will mount up with wings like eagles, they will run and not get tired, they will walk and not become weary.
—Isaiah 40:31

"I have been crucified with Christ; and it is no longer I who live, but Christ lives in me; and the life which I now live in the flesh I live by faith in the Son of God, who loved me and gave Himself up for me."
—Galatians 2:20

The exchanged life is the great exchange that took place at the CROSS. In Christ, during the crucifixion of the Son of God, the entire Adamic race was crucified. Whoever accepts Jesus Christ as life experiences the exchanged life of his or her self-centeredness for Christ-sufficiency.

Paul gets to the heart of what the exchanged life is all about when he writes: "I have been crucified with Christ; and it is no longer I who live, but Christ lives in me; and the life which I now live in the flesh I live by faith in the Son of God, who loved me and gave Himself up for me" (Galatians 2:20). This statement is phenomenal! Paul is conveying that he has been united with Christ on the cross on all aspects: death, burial, resurrection, and ascension. This is not a metaphor, but a deep spiritual reality.

I also like the way Richard F. Hall puts it:

> The exchanged life is the exchange (with Christ at the cross) of a self-centered life lived out of the Christian's own resources, as if he were still in Adam, for a Christ-centered life lived out of Christ's resources because he (the Christian) is in Christ.[38]38

In a nutshell this is the exchanged life.

The Exchanged Life

The term "exchanged life" is taken from the well-known passage in Isaiah 40:31. English translations refer to those who wait on or hope in the Lord as being able to renew their strength. Some commentaries and study Bibles that deal with this verse note that the literal translations of the Hebrew word for renew is exchange. Those who wait on the Lord will exchange their strength for His strength, as stated in verses 25– 30. J. Hudson Taylor made the English term "exchanged life" popular through his testimony of how God made him a new man in chapter 14 of the book titled, Hudson Taylor's Spiritual Secret.[39]

Other Christian authors who wrote on the subject of the exchanged life call it the deeper life with Christ. For example:

- Watchman Nee calls this kind of life the normal Christian life.
- Andrew Murray, a well-known author, calls it the deeper life.
- Hannah Whitall Smith, who wrote at the end of the nineteenth and beginning of the twentieth centuries, calls this kind of life the happy life of a Christian.
- Gene Edwards calls it the highest life.
- Major Ian Thomas refers to it as the saving LIFE of Christ.
- Dr. Charles Solomon, in the mid 60's and early 70's, coined the term Spirituotherapy, which became

known as Exchanged Life Counseling.

- Yet others call it the abiding life, the victorious life, or the abundant life.

No matter what name or title or description you would like to use to describe it, this kind of life is for every born-again believer. This life is not for a special group of elite Christians. Every genuine child of God is destined "in Christ" to experience and live it here on earth and then exponentially more in eternity. As I mentioned above, the first prophetic glimpse of this can be found in the Old Testament in the book of Isaiah:

> But those who wait for the Lord [who expect, look for, and hope in Him] shall change and renew [exchange] their strength and power; they shall lift their wings and mount up [close to God] as eagles [mount up to the sun]; they shall run and not be weary, they shall walk and not faint or become tired (Isaiah 40:31 AMP).

Paul explains this in New Covenant terms in Galatians 2:20:

> I have been crucified with Christ; and it is no longer I who live, but Christ lives in me; and the life which I now live in the flesh I live by faith in the Son of God, who loved me and gave Himself up for me.

The first "I" references the "old Paul" he used to be in Adam. That old "I" died with Christ. It was a real crucifixion of heart and will. But Christ did not remain in the tomb. Everybody knows that! He was raised from the dead. Then, at the resurrection, Paul, who was in Christ, came to life too. In Romans he writes: "For if we have become united with Him in the likeness of His

Every genuine child of God is destined to experience the Exchanged Life.

death, certainly we shall also be in the likeness of His resurrection" (Romans 6:5). Furthermore, he can enjoy a brand-new life now. Paul explains: "so that as Christ was raised from the dead through the glory of the Father, so we too might walk in newness of life" (Romans 6:4).

Based on this fact Paul declares: "Christ lives in me." This new life is not like the old one, dependent on the personal struggling efforts of a religious person trying to draw near to God in his own righteousness. This is a completely new life having its source in the True Vine— Christ Himself. Jesus tells us: "I am the vine, you are the branches" (John 15:5).

Paul continues: "and the life which "I" now live in the flesh "I" live by faith in the Son of God, who loved me and gave Himself up for me." The second "I" here refers to the "new Paul," not an "improved Paul" or Paul who is now "converted to the Way." No. The second "I" means a new creation in Christ—the "new Paul" who, spiritually speaking never existed before.

In 2 Corinthians 5:17, he captures this concept very well: "Therefore if anyone is in Christ, he is a new creature; the old things passed away; behold, new things have come." These are facts and must be known by all Christians. These are part of a past "transaction" which has been recorded in the "heavenly accounting books." Let us look at Romans 6:6: "Knowing this, that our old self was crucified with Him."

The beauty of Galatians 2:20 is that these wonderful truths hidden in this Scripture are for us as well.

I—the "old Valy" have been crucified with Christ, the "old Valy" is dead. I—the "new Valy," has Christ as the source of life and now I live by the faith of the Son of God. Isn't that what Paul is saying?

In the second letter to the Corinthians, Paul explains:

> For the love of Christ controls us, having concluded this, that one died for all, therefore all died; and He died for all, so that they who live might no longer live for themselves, but for Him who died and rose again on their behalf. (2 Corinthians 5:14–15)

As I mentioned earlier, J. Hudson Taylor is the one who, in a sense, coined the term exchange life. In his letter to his sister, Amelia, sent from Chinkiang, China on October 17, 1869, Hudson writes:

> I am no better than before. In a sense, I do not wish to be, nor am I striving to be. But I am dead and buried with Christ—aye, and risen too and ascended. And now Christ lives in me, and *"the life that I now live in the flesh, I live by the faith of the Son of God, Who loved me, and gave Himself for me."*[40]

Those who study the *"exchanged life"* realize that there are some important stages leading to this deeper life in Christ. Based on my own studies and the way I perceived the Holy Spirit's guidance regarding this spiritual reality these stages are as follows:

First, there is a personal realization of the failure (or bankruptcy) of their own flesh. Christians moving towards the deeper and abundant life have to realize first the failure and bankruptcy of their own flesh.

Paul describes this agony in his letter to the Romans. He writes: "For I know that nothing good dwells in me, that is, in my flesh; for the willing is present in me, but the doing of the good is not" (Romans 7:18). When a Christian realizes that no matter what he is doing is falling short of God's expectation for holiness of all that he in his life with Christ.

Second, there is a readiness to surrender and a willingness to embrace the cross. The Christian who is overwhelmed with this "spiritual sense of inadequacy" before God is finally ready to meet the Risen Savior with a surrendered heart at the foot of the cross.

Paul expresses very well this agony of the soul: "Wretched man that I am! Who will set me free from the body of this death?" (Romans 7:24).

These are the words of Taylor before he experienced the exchanged life:

> Every day, almost every hour, the consciousness of sin oppressed me. I knew that if I could only abide in Christ all would be well, but I could not ... I hated myself; I hated my sin; and yet I gained no strength against it.[41]

It sounds pretty similar to Paul's words from Romans 7, doesn't it?

Third, there is an appropriation of the resurrected life of Jesus. At this point, through the abiding presence of the Holy Spirit, the Christian appropriates, by faith, the resurrection life of Christ. Paul writes: That I may know Him and the power of His resurrection and the fellowship of His sufferings, being conformed to His death" (Philippians 3:10). At this stage in walking with Christ the promise of Jesus from John 7:37–39 is experienced. Now: "From his innermost being will flow rivers of living water." This is the exchanged life; this is the deeper life; this is the normal Christian life that these beloved authors experienced and wrote about. And this is exactly the type of life Jesus would like for you and me to experience in the here and now. Christ paid for it: "I came that they may have and enjoy life, and have it in abundance (to the full, till it overflows)" (John 10:10(b) AMP). Why not live it?

Fourth, we need spiritual friends or mentors appointed by God. Many times, ordinary people like you and I need a mentor or a spiritual friend to show us the path towards this deeper life.

In Hudson Taylor's case God used John McCarthy to help Hudson move to the stage of rest in Christ despite the life of struggle and turmoil.

Regarding this experience Taylor writes:

> When my agony of soul was at its height, a sentence, "*abiding, not striving not struggling,*" in a letter from dear McCarthy was used to remove the scales from my eyes, and the Spirit of God revealed the truth of our *oneness with Jesus* as I had never known it before."[42]

The secret is in abiding, not in struggling; in trusting and resting. From this position of abiding in Christ, trusting Him, and resting in Him flows all power to serve Him and rejoice in Him.

After Hudson experienced this exchange his fellow-missionaries stated about him: "Mr. Taylor went out, a new man in a new world, to tell what the Lord had done for his soul."[43] Powerful, isn't it?

This is what true oneness with Christ causes in a disciple who reads Galatians 2:20 for the first time from this perspective. There is a special rest that comes from the full identification with Christ in His death, burial, resurrection, and ascension. This is our true life— Christ's life.

Paul writes:

> For you have died and your life is hidden with Christ in God. When Christ, who is our life, is revealed, then you also will be revealed with Him in glory. (Colossians 3:3– 4)

Taylor writes:

> The sweetest part, if one may speak of one part being sweeter than another, is the rest which full identification with Christ brings. I am no longer anxious about anything, as I realize this; for He, I know, is able to carry out His will, and His will is mine.[44]

This is a full consecration of the thoughts and affections to Christ. This is a complete surrender of the whole being to Him. This is constant looking to Him for grace. This is the exchanged life, the abiding life, the fruitful life in Christ. This is the abundant life Christ promises in John 10:10. Would you receive it?

Taylor continues:

> And further—walking more in the light, my

> conscience has been more tender; sin has been instantly seen, confessed, pardoned; and peace and joy (with humility) instantly restored.[45]

Hudson Taylor experienced this by faith more than one hundred years ago in China. Why not make it, by faith, your experience too? My fervent prayer is that all of my readers, in God's timing, will experience this kind of exchanged life, abiding life, and fruitful life in Christ. Remember, this is the birthright of every child of God.

Reflection Questions

Please reflect upon the following questions, briefly elaborate, and then share your thoughts with a friend or your small group.

1. What did the Holy Spirit whisper to your heart through this chapter? What did you like the most in this chapter?

2. What new concepts did you learn from this chapter? Which idea are you committed to implementing in your life?

3. Based on Galatians 2:20 and the author's explanations, please explain in your own words the concept of a changed life.

4. Please read Hudson Taylor's testimony carefully, then share your thoughts and heart impressions about Taylor's experience.

5. List the best aha moments you had while reading this chapter.

Endnotes:

[38] Richard F. Hall, *Foundations of Exchanged Life Counseling,* (Aurora, CO: Cross-Life Expressions, 1993), 57.
[39] *Grace Life Conference Manual,* (Aurora, CO: Cross-Life Expressions, 2000), 45.
[40] Dr. & Mrs. Howard Taylor, *Hudson Taylor's Spiritual Secret,* (Chicago, IL: Moody Press, 1989), 163.
[41] *Hudson Taylor's Spiritual Secret,* 158, 159.
[42] V. Raymond Edman, *They Found the Secret,* (Grand Rapids, MI: Zondervan, 1984), 20.
[43] *They Found the Secret,* 19.
[44] *Hudson Taylor's Spiritual Secret,* 162, 163.
[45] "A Letter from J. Hudson Taylor to his sister, Mrs. Broomhall, Amelia), CHINKIANG, October 17, 1869. www.wholesomewords.org.
Accessed on June 18, 2014.
https://www.wholesomewords.org/missions/biotaylor11.html.

-8-

Biblical Anthropology

When I consider Your heavens, the work of Your fingers, the moon and the stars, which You have ordained; what is man that You take thought of him, and the son of man that You care for him?
—Psalm 8:3–4

How did life begin? This question has generated many debates. I am not going to engage in any of those controversial debates, but before diving into this topic, let me set the stage by sharing a joke with you.

A scientist challenges God to a *"Who can make a better human being"* contest. God agreed to engage in this contest. The scientist, with great delight, bends over to pick up some dust to make his human being. Then God says, "No, no … you create your own dirt." I laugh every time I think about this joke.

The origin of life

I hold a biblical world view and I don't think God needs me to defend Him. When considering the origin of life, we have only two main options:

1. Either life was created by an intelligent source (God)

2. It began by natural processes

However, a very big question remains unanswered: Where does the matter come from?

All theories assume that the matter existed for eternity as the cosmic egg, primeval atom, condensed mass, or primordial soup.[46]

I don't have enough faith to believe all this nonsense. The biblical account makes more sense. I believe that the entire universe (all matter) and life (all forms of life) were created by God. Where does matter and life come from? God Himself created it: "In the beginning God created the heavens and the earth" (Genesis 1:1).

Isaiah writes: Everyone who is called by My name, and whom I have created for My glory, whom I have formed, even whom I have made. (Isaiah 43:7)

John writes:

> In the beginning was the Word, and the Word was with God, and the Word was God. He was in the beginning with God. All things came into being through Him, and apart from Him nothing came into being that has come into being. (John 1:1–3)

How about the universe in all its complexity? The Bible answers this question too. Isaiah tells us: "Lift up your eyes on high and see who has created these stars, the One who leads forth their host by number, He calls them all by name; because of the greatness of His might and the strength of His power, not one of them is missing" (Isaiah 40:26).

Not only is the entire universe created by God, but I also believe that it is sustained by Jesus Christ.

Paul writes:

> For by Him all things were created, both in the heavens and on earth, visible and invisible, whether thrones or dominions or rulers or authorities—all things have been created through Him and for Him.

> He is before all things, and in Him all things hold together. (Colossians 1:16–17)

As I said, I don't have enough faith to believe in the big bang[47] or in the theory of evolution[48]. I cannot accept that life generated itself from non-organic matter. When looking around, all of us are mesmerized by the complexity of life. Everything in nature is very organized and speaks loudly of the Creator who sustains it. This is exactly what the Bible asserts: "For since the creation of the world His invisible attributes, His eternal power and divine nature, have been clearly seen, being understood through what has been made, so that they are without excuse. (Romans 1:20)

I don't have enough faith to believe all of this nonsense. The biblical account makes more sense.

It is extremely difficult to accept that the universe, in its splendor, life, and beauty, is the result of a cosmic accident. However, this is exactly what evolutionary theory proclaims—*organic life appeared from non-organic matter through natural processes*. Then, after billions and billions of years, through random mutations and natural selection we arrived where we are today. It does not make any sense to me whatsoever.

As an engineer, I have great respect and appreciation for science; I am bewildered that such a thing, described above, is called "*science.*" No wonder Paul warned Timothy to be on guard:

> O Timothy, guard what has been entrusted to you, avoiding worldly and empty chatter and the opposing arguments of what is falsely called "knowledge" (science in KJV)—which some have professed and thus gone astray from the faith. Grace be with you (1 Timothy 6:20–21 emphasis mine).

Biblical Anthropology

The term anthropology is a compound word that derives

from Greek. Anthropos means "man" and logos means "word, matter, or thing." Putting the two words together we get anthropology. Merriam Webster provides this definition:

> The science of human beings; especially the study of human beings and their ancestors through time and space and in relation to physical character, environmental and social relations, and culture, and Theology dealing with the origin, nature, and destiny of human beings.[49]45

Biblical anthropology is the study of man from the Scripture's point of view.

What is man?

A comprehensive answer to this question would require volumes. I will share a few characteristics of the crown of God's creation. The creation of man is so wonderful that the Holy Spirit inspired David to write: "What is man that You take thought of him, and the son of man that You care for him?" (Psalm 8:4).

I remember a particular course in college in ferrous metallurgy. In this class we learned about the internal composition of various alloys[50]46. The lab section of this class was interesting because small pieces of various alloys were handed over to the students. We polished one end of the bar, applied a special solution on the shiny surface, and then placed the sample under a special microscope. To our amazement we were able to see the main components, the internal makeup, of that particular alloy.

The Word of God is that special microscope that shows us the internal makeup of a human being.

The Bible tells us:

> For the word of God is living and active and sharper than any two-edged sword, and piercing as far as the division of soul and spirit, of both joints and marrow,

> and able to judge the thoughts and intentions of the heart. (Hebrews 4:12)

From this passage alone we notice some distinct elements that make up our being: spirit, soul—thoughts and intentions, and body—joints, indicating the connections of bone structures, and marrow—suggesting our nervous system.

Made in the image of God

Let's go back to the creation account described in Genesis. God called in existence the entire universe by speaking things out. The Scripture tells us that for five days in a row, "God said" followed by "and there was" or "it was so"; light, firmament, dry land, vegetation, stars (including the sun and the moon), and animals and birds were spoken into existence by the Almighty God. But on day six, when it came to the creation of Adam, God said: "Let us make man in our image, after our likeness" (Genesis 1:26).

This time, the Triune God (Father, Son, and Holy Spirit) used the dust of the earth He just created a couple of days before. He fashioned with His own hands this special creature called man. The clay form, more beautiful than any statue sculpted by the famous Michelangelo, was laying lifeless on the ground. God stooped down and breathed the breath of life into Adam's nostrils. Suddenly, the lifeless clump of clay became a living soul. "And the LORD God formed man of the dust of the ground, and breathed into his nostrils the breath of life; and man became a living soul" (Genesis 2:7 KJV).

The intersection of God's Spirit and the clay form generated a fully functioning adult human being with all his faculties in place: spiritual, volitional, emotional, and physical (including the five senses). ***No wonder the creation of man is considered the crown of God's creation.***

I know that the subject matter gets heavier, and another joke might lighten us up. I heard this and it made me laugh so hard!

A little girl asked her mother: "How did the race appear?" The mother answered: "God made Adam and Eve and they had children and so was all mankind made."

Two days later the girl asked her father the same question. The father answered: "Many years ago there were apes from which the human race evolved."

God stooped down and breathed the breath of life into Adam's nostrils. Suddenly, the lifeless clump of clay became a living soul.

The confused girl returned to her mother and said: "Mom how is it possible that you told me the human race was created by God, and Dad said they developed from apes?" The mother answered: "Well, dear, it is very simple. I told you about my side of the family and your father told you about his."

Man is a triune being

God is a Triune God: God the Father, God the Son, and God the Holy Spirit. Since He created man in His likeness, we must also be a triune person: spirit, soul and body. The apostle Paul writes: "Now may the God of peace Himself sanctify you entirely; and may your spirit and soul and body be preserved complete, without blame at the coming of our Lord Jesus Christ" (Thessalonians 5:23).

The English word *spirit* was translated from the Greek word *pneuma.* In the original language it means wind, breath, or spirit. From the word "pneuma" derives pneumatology which refers to the study of the biblical doctrine of the Holy Spirit.

The word *soul* came from the Greek word *psuche.* Most Christian thinkers believe that the soul part of human beings includes *mind, emotions,* and *will.* From the word psuche we get the word psychology. Psychology is the science of mind, behavior, and characteristics of an individual.

Finally, the English word flesh comes from the Greek word *sarx.* Flesh means bodily desires, not the body itself.

Flesh is generally read with a negative connotation. The Greek word for body is *soma*. It is used in such places as "Now may the God of peace Himself sanctify you entirely; and may your spirit and soul and body [soma] be preserved complete, without blame at the coming of our Lord Jesus Christ" (1 Thessalonians 5:23), "and He Himself bore our sins in His body [*soma*] on the cross, so that we might die to sin and live to righteousness; for by His wounds you were healed" (1 Peter 2:24), and "But Peter sent them all out and knelt down and prayed, and turning to the body [*soma*], he said, "Tabitha, arise." And she opened her eyes, and when she saw Peter, she sat up'" (Acts 9:40).

I like the statement quoted by Jessie Penn-Lewis, in her book, *Soul & Spirit*:

> Tertullian, one of the Fathers of the Church who wrote in the early centuries of the Christian era, calls the flesh—or physical being—the body of the soul, and the soul—the vessel of the spirit. The soul stands between the spirit and the body. "Direct communication between spirit and flesh is impossible; their communication can be carried on only by mend of a medium— the soul being that medium.[51]

Andrew Murray also says:

> The spirit is the seat of our God's consciousness; the soul is the seat of our self-consciousness; the body of our world- consciousness. In the spirit, God dwells; in the soul, self; in the body, sense.[52]

I also like the ideas Watchman Nee brings to us. He writes:

> According to the teaching of the Bible and the experience of believers, the human spirit has three main functions. These are conscience, intuition and communion (or worship).[53]

- Man is a spiritual being called to worship God

"God is Spirit" (John 4:24a). God created man in His own image. Therefore, man is a spiritual being able to worship God. He was created for an intimate fellowship with Him. Nobody can relate to God or communicate with Him without having this spiritual dimension. Jesus explains, "And those who worship Him must worship in spirit and truth" (John 4:24b).

- Man is created for work and creativity

Man is created not only to worship God, but to work for Him and take care of God's creation. The book of Genesis tells us: "Then the LORD God took the man and put him into the Garden of Eden to cultivate it and keep it" (Genesis 2:15). When human beings are working and creating things, they experience a sense of fulfillment. The capacity to work and be creative is God's special gift to humanity.

- Man is created for community

At the end of each act of creation, God declared that it was good, even very good: "God saw all that He had made, and behold, it was very good. And there was evening and there was morning, the sixth day" (Genesis 1:31). However, when it came to Adam, God said: "It is not good for the man to be alone" (Genesis 2:18a).

With this thought in mind, God established the institution of marriage. Marriage, family, and community are God's ideas, not peoples' ideas. God said: "I will make him a helper suitable for him" (Genesis 2:18b).

- God establishes marriage as the first institution

The Bible tells us:

The LORD God fashioned into a woman the rib which

> He had taken from the man and brought her to the man. The man said, "This is now bone of my bones, and flesh of my flesh; She shall be called Woman, because she was taken out of Man." For this reason, a man shall leave his father and his mother, and be joined to his wife; and they shall become one flesh. And the man and his wife were both naked and were not ashamed. (Genesis 2:22–25)

The current status of humankind

For an accurate understating of the current spiritual status of humanity we must go back to the book of Genesis to the fall of Adam and Eve. They were created for God and each other. They were created as persons with free will. At the soul level they could exercise their capacity to choose:

- To obey, love, and commune with God.
- To listen and obey the voice of the enemy.

I will not describe all the details about the origin of sin, the devil, and why all of these were allowed to take place, but I will briefly present the context of the fall.

God designed and planted the most beautiful Garden we can imagine for the first family. In that perfect environment, God placed only one restriction to Adam:

> The LORD God commanded the man, saying, "From any tree of the garden you may eat freely; but from the tree of the knowledge of good and evil you shall not eat, for in the day that you eat from it you will surely die." (Genesis 2:16–17)

Instead of choosing love and communion with God, Adam exercised his free will to rebel against God. Adam and Eve died the moment they ate from the forbidden fruit. By this very act of willful disobedience, Adam let sin enter into the world and, with it, death and destruction.

Paul explains: "Therefore, just as through one man sin entered into the world, and death through sin, and so death spread to all men, because all sinned" (Romans 5:12).The question is: What exactly died?

Since man is a triune person (spirit, soul and body) and since Adam and Eve continued to live for hundreds of years after they sinned, we can conclude that something happened with their spirit. Theologians tell us that they died spiritually. How can I illustrate this complex concept in very simple terms? I prayed and this illustration came to mind.

Imagine a beautiful candle skillfully crafted and placed in a candleholder by the Master Chandler. The candle wick, at its fullest strength, is fully lit. The light it produces is magnificent, glorifying the Great Artist. The wax needs the holder to keep it straight. The wick needs wax around it. Everything works so harmoniously! The Master enjoys being around it. The candleholder shines, it does not become old or outdated. The wax, even though it is melting by the heat of the light, reconstructs itself. The wick burns but it does not get consumed. Master Chandler constructed them this way. Such a unique masterpiece.

After a while, an envious pseudo-Craftsman sneaks into the room and blows out the light. The darkness settles in the room. The candle gets uglier by the day, just a clump of melted wax. The holder gets old and outdated. Everything is now ruined.

Since Adam and Eve continued to live for hundreds of years after they sinned, theologians tell us that they died spiritually.

Spiritual death is like putting out a candle. In simple terms, spiritual death alienated Adam and Eve from God. They lost communion with their Creator. They were cut off from the real source of life—God's Spirit. At the soul level they became rebels. Their bodies lost the divine purpose of housing the Holy Spirit of God. Their bodies started to decay and become full of all sorts of lusts: "lust of the flesh," "lust of the eyes," and "the boastful pride of life" (see 1 John 2:16). From that point onward, Adam and Eve and all of their descendants, including us, lived only at the soul level and became spiritually enslaved to God's enemy—Satan.

The Bible states:

> And you were dead in your trespasses and sins, in which you formerly walked according to the course of this world, according to the prince of the power of the air, of the spirit that is now working in the sons of disobedience. (Ephesians 2:1)

God's marvelous plan

Despite their rebellious state, God continued loving and pursuing His high-prized creation. God was not surprised by Adam's disobedience. Before the foundation of the universe the Triune God knew that this would be a painful experience for all.

Before time and space, the Trinity envisioned the Cross.

Before time and space, the Trinity envisioned the Cross. God reconciles us, the rebellious sons, and daughters of Adam, through Christ on the Cross. According to the Bible, at the Cross "God was in Christ reconciling the world to Himself" (2 Corinthians 5:18).

Wow! What a marvelous, indescribable, and amazing love! What a wonderful Father we have! What a magnificent Big Brother we have who was willing to lay down His own life for us!

A new creation

Every human being qualifies for a complete makeover because of the amazing work that took place at the Cross. Sin was and is a terrible thing done against God. Sin has terrible consequences. The good news is that the Son of God is the propitiation for our sins. John writes: "And He Himself is the propitiation for our sins; and not for ours only, but also for those of the whole world" (1 John 2:2). Whoever responds in faith to the message of salvation has the opportunity to be reconciled to God. Paul teaches us: "For if while we were enemies we were reconciled to God through the death of His Son, much more, having been reconciled, we shall be saved by His life" (Romans 5:10).

Through Christ, we not only are reconciled but we are also declared righteous. The Bible reveals: "For as through the one man's disobedience (Adam) the many were made sinners, even so through the obedience of the One (Christ) the many will be made righteous" (Romans 5:19).

Moreover, through the power of the Holy Spirit, whoever accepts God's solution for salvation becomes a new creation. This spiritual reality is stated in 2 Corinthians 5:17: "Therefore if anyone is in Christ, he is a new creature; the old things passed away; behold, new things have come."

Being born again means becoming a new creature. It is like the Master Chandler lights the wick again, restores the wax, and promises to design a brand-new candleholder that will never get ruined.

Let me briefly explain the meaning of a new creation. When you accepted Jesus Christ as your personal Savior by faith (Romans 10:9–10), a few things took place:

- The Holy Spirit *regenerated* you—created a new spirit in you (John 3:3, 6; Titus 3:5)
- He *baptized* you in Christ (Romans 6:3)
- God's Spirit supernaturally *immersed* you into God's Church (1 Corinthians 12:13)
- And He united you with God (1 Corinthians 6:17)

After you are born again, God is committed to sanctify you entirely: *spirit, soul,* and *body* (see 1 Thessalonians 5:23–24). As a new creation in Christ, we can exercise our free will and invite God to progressively sanctify our whole being. As this amazing process gradually takes place deep inside our inner person, we are experiencing new things that not even Adam in his state of innocence experienced. Wonderful!

Reflection Questions

Please reflect upon the following questions, briefly elaborate, and then share your thoughts with a friend or your small group.

1. What did the Holy Spirit whisper to your heart through this chapter? What did you like the most in this chapter?

2. What new concepts did you learn from this chapter? Which idea are you committed to implementing in your life?

3. What does it mean to be made in the "image of God"? Please elaborate.

4. In your own words, please explain the concept of man as tripartite or triune being.

5. List the best aha moments you had while reading this chapter.

Endnotes:

[46] Primordial soup, or prebiotic soup, is a hypothetical condition of the Earth's atmosphere before the emergence of life. It is a chemical the theory, simple organic compounds were created from non-living inorganic molecules (abiogenesis) through physical and chemical reactions on the Earth's surface. The so formed organic molecules accumulate into a rich organic ocean, or a "soup." In this soup, simple organic molecules reacted with each other (polymerise) to form more complex molecules, including nucleic acids environment in which the first biological molecules (organic compounds) were formed under natural forces. According to and proteins, which are the central structural and functional components of all organisms. These molecules then aggregate to become the first forms of life. Accessed on February 27, 2018. https://en.wikipedia.org/wiki/Primordial_soup.
One of the biggest questions physicists are striving to answer is what happened moments after the Big Bang. How the universe as we know it now evolved is a complex question involving study by vastly different branches of physics including particle physics, nuclear physics, and cosmology. A few seconds after the Big Bang, the universe was made of a thick, 10-billion degree 'cosmic soup' of subatomic particles. As the hot universe expanded, the interactions of these particles caused the universe to behave like a cooling thermonuclear reactor. This reactor produced light nuclei, such as hydrogen, helium, and lithium, found in the universe today." Accessed on February 27, 2018.
http://www.dailymail.co.uk/sciencetech/ article-3554010/Capturing-universe-looked-seconds-Big-Bang-Model-simulates-conditions-cosmic-soup-particles.html.
[47] The Big Bang Theory is the leading explanation about how the universe began. At its simplest, it says the universe as we know it started with a small singularity, then inflated over the next 13.8 billion years to the cosmos that we know today. Accessed on February 27, 2018. https://www. space.com/25126-big-bang-theory.html.
In 1927, an astronomer named Georges Lemaître had a big idea. He said that a very long time ago, the universe started as just a single point. He said the universe stretched and expanded to get as big as it is now, and that it could keep on stretching. Accessed on February 27, 2018. https://spaceplace.nasa.gov/big-bang/en/.
A Belgian priest named Georges Lemaître first suggested the big bang theory in the 1920s when he theorized that the universe began from a single primordial atom. Accessed on February 27, 2018.
https://www.nationalgeographic.com/science/space/universe/origins-of-the-universe/.
[48] In 1858, when English naturalist Charles Darwin (1809–1882) proposed

his theory of evolution by natural selection, most of the scientific world believed that the account of the creation of the world as written in the biblical book of Genesis was true. https://www.encyclopedia.com/social-sciences/ applied-and-social-sciences-magazines/evolutionary-theory. The theory of evolution by natural selection, first formulated in Darwin's book On the Origin of Species in 1859, is the process by which organisms change over time as a result of changes in heritable physical or behavioral traits. Changes that allow an organism to better adapt to its environment will help it survive and have more offspring. Accessed on February 27, 2018. .https://www.livescience.com/474-controversy-evolution-works.html. Evolution, theory in biology postulating that the various types of plants, animals, and other living things on Earth have their origin in other preexisting types and that the distinguishable differences are due to modifications in successive generations. The theory of evolution is one of the fundamental keystones of modern biological theory. Accessed on February 27, 2018. https://www.britannica.com/science/evolution-scientific-theory (Accessed on February 27, 2018).

[49] Anthropology. www.merriam-webster.com. Accessed on February 26, 2018. https://www.merriam-webster.com/dictionary/anthropology.

[50] An alloy is a mixture of metals or a mixture of a metal and another element. ... Examples of alloys are steel, solder, brass, pewter, duralumin, bronze, and amalgams. Accessed on December 26, 2017. https://en.wikipedia. org/wiki/Alloy.

[51] Jessie Penn-Lewis, *Soul & Spirit,* (Christian Literature Crusade, Fort Washington, PA: 1992-93), 11,12.

[52] *Soul & Spirit,* 12,13.

[53] Watchman Nee, The Spiritual Man, 35. Accessed on February 26, 2018. www.biblesnet.com.

-9-

Your New Identity

See how great a love the Father has bestowed on us, that we would be called children of God; and such we are. For this reason, the world does not know us, because it did not know Him. Beloved, now we are children of God, and it has not appeared as yet what we will be. We know that when He appears, we will be like Him, because we will see Him just as He is.

— 1 John 3:1-2

In 1994, Disney released an animated movie called The Lion King. My wife and I took our children to watch the movie. The story revolves around Simba, a lion cub and heir to the throne. Simba was tricked into thinking he killed his father. As a result of the tragedy in his life Simba abandons his identity as the future king and runs far away.

You have forgotten who you are!

A wise monkey, Rafiki, convinces Simba, now an adult lion, to face his past. He told Simba, "Oh yes, the past can hurt. But from the way I see it, you can either run from it, or learn from it." A radical change takes place in Simba's heart after a mysterious conversation with his father. The dialogue between father and son was an absolute game changer for

Simba. His father, Mufasa, told his son, "Simba, you have forgotten me." Simba tried to defend himself, "No! How could I?" Then his father told his son these heart-penetrating words: "You have forgotten who you are, and so forgotten me. Look inside yourself, Simba. You are more than what you have become."

More often than not, we as Christians do not know our true identity. We run away forgetting our calling and destiny. As Simba was challenged to face his past despite the hurt, we too must look inside and rediscover our identity.

Who are you? Who am I?

These are simple questions, but when it comes to our spiritual identity these questions are not that simple. Let me ask you again: Who are you? Or, I ask myself: Who am I? My immediate response would be based on my earthly and cultural roots:

- I am the son of Dumitru and Paraschiva.
- I am the husband of Elena.
- I am the father of Evelina, Timotei, Dorian, and Cristina.
- I am a former engineer.
- I am a minister and a writer.

Do you see what I did? I addressed the inquiry about my identity using various roles of my earthly existence defined by the culture: family of origin, education, type of work, etc.

How would you answer that question?

How about your spiritual identity? How about my spiritual identity? In other words: Who am I in Christ? That is a tough question, isn't it? I agree. I hope that this chapter will address this question.

Looking closely at 1 John 3:1–2, we can clearly see that, first and foremost, we are God's children. This passage alone speaks volumes. More importantly, it is indicating that we are God's children right now, not sometime in the future. Hear

John's words: "Beloved, now we are children of God." This truth and spiritual reality should be the starting point of our new identity. It starts with God's love, the heart of Jesus, and the testimony of the Holy Spirit. Praise the Lord.

The author of Hebrews tells us:

> For it was fitting for Him, for whom are all things, and through whom are all things, in bringing many sons to glory, to perfect the author of their salvation through sufferings. For both He who sanctifies and those who are sanctified are all from one Father; for which reason He is not ashamed to call them brethren, saying, "I will proclaim Your name to My brethren; in the midst of the congregation, I will sing Your praise." Again, "I will put my trust in him." And elsewhere, "Behold, I, and the children whom God hath given me." (Hebrews 2:11–13)

Wow! Did you hear that? Christ suffered for us to bring us, former sinners, to glory. What is the opposite of glory? The opposite of glory is shame. Jesus despised the shame and endured the cross to bring us to His glory. Jesus calls us His brothers. The humblest thing we can do is to agree with the Bible.

Why would an innocent, perfect, sinless human being suffer? This is a mystery! Only in heaven will we understand. One thing is clear: God made Christ sin on our behalf "so that we might become the righteousness of God in Christ" (2 Corinthians 5:21). This statement has profound implications! Simply put, because of Christ, we share His righteousness.

Understanding our spiritual identity requires a deeper comprehension of God's righteousness. Christ's righteousness is the foundation of the believer's identity.

If we desire to experience God, we will have to leave our religious comfort zone. This is the only way we can learn about our true identity. We must leave the old, worldly or religious ways of looking and thinking of our identity. We must let the Scriptures communicate to us in ways that only the Scriptures can. We must invite the Holy Spirit to be our True Counselor and reveal to us who we really are.

Let's start by looking closely at Colossians 3:3–4:

> For you have died and your life is hidden with Christ in God. When Christ, who is our life, is revealed, then you also will be revealed with Him in glory.

Oh, if only the people of God would realize they have access to the very life of Christ. Christ gave His very life to you and me. I hope you see this in the Bible and pray that you realize the implications of this truth!

Do you see why it can be so difficult for us to address the question of identity? When we get asked: "*Who are you?*" We think of all sorts of ways to answer that question from an earthly perspective.

We have to invite the Holy Spirit to be our True Counselor and reveal to us who we really are.

"*Well, I am Valy Vaduva.*" No, that is your name. "Who are you?" "*I am a Romanian American.*" No, Romania is the country of origin, and America is the country you live in now. "Who are you, Brother Valy?" "*Well, I'm a former engineer, now a minister, and a writer.*" That is your occupation. Brother Valy, I did not ask you what you did, or what you do now. So, let me ask you again, "Who are you?" "*Well, I live in Livonia.*" No, that is your home city.

Do you see? We attempt to identify ourselves around ourselves. *Who are you?* is the hardest question. We probably never took the time to analyze our identity through the lens of Scripture alone. Therefore, our natural tendency is to define and establish our identity, personal image, and self-esteem based on what we do, where we come from, our possessions, reputation, education, and how many letters we have accumulated after our name.

To understand our new identity, we must learn and know the right identifiers outside of ourselves. My dear friend, the aspect of spiritual identity in the believer's life is equally important to the issue of victory. Every believer wants to have spiritual victory in his or her life. Every believer needs to know who he or she is in Christ.

If Christians see themselves only as forgiven sinners, they will naturally consider sinful behavior as something normal and to be expected. However, David Needham asserts that for a genuine Christian, continuing sinning is *"choosing to act as temporarily insane."*[54] Ouch!

If this is the case, we will continue sinning and asking for forgiveness. However, based on New Testament teaching, this is a faulty view. As a result of this wrong view, we are in a vicious cycle of sinning, confessing, repenting, and trying harder.

To understand our new identity, we have to learn and know the right identifiers outside of ourselves.

Christ desires for us to know Him by revelation but He cannot impose His will on us. We must desire to build a genuine intimacy with Him. This requires walking by faith and looking at Him, not at our circumstances. The spiritual concepts we believe have a great influence in our lives. It is so important to know and to believe who we are in Christ. When we fully embrace our new identity, in time, our behavior will get into alignment with who we truly are. We are not going to reach perfection, but we will live a more fulfilled and victorious Christian life.

Self-esteem

The term self-esteem gained popularity with the rise of psychology in the 1960s. Schools and churches alike developed curriculum to address the issue of self-esteem. A simple definition of self-esteem states that it is: *"a confidence and satisfaction in oneself."*[55]

I like the quote cited by Dr. Seamands in his book, *Healing for Damaged Emotions:*

> Dr. Maurice, a professional Christian counselor in his excellent book *The Sensation of Being Somebody,*

> explained that there are three essential components of a healthy self-image:
>
> *Belongingness*—A sense of belongingness, of being loved.
> *Worthwhileness*—A sense of worth and value. This leads to the inner belief that we count and have value.
> *Competence*—A sense of being competent. This leads us to the feeling that we can accomplish the task at hand. We are well equipped to meet life's demands.
> Put them all together, Dr. Wagner says, and you have a triad of self-concept feelings: *belongingness, worthwhileness, and competence*.[56]

Interesting, isn't it? We live in a world of Facebook, Instagram, Snapchat, and many other social media tools that concentrate on selfies.[57] Under these circumstances how a genuine Chrit's disciple is supposed to deal with the concept of self-esteem?

Taking a selfie and posting it on social media with the caption: "Look at me: I am a casual Christian" will not be enough. Is there such a thing as a biblical self-worth?

But first, let us look at some of the methods used by the secular world to determine self- esteem. This is by no means an exhaustive list.

1. The attitude of parents towards children

Not everybody has the privilege of being born in a loving, Christian family. God knows all the details. The truth is that parents can influence their children with their words, attitudes, and behaviors.

If parents criticize their children, then they have diminished chances to stand up against the world. They would most likely have the tendency to go with the flow or fail under pressure.

If the church puts down children and teenagers using criticism, judgment, and disapproval, they have diminished chances to succeed as Christians. In their college years, they would most likely, fail to stand up for their faith.

2. Successes or failures in carrying out tasks

Failures in life can paralyze us. Success may lead us to pride and self-centeredness. Some people can tolerate failure and with persistence can succeed. Henry Ford, the founder of Ford Company, had many financial failures. On one occasion he said: "Failure is simply the opportunity to begin again, this time more intelligently."[58] The reality is that not everybody has this attitude. Others might view failure as a steppingstone toward the desired end result. Take Thomas Edison as an example—the inventor of the electrical bulb and light that all of us now enjoy. I read somewhere that Edison made 1,000 unsuccessful attempts. When a reporter asked: "How did it feel to fail 1,000 times?" Edison responded: "I didn't fail 1,000 times. The light bulb was an invention with 1,000 steps."[59] Despite his failures, Edison pressed on until he reached the desired result, which led to economic success. Again, not everyone is an inventor like Edison. Depending on the personality and mindset, successes or failures have a major impact on the way one views himself or herself.

3. Individual perception of God's attitude towards him or her

When it comes to the concept of self-esteem, our perception of God's attitude toward us is crucial. I like the way A. W. Tozer links the self-concept with our God-concept. He writes:

> What comes into our minds when we think about God is the most important thing about us … For this reason, the gravest question before the Church is always God Himself, and the most portentous fact about any man is not what he at a given time may say or do, but what he in his deep heart conceives God to

be like.[60]

If our conception of God is not biblically correct, then our perception of God's attitude toward us is also incorrect. As a result, the way in which we establish our personal image is deformed.

4. Approval or rejection from friends

In the process of growing up, there was a period in our lives when the opinion of our friends meant everything. If our friends told us something, we believed them. If our parents and teachers were telling us something different, we were ready to argue with them and side with our friends. However, as adults, if we are still influenced by our friends more than God then we are in a very dangerous situation.

Our thinking is clouded and our view of others and ourselves is not biblical.

5. Lies from Satan—the enemy of our soul

Over the span of our lives, we have accumulated many lies about ourselves, others, and God. They are coming directly from Satan—"he is a liar and the father of lies" (John 8:44b). These lies have influenced our view about God, others, and ourselves. The things we believe are now part of our mental and emotional lens through which we interpret reality.

According to Robert S. McGee, there are four major false beliefs that contaminate the hearts and minds of people. These are:

1. I must meet certain standards in order to feel good about myself.
2. I must be approved by others to feel good about myself.
3. Those who fail (including myself) are unworthy of love and deserve to be punished.
4. I am what I am. I cannot change. I am hopeless.[61]

As a result of these false beliefs, McGee asserts that people are caught in all sorts of destructive behaviors such us: *performance trap, addiction to approval, the blame game, and shame.* The good news is that God has answers for every false belief:

- For the *Performance Trap*, God's answer is *justification* in Christ alone.
- For the *Approval Addict*, God's answer is *reconciliation* through the blood of Christ.
- For the *Blame Game*, God offers *propitiation* through His Son Jesus Christ.
- For *Shame*, God provides *regeneration* through the power of the Holy Spirit.

These are just some of the methods by which the world shapes people's self-esteem. The trouble is that, more often than not, Christians also use these same methods to establish their personal image and self-esteem. This leads to emotional conflict and spiritual failures in their lives.

The immeasurable value of your soul

What is the value of your soul? I will use an illustration to address this question. According to CNN Money magazine, Yusaku Maezawa, a Japanese billionaire, founder of Japan's largest online fashion mall, paid $110.5 million for the "Untitled," a painting depicting a skull-like head, of Jean-Michel Basquiat.[62] This is the highest price ever paid at an auction for a painting by an American artist. Can you imagine that? One hundred and ten million dollars for a painting!? I can't. Maezawa's collection already includes works from Pablo Picasso, Alberto Giacometti, and Jeff Koons. In an interview taken at home, the Billionaire was

God is the Buyer who redeemed our souls and the price He paid is Jesus Christ.

asked: "Why spend $110 million on a Basquiat?" He responded: "I decided to go for it."

Do you see this? The value of the painting is more than just the price of the canvas, the brushes and paints used in the process, the time the artist spent making it, and the frame used to assemble the final product. The value of the painting at an auction is the price that one particular buyer wants to pay for it. Imagine that I would paint a similar painting. I am sure that no one would pay to cover the cost of the supplies or my time unless my name was Leonardo Da Vinci, Vincent Van Gogh, Rembrandt, Michelangelo, Claude Monet, or Pablo Picasso.

So, back to our question: *"What is the value of your soul?"* The value of your soul and mine is determined by the price the Buyer wants to pay for it. God is the Buyer who redeemed our souls and the price He paid is Jesus Christ. You and I are extremely valuable! In His love, the Father paid the highest prices possible—His only begotten Son. That is why John 3:16 is the premier verse of the entire Bible: "For God so loved the world, that He gave His only begotten Son, that whoever believes in Him shall not perish, but have eternal life."

Our redemption cost the blood of God's own Son. The author of Hebrews explains that our redemption was accomplished: "not through the blood of goats and calves, but through His own blood, He entered the holy place once for all, having obtained eternal redemption" (Hebrews 9:12). Dear beloved, we have been redeemed by the precious blood of the Lamb. This redemption is not for a day or even a year; this redemption is for eternity.

Biblical self-worth

When it comes to our biblical self-worth or spiritual identity the most critical aspect has to do with the doctrine of righteousness.[1]

---

[1] AN: For more about *righteousness* please refer to the section called "Spiritual Identity Ignorance" in the Appendix A: "The Danger of Spiritual Immaturity."

As I alluded previously, that depending on the religious background in which we were raised, over the years our experiences tinted our spiritual glasses. Now, every time we read the Bible and listen to sermons, we interpret the messages through our own lenses. As a result, we have accumulated a series of deformed expectations of God. In time, these perceptions became standards of living or laws for us.

If our perceived identity is that of just forgiven sinners, we are going to have a continuous struggle with the concept of righteousness. We continue to live under pressure to meet certain expectations, standards, and comply with the laws that we have fabricated to achieve righteousness and maintain it. This is not the Christian life Jesus intends for His disciples. If we fail repeatedly, we are likely to feel inferior. Since we don't see much progress in our lives, we start feeling insecure and develop a critical attitude. If we notice others who perform better than us, we become jealous. We start focusing on the obstacles in our lives which prevent us from having success. As a result, we increase our striving. In the process we become more and more controlling. In our skewed view, these things are supposed to give us success and provide us with a sense of significance. However, the opposite happens; they become major barriers that prevent God's breakthrough. It is hard to give up control and start walking by faith. We are afraid to walk on an unknown path; but, more often than not, the unknown path is the only way to freedom and victory.

According to Pia Mellody:

> Healthy self-esteem is the internal experience of your own value and preciousness. When you cannot experience healthy self-esteem, you experience esteem in two inappropriate ways. At one end of the spectrum is the experience of low or no self-esteem. At the other end is the experience of arrogance and grandiosity, of being better than others.[63]

If you are a parent, please encourage your children with

the Word of God. Be there for them. When they do not see anything good in themselves, be the one who affirms them. Look for something good in them and tell them: "You are so talented!" "I see that you are disciplined." "It looks like you like to read. Keep on keeping on." Parents have a lot of influence over the development of their children.

According to the essay, "Parental Influence on the Emotional Development of Children," by Bethel Moges and Kristi Weber:

> Parents have a significant influence on how children turn out, including their personality, emotional development, and behavioral habits, as well as a host of other factors.[64]

Scripture teaches that parents sanctify their children (see 1 Corinthians 7:14). In reference to parenting, Scripture tells us: "You shall teach them diligently to your sons and shall talk of them when you sit in your house and when you walk by the way and when you lie down and when you rise up" (Deuteronomy 6:7). A much clearer verse is found in the book of Proverbs: "Train up a child in the way he should go, even when he is old he will not depart from it" (Proverbs 22:6)

If our parents did not build us up, we need spiritual parents who know how to encourage us with the Word. There is power in the Word of God, especially the teaching about our new identity in Christ. Faith is strong because God is strong. Therefore, whoever believes in God has access to the power of God.

I like the way Robert S. McGee, views self-esteem:

> An accurate biblical self-concept contains both strength and humility, both sorrow over sins and joy about forgiveness, a deep sense of our need for God's grace, and a deep sense of the reality of God's grace.[65]

Above all I appreciate the simplicity and clarity of the Word of God.

In Romans, Paul writes:

> For through the grace given to me I say to everyone among you not to think more highly of himself than he ought to think; but to think so as to have sound judgment, as God has allotted to each a measure of faith. (Romans 12:3)

You are a swan not a duck

Speaking about our new identity, let me share with you an illustration. I don't remember exactly where I read this, but I still like it:

> Once upon a time, when wise men talked to birds and animals, there was an interesting situation. A swan, in a hurry flying south for the winter, laid her egg into a domestic duck nest. Domestic ducks do not fly to warm regions. The mother duck cared for this egg along with her own eggs until all of them hatched. The ducklings, one after another, came out of the broken eggs, and so did the cygnet (baby swan).
>
> Things were good for a while. There was almost no difference between them. All of them were covered in a downy coat. They were eating together just fine. All things were good until they started growing and maturing.
>
> Now the cygnet grew taller and stronger. He had beautiful feathers, a long neck, bigger beak, and wider wings. He got so depressed because he was so different than his brothers and sisters. His perceived "family" were smaller, had shorter legs, short beaks, short necks, colorful feathers, and smaller wings.
>
> The young swan wanted so much to resemble the other ducks. He even tried to walk on his knees in order to fit in.
>
> The swan reached the highest point of his crisis—his depression almost led him to suicidal thoughts. The

cold season had come and gone in that area. Spring came and the summer was approaching.

A wise man happened to travel through that area. He saw the young swan among the family of ducks. Then the wise man said to him: "I noticed that you look disturbed and depressed. I am wondering why that is?"

The young swan relayed in a low and sad tone of voice: "I don't know what is wrong with me. I don't fit it. I tried and I tried to be like my fellow brothers and sisters, but with no avail. I am so depressed. I even tried many times to imitate the behavior of my siblings, but nothing happened. All of this does not suit me. I was born in this family, but, apparently, I am totally different from the rest of my family. Everyone laughs at me. They make fun at my attempts to fit in. Obviously, I am not accepted. I do not know what to do! I am puzzled! Do you know what is going on? Please tell me?"

And the wise man, said to him: ***"My dear, you are not a duck. You are a swan."*** The young swan responded: *"What are you talking about? What do you mean by this?"* The wise man, pointing towards the sky, said to him: "Do you see these great and beautiful birds flying high up in the sky with their wings widely spread? You are part of that family." "I am confused. I don't understand! What happened to me?"

Our identity must be established on the Word of God and what our heavenly Father tells us.

The wise man continued: "It appears that your mother did not have time to wait for her egg to hatch, and so she let you be born into a family of ducks. They adopted you but you are not a duck; you are a swan. Spread your wings as wide as you can and fly with your true bird kin."

The swan started running, spread his beautiful wide

white wings, and started flapping them. He flew higher and higher. After a while he reached his family. What a relief! What freedom! Welcome to the family! What a joy!

My dear friend, the moral of this story is simple and straightforward. It is in vain to try to draw our identity based on what the world tells us or on what other people say to us. Our identity must be established on the Word of God and what our heavenly Father tells us. As believers, our identity is so critical to our worship, our vision, and our victory. The fact that we do not completely understand and don't experience these realities makes us reluctant to enjoy the relationship we have with our Lord Jesus Christ and with the Holy Spirit. Let's consistently pray that God will cause us to comprehend our true spiritual identity.

Conclusions:

1. You are God's masterpiece! You are the crown of God's creation! You are the apple of God's eye! You are extremely valuable! The Father God could not foresee the eternity without you. Therefore, in the most harmonious consensus the Trinity decided to send the only Begotten Son to pay the price of redemption for the Adamic race. Not only that, but God will create a
anew race altogether with Christ as the Head.
2. You are anew creation in Christ. As a new creation: "you now have a new identity, new nature and life, and are endowed with new resources, power, attribute, family, heritage, security, position, purpose, and destiny."[66]
3. Embrace what your Father God says about you. From now on, the humblest thing you can do is to agree with the Word of God regarding who you are.

As Christ disciples, let's affirm and declare these 12 powerful truths:

1. I am a new creature in Christ (2 Corinthians 5:17)
2. I am God's workmanship (poem, unique art) (Ephesians 2:10)
3. I am a partaker of His divine nature (2 Peter 1:3–4)
4. I am God's child, born again of the incorruptible seed of the Word of God (1 Peter 1:23)
5. I am born of God, and the evil one does not touch me (1 John 5:18)
6. I have the righteousness of Christ (Philippines 3:9)
7. I am alive with Christ (Ephesians 2:5)
8. I am holy and without blame before Him in love (Ephesians 1:4; 1 Peter 1:16)
9. I am the temple of the Holy Spirit; I am not my own (1 Corinthians 6:19)
10. I can do all things through Christ Jesus (Philippians 4:13)
11. I am an ambassador for Christ (2 Corinthians 5:20)
12. When He returns, I will be like Him (1 John 3:1–3)

This is your *New Identity*. When the enemy whispers into your ears: "Don't trust the Word of God," tell him out loud:

Depart from me Satan, I am a precious child of God and there is nothing that can separate me from my Father's love.

Then declare with conviction Romans 8:28–39. I guarantee you that the devil will not bother you anymore about identity.

Reflection Questions

Please reflect upon the following questions, briefly elaborate, and then share your thoughts with a friend or your small group.

1. What did the Holy Spirit whisper to your heart through this chapter? What did you like the most in this chapter?

2. What new concepts did you learn from this chapter? Which idea are you committed to implementing in your life?

3. After reading the section titled Self-Esteem, jot down the most important ideas.

4. After reading the section titled Biblical Self-Worth, write the most important concepts.

5. List the best aha moments you had while reading this chapter.

Endnotes:

[54] David Needham, *Alive for the First Time,* (Sisters, OR: Questar Publishers, 1995), 92.
[55] Self-esteem. www. merriam-webster.com. Accessed on February 12, 2018, https://www. merriam-webster.com/dictionary/self-esteem.
[56] Cited by Dr. Seamands in, *Healing for Damaged Emotions,* (David C Cook, Colorado Springs, CO: 1981, 2015), 85.
[57] According to Wikipedia: "A selfie is a self-portrait photograph, typically taken with a smartphone which may be held in the hand or supported by a selfie stick. Selfies are often shared on social networking services such as Facebook, Instagram and Snapchat. They are for vanity usually flattering and made to appear casual." www.en.wikipedia.org. Accessed on February 19, 2018. https://en.wikipedia.org/wiki/Selfie.
According to BBC news, "selfie" was named by Oxford Dictionaries as the word of 2013. www.bbc.com. Accessed on February 19, 2018. http://www.bbc.com/news/uk-24992393.
[58] www.quotespedia.org. Accessed februarie 20, 2018. https://bit.ly/3srgwgk.
[59] Thomas Edison. www.medium.com. Accessed on February 19, 2018. https://bit.ly/3sttBFP https://medium.com/cry-mag/thomas-edisons-theorem-for-success-b96591bf7dd1.
[60] A. W. Tozer, *The Knowledge of the Holy,* (New York: Harper & Row, 1961), 9.
[61] Robert S. McGee, *The Search for Significance,* (Thomas Nelson, Nashville, TN: 1998, 2003), 26.
[62] Untitled painting auction record. www.money.cnn.com. Accessed on January 23, 2018. http://money.cnn.com/2017/05/18/luxury/jean-michel-basquiat-untitled-painting-auction-record/index.html.
[63] Pia Mellody, *Breaking Free* (New York: Harper & Row, 1989), 29-30, cited by David Seamands in *Healing for Damaged Emotions: Workbook,* (David C Cook, Colorado Springs, CO: 1981, 2015).
[64] Bethel Moges and Kristi Weber, "Parental Influence on the Emotional Development of Children." www.my.vanderbilt.edu. Accessed on February 13, 2018. https://my.vanderbilt.edu/developmentalpsychologyblog. /2014/05/parental-influence-on-the-emotional-development-of- children/.
[65] *The Search for Significance,* 10, 11.
[66] Dr. Lewis Gregory, *Introducing the New You,* (Source Ministry International, Snellville, GA: 2005), 151.

-10-

The Power of Forgiveness

Be kind to one another, tenderhearted, forgiving each other, just as God in Christ also has forgiven you.
— Ephesians 4:32

Many years ago, I was overseas on a mission trip to teach about spiritual growth. The family who hosted me invited me to go to their church. The local pastor invited me to the podium to preach. As I waited for my turn, I sensed inside my heart that the Holy Spirit wanted me to speak about forgiveness, not on *spiritual growth* as I was previously planning.

As Christ's disciple, I learned early on in life to go with the leading of the Holy Spirit. The Scripture that came to my mind was from Matthew 18:21–35. As I delivered my message there was a deep silence within the audience. On the way back to their house, the hosts asked me: "Do you know what happened during the church service?" I said: "I have no idea. What happened?" The hosts said: "Your message deeply touched our hearts." They continued: "For several years now we have been hurt and wounded by some people in leadership in this church. There were a lot of unfounded and unjust accusations against us. We have been humiliated and put down. We were not allowed to minister though music anymore in that church. It has been very hard for the entire family. The Holy Spirit convicted us, and we are committed to follow the steps you taught us in your sermon."

The next day I went to a different town to preach. When I returned to my host family, they told me that they went to a leader's house. They humbled themselves, and even though they were the victims in this entire situation, they extended their forgiveness for all that had been done to them. Of course, as in many similar occasions, the offenders did not admit anything. Therefore, there was no reconciliation, but the Holy Spirt was present and did what only God can do—liberated and healed these victims. They returned home very happy.

We praised God for this. We prayed and thanked the Lord for His goodness and faithfulness. At the end the sister who was deeply hurt said, "I feel so light. I am so happy and free. I was not able to pray and rejoice in the Spirit like this since the whole ordeal took place years ago. I praise God for everything!"

I returned to the States. After a short while I received a message from this family. Here is the message:

> Did God have to send people from overseas to teach us and make us understand His will in our lives? Apparently so. For quite some time, we have been experiencing various trials. God's school is sometimes incomprehensible to us. We were often knocked to the ground. We were trampled over. We have been defamed and slandered many times by so- called men of God. We were brokenhearted by the hypocrisy and lack of compassion that exists in God's House. All of these, because we have not fully understood the teaching on forgiveness from Matthew 18:21-35—the parable of the unmerciful servant. But God, who is full of mercy and grace, spoke to us, particularly to my wife. The Lord performed a miracle in our family through the message that you preached here. A great burden which pressed so hard on us for many years has been lifted up.

Let's be reminded that we live in a culture infected by sin. We came from various subcultures, certain families, specific church backgrounds, and specific communities. Let's be honest, we are imperfect people too and we live among other imperfect people. Therefore, it's impossible not to encounter various offenses. Jesus told His disciples: "It is inevitable that stumbling blocks come, but woe to him through whom they come!" (Luke 18:1, see also Matthew 18:7). Despite all of these, our attitude must be already established: *"I will not let myself be offended by this. I will forgive immediately. For me, practicing forgiveness is a lifestyle."*

Often, it is much easier to bring sacrifices to the Lord rather than showing and practicing mercy. But God clearly tells us: "I desire compassion, and not sacrifice" (Matthew 9:13). Even in the Old Testament we can read: "He has told you, O man, what is good; and what does the LORD require of you, but to do justice, to love kindness, and to walk humbly with your God?" (Micah 6:8). It seems so simple, but something keeps us from being compassionate. Maybe we consider compassion and forgiveness a sign of weakness, but it is quite the opposite. Jesus came into our world not because we deserved it, but because He had compassion for us. God loved us so much that He sacrificed His only begotten Son for us so we can be set free.

The Parable of the Unmerciful Servant, from Matthew chapter 18, tells us that the king forgave a slave of the debt of ten thousand talents[67] of gold just because he was moved with compassion. The Bible tells us: "And the lord of that slave felt compassion and released him and forgave him the debt" (Matthew 18:27).

The king represents God. This servant owed the king a huge sum of money,[2] an unpayable debt. No matter how much and how hard he would work, his entire family could not save ten thousand talents of gold in a lifetime. This unpayable debt refers to our sinfulness. This parable also shows how full of evil, deceitful, and ungrateful the human

---

[2] AN: See endnotes for more details.

heart can be towards others and God and how disregarding and disrespectful towards His forgiveness.

The servant, who was forgiven the unpayable debt, has a dispute with a fellow servant over an insignificant amount of money. His colleague owed him one hundred denarii[68]. This represents the wages from one hundred days of work. This is a derisory sum of money compared to the huge amount that the king forgave him. The forgiven slave was not willing to forgive his fellow servant.

Matthew writes:

> But that slave went out and found one of his fellow slaves who owed him a hundred denarii; and he seized him and began to choke him, saying, "Pay back what you owe." So his fellow slave fell to the ground and began to plead with him, saying, "Have patience with me and I will repay you." But he was unwilling and went and threw him in prison until he should pay back what was owed. (Matthew 18:28–30)

This scene seems unbelievable! But unfortunately, this happens in life almost all the time: broken families, relatives disenchanted with each other, churches in conflict, assemblies in chaos and disunity. Why? There is a lack of mercy, compassion, and forbearance and instead there is stubbornness, evil hearts, and unforgiving spirits.

I like the fact that the "Parable of the Unmerciful Servant" is interpreted by Jesus Himself.

Matthew writes:

> Then summoning him, his lord said to him, "You wicked slave, I forgave you all that debt because you pleaded with me. Should you not also have had mercy on your fellow slave, in the same way that I had mercy on you?" And his lord, moved with anger, handed him over to the torturers until he should repay all that was owed him. My heavenly Father will also do the same to you, if each of you does not forgive his brother from

your heart." (Matthew 18: 32–35)

Based on many years of pastoral counseling, Dr. Charles Stanley explains that there are certain stages[69] through which people come to have an unforgiving spirit and offers some steps to deliverance. The following section is my adaptation based on Dr. Stanley's book, *The Gift of Forgiveness*:

We get hurt—we start to develop an unforgiving spirit when we get hurt. All our hurts are in fact some form of rejection. The seeds of an unforgiving spirit are planted when the incident happens. Often this occurs at a very early age. Usually the people around us, who are supposed to love, care and nurture us, knowingly or unknowingly hurt us. This scars us for the rest of our lives.

We become confused—we are not sure what exactly happened, and we are not sure how to respond. We naively rationalize in our minds: "This is not really happening."

We look for detours—we take mental and physical detours. Our desire is to avoid pain at all costs. So, we avoid bringing up that topic or we avoid seeing that person. Some people move, change jobs or churches, or divorce their wives or husbands.

We dig a hole—we bury our pain and hurt so deep that we never talk or think about it. We think that this will resolve it. We hope that in this way the pain caused by rejection will just disappear. But it doesn't.

We deny it—we deny that it ever happened or that it affected us. We cover it up with a smile, justifying it by saying: "Well, that happened so long ago that I have forgotten about it." Or: "I addressed that in the past." But denial is not the solution to the problem.

We become defeated—we might deny the fact that it affected us, but it starts to show up in our lives. We become short-tempered, overly sensitive, shy, jealous, or develop a critical spirit. These flesh patterns are clear indicators that we have not resolved it. We are still carrying the burden and it brings us down.

We become discouraged—this is the critical stage. At this point some of us may seek professional help, which could lead to a happy ending. Unfortunately, many people consider it too difficult, too painful to deal with the issue, so they try to calm down their pain with alcohol or prescription drugs. Husbands leave their wives. Tragically, some people end their own lives.

We discover the truth—through God's help or someone else's help we discover the root of the bitterness. It requires the Holy Spirit's intervention (see 2 Timothy 2:24–26).

We take responsibility—we reach the stage when we no longer blame others. We take responsibility for our own actions. Regardless of the cost, we are now ready to open our hearts to God to deal with our hurts and the emotional pain we have been carrying inside for so long.

We are delivered—when we are ready to deal with the unforgiving spirit we are delivered. Yes, God is still in the business of deliverance. Jesus Christ promised to set us free (see John 8:31–32, 36).

We cannot play with the spirit of unforgiveness! It is extremely dangerous! It leads to a deep root of bitterness. As believers, we must practice forgiveness as a lifestyle. Peter asked: "Lord, how often shall my brother sin against me and I forgive him? Up to seven times? (Matthew 18:21). The rabbis of his day thought that people were supposed to forgive up to three times. Peter, wanting to look super-spiritual, showed a lot of generosity. Three times two plus one … seven times! Exceeding the practice of his day!

The answer he received from the Lord is mindboggling! "I do not say to you, up to seven times, but up to seventy times seven" (Matthew 18:22). If we would like to play with numbers, although this is not what Jesus had in mind, this means four hundred and ninety times per day. Think about it. This means that every three minutes someone is doing something wrong against us and we are supposed to forgive them. What Jesus wanted to communicate is forgiveness as a lifestyle. In other words, we will not allow anyone or anything to offend us.

We need to understand the true meaning of forgiveness from the biblical perspective. Many times, it is easier to understand a particular concept by understanding the opposite of it. Let me briefly explain what forgiveness is not.

Forgiveness does not mean reconciliation

Reconciliation is a step further. Forgiveness is a change in ourselves. Reconciliation involves a change in someone else. Forgiveness is a unilateral step towards reconciliation, but reconciliation must be bilateral and reciprocal. In other words: Reconciliation requires that both sides agree on the facts, pain caused to the other, motivation, and that each party can understand the other's point of view. It requires both parties to understand what happened as well as the consequences of what happened.

Reconciliation requires starting a friendly dialogue, discovering the truth and showing empathy. Each party must be allowed to tell his or her history to establish the truth. Reconciling the pain caused by the offense requires assuming personal responsibility to restore confidence. In some cases, it requires reversal of roles and power. Detecting true remorse is essential in this process. Then you offer a sincere apology for a significant transformation to really take place in the relationship.

On a case-by-case basis, reconciliation may require a debt to be paid to compensate for the loss (or losses) caused to the victim (or victims). The goal is to prevent recurrence of the same harmful conduct and to ensure healing and to further promote a healthy relationship. True reconciliation, if it is properly done, leads to a mutual benefit.[70]

Forgiveness does not mean tolerance

Forgiveness does not mean that we agree with intentional

abuse and mistreatment. Abuse cannot be tolerated; it must be prevented and stopped. To overlook an offense is to disregard a harmful action without protest or disapproval. Forgiveness does not mean excusing a crime or an illegal act. Forgiveness does not mean accepting the unacceptable.

Forgiveness, though, is absolutely necessary for healing and releasing of our own destructive emotions and painful past. We must keep in mind that: "The cross makes forgiveness legally and morally right. Jesus died, once for all our sins. We must forgive as Christ has forgiven us."[71]64 We have the power to forgive those who have wronged us without them asking for forgiveness.

Forgiveness is not forgetting

We cannot forget the pain from the past. By forgiving others, we allow Christ to heal our wounds. God does not have amnesia about our sins. He decided, for His own sake, that, "I will not remember your sins" (Isaiah 43:25). In other words, He is not using our past against us. "Forgetting is a long-term by-product of forgiveness, but it is never a means toward it … we don't heal ourselves to forgive; we forgive in order to heal."[72] It is very likely that we will never forget some of the wounds of the past, but through forgiveness, we will not be slaves to them.

Forgiveness is not easy

In the essay titled, "The Deep Oil of Forgiveness," published on www.aacc, Dr. Tim Clinton writes:

> Forgiveness isn't easy, but it's always necessary. And it only takes one to forgive. When you get to the heart of the matter, our ability to forgive is rooted in the fact that we have been forgiven by God, in Christ (2 Corinthians 5:18–20).[73]

In fact, to forgive is excruciatingly painful and

emotionally difficult. Why? In a sense, forgiveness is accepting to live with the consequences of another's sins. All of us are already in this situation because of Adam's sin. However, we shall never forget that Christ paid for all injustices, from the first man to the last human being who will be born on this planet. Shakespeare wrote: "It is not the wrongdoer's repentance that creates forgiveness, but the victim's forgiveness that creates repentance."[74] Powerful statement, isn't it?

The Bible clearly teaches us:

> Never take your own revenge, beloved, but leave room for the wrath of God, for it is written, 'Vengeance is Mine, I will repay,' says the Lord. "But if your enemy is hungry, feed him, and if he is thirsty, give him a drink; for in so doing you will heap burning coals on his head." (Romans 12:19–20)

Forgiveness is for our own good

Augustine said: "Resentment is like taking poison and hoping the other person dies."[75] Pause for a moment. Let this statement sink in. Let us realize that forgiveness is for our own spiritual, emotional, and physical well-being. Forgiveness is not primarily about the offender; it is about us. We are the first beneficiaries of forgiveness.

In an article called, "Forgiveness: Your Life Depends Upon It," published by Family Therapy magazine, psychiatrist Loren Olson noted that:

> Those more inclined to pardon the transgressions of others have been found to have lower blood pressure, fewer depressive symptoms and, once they hit late middle age, better overall mental and physical health than those who do not forgive easily.[76]

Forgiveness gives the past another meaning

Paul Boese says: "Forgiveness does not change the past, but it does enlarge the future."[77] Through forgiveness we earn the freedom from our past and from those who have abused us. "To forgive is to set a prisoner free and discover that the prisoner was you."[78] More importantly, we cannot change the facts of the past, but we can change the meaning of the past.

After many years of counseling David A. Seamands realized that there are two major causes of the psychological conditions and emotional problems of many evangelicals.

These causes are:

> The failure to understand, receive, and live out God's unconditional grace and forgiveness. The failure to give out that unconditional love, forgiveness, and grace to other people."[79]

Let's briefly look at these two causes:

1. The failure to understand, receive, and live out God's unconditional grace and forgiveness.

The misunderstanding of God's unconditional grace and how it operates causes the inability to receive it fully. This misunderstanding leads many Christians to a performance-based acceptance. Seamands writes:

> "Many of us are like that. We read; we believe a good theology of grace. But that's not the way we live. We believe grace in our heads but not in our gut-level feeling or in our relationships."[80]

To forgive is to set a prisoner free and discover that the prisoner was you.
—Lewis B. Smedes

Therefore, experiential knowledge of the Trinity is the most important aspect in our lives as disciples of Jesus.

I like the way A. W. Tozer writes:

What comes into our minds when we think about God is the most important thing about us. For this reason, the gravest question before the Church is always God Himself, and the most portentous fact about any man is not what he at a given time may say or do, but what he in his deep heart conceives God to be like."[81]

2. The failure to give unconditional love, forgiveness, and grace to other people

Many of us think that we can earn God's grace and forgiveness. This is a lie from the pit of hell. As a result of this misconception, we fail to accept and receive God's love, forgiveness and His wonderful grace. When we fail in this important area, we also fail to give grace and extend forgiveness to others.

David Seamands writes:

> And this results in a breakdown in our interpersonal relationships. It results in emotional conflicts between us and other people. The unforgiven are the unforgiving, and the unforgiving complete the vicious circle because they cannot be forgiven … The vicious circle becomes more vicious. The unaccepted are the unaccepting. The unforgiven are the unforgiving. The ungraced are the ungracious. In fact, their behavior is sometimes positively disgraceful. And emotional conflicts and broken-down relationships are the result.[82]

Now let's explore what forgiveness really means.

- Pardon of sins

Aphesis, rendered "forgive." According to *the Greek New Testament,* it literally means "to send away." See the New Testament's examples in Matthew 26:28 and Acts 2:38 that are associated with the pardon of sins.

- To show kindness

Charizomai signifies "to bestow a favor" or to "show kindness" (see Romans 8:32). Charizomai is rendered "shall freely give."

- To wash away (our sins)

Apolouo means to "wash away." Luke writes: "Now why do you delay? Get up and be baptized, and wash away your sins, calling on His name" Acts 22:16.

- To set free or to redeem

Apolutrosis means redemption. The Bible uses the word redemption as an equivalent for forgiveness. In Ephesians chapter 1 verse 7 we read: "In Him we have redemption through His blood, the forgiveness of our trespasses, according to the riches of His grace."

Moreover, the Lord Jesus started His earthly ministry by declaring:

> The Spirit of the Lord is upon Me, because He anointed Me to preach the Gospel to the poor. He has sent Me to proclaim release to the captives, and recovery of sight to the blind, to set free those who are oppressed, to proclaim the favorable year of the Lord. (Luke 4:18–19)

Forgiveness defined:

Biblical forgiveness is the action and attitude of the Holy and Righteous God according to the richness of His mercy and the fullness of His grace. This kind of forgiveness is based on the Holy and Blameless sacrifice of Jesus Christ on the Cross of Calvary. God decided to pay for all the sins of humanity, past, present, and future, and to give new life eternal to all who come to Him through faith in Jesus Christ. In addition, He covers all the forgiven saints with Christ's righteousness and grants them the unthinkable privilege of living in God's presence for eternity.

Forgiveness from God's perspective

God's forgiveness is a total and complete coverage of our debt forever. We all have heard the story of forgiveness from Matthew 18:27: "And the lord of that slave felt compassion and released him and forgave him the debt."

I like the way Micah writes:

> Who is a God like You, who pardons iniquity and passes over the rebellious act of the remnant of His possession? He does not retain His anger forever, because He delights in unchanging love. He will again have compassion on us; He will tread our iniquities under foot. Yes, You will cast all their sins into the depths of the sea. (Micah 7:18–19)

Do you hear that? God will cast all our sins into the depths of the sea! Wow!

Paul also writes:

> When you were dead in your transgressions and the uncircumcision of your flesh, He made you alive together with Him, having forgiven us all our transgressions, having canceled out the certificate of debt consisting of decrees against us, which was hostile to us; and He has taken it out of the way, having nailed it to the cross. (Colossians 2:13–14)

Corie Ten Boom[83] said: "When we confess our sins … God casts them into the deepest ocean, gone forever … Then God places a sign out there that says: 'No Fishing Allowed!'"[84]

Secular definition

a: to give up resentment of or claim to requital for, (forgive an insult); b: to grant relief from payment of, (forgive a debt). To cease to feel resentment against (an offender), (pardon—forgive one's enemies).[85]

David A. Seamands recommends we take three tests in reference to forgiving others. The following section is my adaptation based on his book, *Healing for Damaged Emotions.*

The resentment test: Take the teaching on forgiveness very seriously. Ask yourself an important question. "Is there someone you resent; someone you've never let off the hook?" Ask the Holy Spirit to bring to your mind people who you need to forgive.

The responsibility test: Do you take responsibility for your own actions? Or is it easier to continue to blame others for what is going on? As we find freedom and healing through forgiveness, we need to learn and practice extending forgiveness to others. We need to assume responsibility for our own faults and failures.

The reminder and reaction test: This question in this case sounds like this: "Do you find yourself reacting against a person because he or she reminds you of someone else?" If this is the case, it means that you have not really forgiven that person from the heart.

Almost two thousand years ago the greatest injustice in the whole universe occurred, Jesus' crucifixion on the Cross of Calvary. In His wonderful wisdom, compassion, mercy and grace, God took the most evil act that was done and turned it into the most sublime gift for humankind—salvation.

Freedom through Forgiveness[86]

God saved us. Our Heavenly Father forgave us, not because we deserve forgiveness, but because He is full of mercy and His lovingkindness endures forever. The psalmist declares, "Oh give thanks to the LORD, for He is good, for His lovingkindness is everlasting." (Psalm 107:1). We are invited to imitate our Lord. We all have been hurt, one way or another, neglected, rejected, betrayed, put down, and offended. However, we are called to extend forgiveness to others who don't deserve it. If we don't do it we are in real danger of giving Satan an opportunity.

Paul writes:

> But one whom you forgive anything, I forgive also; for indeed what I have forgiven, if I have forgiven anything, I did it for your sakes in the presence of Christ, so that no advantage would be taken of us by Satan, for we are not ignorant of his schemes. (2 Corinthians 2:10–11

Anderson recommends that people who are willing to process forgiveness turn to prayer. I invite you to pray the following prayer:

> *Dear heavenly Father, I thank You for the riches of Your kindness, forbearance, and patience toward me, knowing that Your kindness has led me to repentance. I confess that I have not shown that same kindness and patience toward those who have hurt or offended me (Romans 2:4). Instead, I have held on to my anger, bitterness, and resentment toward them. Please bring to my mind all the people I need to forgive in order that I may now do so. In Jesus' name I pray. Amen.*

Let's continue the process. Ask the Holy Spirit to reveal any painful memories that you may have forgotten or buried. Make a list of all the people who have hurt you and all of the wrongs they have done to you. Wait, listen, and complete the list.

From Adam and Eve forward, all people offended others. Nobody is innocent. Paul writes: "for all have sinned and fall short of the glory of God." All of us have been conceived in sin and are prone to sin. The Psalmist cries out, "Behold, I was brought forth in iniquity, and in sin my mother conceived me" (Psalm 51:5). So, according to Anderson: "Forgiveness is agreeing to live with the consequences of another person's sin."[87]

Let's keep in mind that only the cross makes forgiveness legally and morally right. Maybe you are very hard on yourself. You need to forgive yourself too. Remember: God has already forgiven you.

Maybe you are mad at God. You raised your fist towards heaven shouting: "God, where are You? Don't You see what is happening to me?" And you are angry and upset with the Lord. Jot down all the negative feelings about God. All those emotions must be released in order for you to experience emotional healing and receive complete peace from God.

We should initiate forgiveness right away. We should not wait for the offender to come and beg us for forgiveness. It may never happen. Instead, we should follow in the footsteps of Jesus who forgave those who crucified Him without expecting them to ask for forgiveness. Luke records: "Father, forgive them; for they do not know what they are doing" (Luke 23:34).

We should not wait until we feel ready to forgive. Remember: *Forgiveness is a choice.* Therefore, choose to forgive. Start with the first person from your list. One by one, bring each person, each hurt, each wrong to the Cross. Visualize standing before Jesus. Make sure you are being emotionally honest. Express your anger, pain, and hurt openly to God for each person and situation. Spend time in prayer for each person you need to forgive until you have dealt with all the pain and the hurt.

When processing forgiveness, it is important to do it from the heart. Remember Christ's interpretation of the Parable of the Unmerciful Servant? He said: "My heavenly Father will also do the same to you, if each of you does not forgive his brother from your heart" (Matthew 18:35).

If we just process it intellectually and do not let the emotional pain come to the surface, it is almost impossible to experience emotional healing. Invite Jesus to the place where you hurt, ask Him where He was when this happened. Wait and visualize. Ask Jesus to heal this wound. Ask Jesus to forgive this person for their wrongdoing. According to Dr. Anderson: "If your forgiveness doesn't touch the emotional core of your life, it will be incomplete."[88] We should be intentional about forgiving from the heart. We should pray to God to give us emotional strength so we can face the pain, anger and disappointment.

Let go of any desire to avenge yourself or pay the offender back. Give up your right to retaliate or seek revenge. Don't hang on to this issue any longer. Pardon the person by releasing him or her and the situation to Jesus. Ask for compassion, mercy and understanding for this person and the situation. Exchange your anger for God's love and mercy. Bless the person in the very area where they hurt you.

Cooperate with the Holy Spirit. He may bring to the surface many hurts and painful memories. Stay there before the Cross until grace, mercy and forgiveness invade your heart and mind.

When you are done with all the people from the list, pray out loud the following prayer:

Lord Jesus, I choose to forgive (name the person) for (what they did or failed to do), because it made me feel (share the painful feelings, i.e. rejected, dirty, worthless, inferior, etc.)[89]

Make a conscious decision to let go of any resentments. Then pray this prayer:

Lord Jesus, I choose not to hold on to my resentment. I relinquish my right to seek revenge and ask you to heal my damaged emotions. Thank You for setting me free from the bondage of my bitterness. I now ask You to bless those who have hurt me. In Jesus' name I pray. Amen.[90]

A Powerful Story of Forgiveness

Corrie ten Boom, a devout Christian woman, and a holocaust survivor, tells her story in a book called, *The Hiding*

Place. Corrie and her sister Betsy were put in prison. They were placed in a horrible place—a dorm in Ravensbruck. This was a place built for 200 people, but they jammed more than 1,200 women in there. Despite this terrible situation, she recalls that God watched over them and protected them from various harmful situations. Due to a clerical error, Corrie was released from prison after several years. The very next day, all the women her age were exterminated. She got home and started telling her story. There is a movie with the same title based on her book. Corrie ten Boom's testimony is forgiveness and love. The point is that God can carry us through any situation.

Compelled by the love of Jesus, Corrie went to defeated Germany to share with people the message of forgiveness and love. After one of the meetings, one of the cruelest guards of Ravensbruck was there too. Betsy, Corrie's sister, suffered a lot because of him before she died in that camp. He told Corrie that he was a child of God, that he had asked Jesus to come into his heart. He had asked God to forgive him of the cruel sins he had committed. He even prayed that God would give him the opportunity to ask for forgiveness from at least one of his very own victims. And there was the answer to his prayer; Corrie ten Boom was in front of him. So, he asked: "Fraulein ten Boom, I want to be forgiven." He wanted to shake hands with her. But at that very moment she froze; she could not do that. The memory of her dying sister was still vivid in her mind.

In that moment she had to pray for God's help to overcome the hatred and unforgiveness towards this former concentration camp guard. She claimed the love of God as promised in Romans 5:5. Then at that very moment she could forgive him and call him brother. She felt that the love of God flowed to her arms. Then she shook hands with the former criminal. Isn't this a powerful story of forgiveness?

Benefits of forgiveness

One of the most important benefits of forgiveness is the

peace of God we receive when we obey Christ from the heart. The second one is that we don't give an opportunity to Satan to mess up our lives. The bottom line is that when we forgive from the heart we are more like Jesus.

In addition to the spiritual benefits, there are physical and psychological benefits that forgiveness brings. Based on the findings by Mayo Clinic Staff: "Letting go of grudges and bitterness can make way for happiness, health and peace."[91]84

In one of their articles, they list several benefits:

- Healthier relationships
- Greater spiritual and psychological well-being
- Less anxiety, stress and hostility
- Lower blood pressure
- Fewer symptoms of depression
- Stronger immune system
- Improved heart health
- Higher self-esteem

In the same article they list a few negative effects of unforgiveness:

- Anger and bitterness into every relationship and new experience.
- Consumed by the wrongdoing from the past so that you can't enjoy the present.
- Depression or anxiety.
- Life lacks meaning or purpose, or at odds with spiritual beliefs.
- Loss of valuable and enriching connectedness with others.

Moreover, recent research shows that people who make this important mental shift to forgive have another tremendous benefit: living longer.

Professor Susan Krauss Whitbourne, Ph.D on her article titled, "Live Longer by Practicing Forgiveness," published by

Psychology Today in January 2013. She attested that the benefit of forgiveness is a long and better-quality life. Her claim is supported by the study called "Forgive to Live," published in the Journal of Behavioral Medicine. The study was conducted by psychologist Loren Toussaint and his colleagues from Luther College. They investigated the relationships among forgiveness, religiousness, spirituality, health, and mortality in a national

U.S. sample of 1500 adults age 66 and older. This research is among the first to attest to the benefits of forgiveness to a long life.

Reflection Questions

Please reflect upon the following questions, briefly elaborate, and then share your thoughts with a friend or your small group.

1. What did the Holy Spirit whisper to your heart through this chapter? What did you like the most in this chapter?

2. What new concepts did you learn from this chapter? Which idea are you committed to implementing in your life?

3. What are your thoughts on the ten stages that people go through to develop an unforgiving spirit? Please elaborate.

4. After reading the section titled "Freedom though Forgiveness," please jot down some ideas or personal experiences.

5. List the best aha moments you had while reading this chapter.

Endnotes:

[67] How much is a talent of gold one may ask? A Roman talent was 32.3 kilograms (71 lb). https://en.wikipedia.org/wiki/ Talent_(measurement) (Accessed on February 28, 2017).
Then, 10,000 talents equal 323,000 kilograms of pure gold. You do the conversion in US Dollar. Maybe 12,959,406,000 USD. www.goldprice.org. Accessed on February 28, 2017. http://goldprice.org/gold-price-per-kilo.html.
The bottom line is that this is a huge sum of money the slave owed to the king. It represents our sinfulness that cannot be paid for. Only God was able to handle that type of debt by sacrificing His only begotten Son on the Calvary Cross.
[68] How much is 100 denarii one may ask? A small silver coin. www.en.wikipedia.org. Denarius. Accessed on February 28, 201). https://en.wikipedia.org/wiki/.
One denarius was one day's wages in the time of Jesus. If we convert 100 denarii in US dollars in today's market it is estimated to be $3650 USD. "According to the U.S. Census Bureau, the average household income was $73,298 in 2014, the latest year for which complete data is available. However, this doesn't tell the whole story. Depending on your family situation and where you live, average household income can vary dramatically. www.usatoday.com. Accessed on February 28, 2017. http://www.usatoday.com/story/money/personalfinance/2016/11/24/ average-american-household-income/93002252/.
[69] Dr. Charles Stanley, *The Gift of Forgiveness,* (Thomas Nelson, Nashville, TN: 1991), 91-96.
[70] To process reconciliation with someone, seek help from a qualified Christian Counselor or a qualified Pastor or Life Coach.
[71] Neil T. Anderson, *The Bondage Breaker,* (Harvest House Publishers, Eugene, OR: 2000), 222.
[72] Neil. T. Anderson, *The Steps to Freedom in Christ,* (Gospel Light, Colorado Springs, CO, 2004), 11.
[73] Dr. Tim Clinton, "The Deep Oil of Forgiveness." www.aacc.net. Accessed on February 19, 2014. http://www.aacc.net/2014/02/18/ the-deep-oil-of-forgiveness-4/.
[74] William Shakespeare, "The Merchant of Venice," Act 4 scene 1.
[75] Saint Augustine-Quotes. www.sniblit.com.Accessed on February 28, 2017. http://www.sniblit.com/Saint- Augustine-Quotes.html http://www.famousquotefrom.com/saint-augustine/.
[76] Olson, L. A. "Forgiveness: Your Life Depends Upon It." Published on March/April of 2011, by Family Therapy, 10 (2), 28-31.
[77] Forgiveness. www.thinkexist.com. Accessed on February 28, 2017. http://thinkexist.com/quotation/ forgiveness_does_not_change_the_past-

but_it_does/9267.html.
[78] Lewis B. Smedes on forgiveness. www.brainyquote.com. Accessed on February 28, 2017, https://www.brainyquote.com/ authors/lewis_b_smedes.
[79] David A. Seamands and Beth Funk, *Healing for Damaged Emotions Workbook* (David Cook, Colorado Springs, CO: 2015), 45.
[80] Ibid, 46.
[81] A.W. Tozer, *The Knowledge of the Holy*, Chapter 1. www.heavendwellers.com. Accessed on March 29, 2017. http://www.heavendwellers.com/hdt_chapter_1_koh. htm.
[82] Seamands, 49.
[83] Corrie ten Boom, a devout Christian woman and a holocaust survivor, tells her story in a book called, *The Hiding Place*. www.bible.org. Accessed on February 28, 2017, https://bible.org/seriespage/7-corrie-ten-boom-portrait-forgiveness.
[84] Corrie ten Boom quote on forgiveness. www.crosswalk.com. Accessed on March 3, 2017, http://www.crosswalk.com/faith/ spiritual-life/inspiring-quotes/40-powerful-quotes-from-corrie- ten-boom.html/.
[85] Forgive. www.merriam- webster.com. Accessed on February 27, 2017, https://www.merriam- webster.com/dictionary/forgive.
[86] Adapted from Step Three: "Bitterness vs. Forgiveness." Dr. Neil T. Anderson, *The Steps to Freedom in Christ*, (Gospel Light, Colorado Springs, CO: 2004), 11-13.
[87] Anderson, Breaker, 223.
[88] Ibid, 224.
[89] Anderson, Steps, 12.
[90] Ibid, 13.
[91] Mayo Clinic Staff, "Forgiveness: Letting go of grudges and bitterness." www. mayoclinic.org. November 2014. Accessed on February 27, 2017. http://www. mayoclinic.org/healthy-lifestyle/adult-health/in- depth/ forgiveness/art-20047692?pg=1.

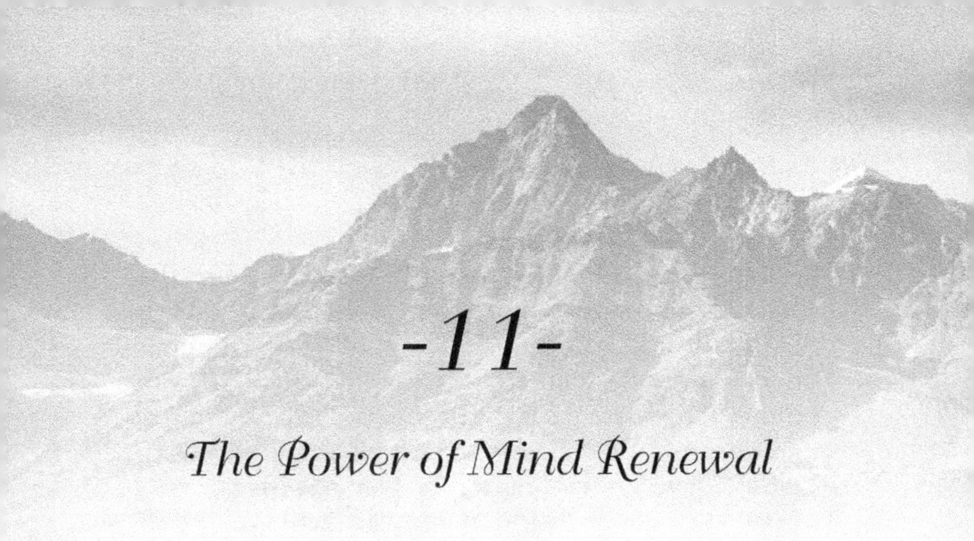

-11-

The Power of Mind Renewal

In reference to your former manner of life, you lay aside the old self, which is being corrupted in accordance with the lusts of deceit, and that you be renewed in the spirit of your mind.
—Ephesians 4:22–23

One morning, some time ago, I woke up with the passage from Ephesians 4:20–32 to 5:1–2 vivid in my mind. Immediately, something deep resonated in my spirit: "*Believers must repent.*" Mind renewal (Gr. metanoia[92]) is a continuous process. I looked more closely at that text in Ephesians. Then, the spiritual impression I received previously made even more sense, especially in the context of chapter four of this epistle. The context of this entire chapter is about spiritual growth and maturity. I wrote extensively about this topic in my previous chapters.

With this context in mind, Paul continues to teach believers, in the most practical terms, what Christian living really is. Things are self-evident when taken in the context in which they were written! Paul, under divine inspiration, just finished his train of thought regarding the building up of the body of Christ: "According to the proper working of each individual part, causes the growth of the body for the building up of itself in love" (Ephesians 4:16). After this powerful statement he contrasts *"the Christian way of living"* with *"the living of the Gentiles."* The key phrase he uses here is ***"walk in the futility of their minds."*** The contrast is so obvious.

Let's listen to this:

> So this I say, and affirm together with the Lord, that you walk no longer just as the Gentiles also walk, in the futility of their mind, being darkened in their understanding, excluded from the life of God because of the ignorance that is in them, because of the hardness of their heart; and they, having become callous, have given themselves over to sensuality for the practice of every kind of impurity with greediness. (Ephesians 4:17–19)

Striking, isn't it? Paul continues with the conjunction "but," which makes the contrast even more obvious. In the next paragraph, he uses another key phrase: *"Be renewed in the spirit of your mind."*

Now let us read this passage:

> But you did not learn Christ in this way, if indeed you have heard Him and have been taught in Him, just as truth is in Jesus, that, in reference to your former manner of life, you lay aside the old self, which is being corrupted in accordance with the lusts of deceit, and that you be renewed in the spirit of your mind, and put on the new self, which in the likeness of God has been created in righteousness and holiness of the truth. (Ephesians 4:20–24).

Brilliant, isn't it?

In other words, spiritual growth and maturity imply continuous repentance—*being renewed in the spirit of our minds.* Wow! The mind of born-again believers has a spiritual dimension. This aspect is crucial in the process of progressive sanctification. In other words, believers, out of obedience, are admonished to exercise the spiritual dimension they possess and renew their minds by the Word of God. This, according to Paul, is part of the ongoing process of spiritual formation. And here is exactly where many Christians have real-life issues—they forget to renew their minds.

I remember the chorus of an old hymn, based on Galatians 3:27, the congregation sang when I was baptized in water many years ago:

All of you who were baptized into Christ,
In Christ, you have also clothed yourselves.
Hallelujah! Hallelujah!

This is absolutely true from the spiritual point of view. This truth is at the very heart of being born again. However, in Ephesians 4:20–24, Paul talks about the manifestation and visibility of Christ in our daily lives. In other words, since it is very true that when I was born again, I was clothed with Christ, this aspect should also be true in how I live my life practically. The nature and character of Christ should be seen in me.

One might ask: *"How am I supposed to deal with my former manner of life, with past corruption, lust, and deceit?"* God's Word tells us exactly how to proceed. How can we do this? By renewing our minds. We must stop permitting the world to shape and form us according to its values. On the contrary, we must be transformed.

Paul tells us very directly: "And do not be conformed to this world, but be transformed (Gr. *metamorphoo—supernaturally transformed*) by the renewing (Gr. *anakaínōsis—a renewal brought about by the power of God*) of your mind" (Romans 12:2a).

Transformation through the renewing of the mind is a daily, lifelong process. It involves putting off the old self and putting on the new self—"which in the likeness of God has been created in righteousness and holiness of the truth" (Ephesians 4:24b).

Everything Paul writes, from Ephesians 4:25 to the end of the epistle, are practical steps for believers in all life areas, i.e:

family, business, church, spiritual warfare, and so on.

Based on the spiritual truths I understood that morning, I would like to share some practical steps for renewing our minds.

1. Transparency in our Christian relationships

Paul writes: "Therefore, laying aside falsehood, speak truth each one of you with his neighbor, for we are members of one another" (Ephesians 4:25). Sometimes, as believers, if we are not careful, we can easily be caught into the spider web woven so carefully by the "god of this world" to tell people what they want to hear so that we can be loved and accepted by them. I know that this sounds so politically correct. But it is wrong.

In the local church context, we become people-pleasers, using words in such a way so we can please the entire congregation. We mask the reality of our hearts to protect ourselves from being hurt. Very soon, we will be so caught in that spider web through various forms of lying that we will no longer see reality. We must stop this! Instead, invite the Holy Spirit into the deep area of hurt that conditioned us to be people-pleasers instead of God-pleasers. Upon proper emotional healing, we can be empowered by the Holy Spirit to speak the truth in love.

No wonder Paul encourages the Lord's servants to be spiritually discerning (2 Timothy 2:24–26).

Remember that spiritual transparency is crucial in the process of spiritual transformation. I am becoming more convinced that spiritual transformation (metamorphosis) is impossible without it.

2. Exercising self-control

Paul writes: "Be angry, and yet do not sin; do not let the sun go down on your anger, and do not give the devil an opportunity" (Ephesians 4:26–27).

Anger is a powerful emotion. Aristotle writes: "Anyone can

become angry—that is easy. But to be angry with the right person, to the right degree, at the right time, for the right purpose, and in the right way—that is not easy."[93] A simple definition of anger is this: "a strong feeling of being upset or annoyed because of something wrong or bad. The feeling that makes someone want to hurt other people, to shout."[94]

I appreciate what Andrew D. Lester, professor of pastoral theology and pastoral counseling at Texas Christian University's Brite Divinity School, explains about anger.

He asserts:

> Anger has its origins in creation, not our sinfulness … Anger is connected to embodiment and is a basic ingredient in the imago Dei, actually a gift from God.[95]

Interesting point, isn't it? In other words, we get angry because God wired us that way. Car designers and automakers equip automobiles with various check engine lights to warn the driver that there is something wrong under the hood; similarly, God wired us with the capacity to get angry when we feel threatened, or face injustices. I also like how pastor and author Ed Chinn said it: "Anger is one of the main "dashboard lights in life."[96] In case there is a real threat (i.e., physical danger) or imaginary threat (i.e., perception of injustice, oppression, or humiliation), or just lack of control over adverse situations or circumstances, it is normal to get angry.

In fact, Paul tells us not to suppress anger. However, he warns us regarding this strong emotion—"*Be angry, and yet do not sin.*" If anger is uncontrolled, it can fester and open the door to the enemy to work in our lives.

Similarly, James admonishes us:

> This you know, my beloved brethren. But everyone must be quick to hear, slow to speak and slow to anger; for the anger of man does not achieve the righteousness of God. (James 1:19–20)

Of course, James does not suggest pretending that we are not angry. He is simply saying that when we act under the influence of this emotion we don't operate in agreement with God's righteousness. This should make us pause and deeply reflect on it.

So, if suppressing our anger is not the solution, how should we handle anger? We acknowledge our emotions before God and pray for His perspective on every situation. If we are willing to let go of the anger, the Holy Spirit is ready to assist us in exploring deeper and more hurtful emotions. In God's timing, this will result in healing and transformation. The truth is that either hidden (covert anger) or out into the open (overt anger), anger perturbs many churches and destroys the fellowship between believers. Moreover, it causes families to break down.

It doesn't have to be this way for God's children. Solomon, the wisest man who ever walked on this earth (besides Jesus), asserted that the ability to handle anger properly is an essential character trait; it is better than the one "who conquers a city." Solomon writes: "He who is slow to anger is better than the mighty, and he who rules his spirit, than he who captures a city" (Proverbs 16:32).

In the same article cited earlier, Professor Lester acknowledges that anger often becomes a tool for evil, yet he insists that anger is a gift from God in at least three ways:

- First, the physiological and psychological ability to become angry prepares our minds and bodies for actions that contribute to our physical and psychological survival.
- Second, the ability to activate our capacity for anger in appropriate situations protects and preserves our physical, mental, and spiritual health.
- Third, proper anger—one that reflects Jesus' occasional angry responses to evil—motivates us to speak and act when we may be tempted to remain silent and unresponsive to the vast needs and troubles

of a world infected with sin.

Positive character traits such as "hope, courage, intimacy, self-awareness, and compassion" are born as we exercise a discerning, holy, loving anger.

As we progress in our Christian maturity and experience the transforming power of the Holy Spirit, we become more and more in tune with our emotions. As a result of the inner healing, we are enabled to discern and decide what makes us angry. We all agree that "anger management" is not the solution here.

The only antidote to such powerful emotion is self-control, which is the fruit of the Spirit (see Galatians 5:22–23). The fruit of the Spirit is not a byproduct of us keeping the law—no matter what law we are talking about— but it is the result of being transformed and then led by the Holy Spirit.

3. Honesty and integrity in business

Paul continues: He who steals must steal no longer; but rather he must labor, performing with his own hands what is good, so that he will have something to share with one who has need. (Ephesians 4:26)

We live in a society whose social dimensions are influenced by money. Status is based on money. Even inside various congregations, religious status most often depends on finances. Popularity, primarily, is influenced by money. King Solomon highlights this fact: "The poor is hated even by his neighbor, but those who love the rich are many" (Proverbs 14:20). We all know that political positions depend on money. Unfortunately, the ecclesiastical position depends on finances as well. The point is that if we are not careful, money, social status, popularity, etc., can lead to favoritism even in the house of God.

James writes without any gloves:

> My brethren, do not hold your faith in our glorious Lord Jesus Christ with an attitude of personal

> favoritism. For if a man comes into your assembly with a gold ring and dressed in fine clothes, and there also comes in a poor man in dirty clothes, and you pay special attention to the one who is wearing the fine clothes, and say, "You sit here in a good place," and you say to the poor man, "You stand over there, or sit down by my footstool," have you not made distinctions among yourselves, and become judges with evil motives? (James 2:1–4)

What is a Christian believer or leader supposed to do? Paul has an answer for us. He urges us to conduct ourselves without any prejudices. He admonishes us: "I solemnly charge you in the presence of God and of Christ Jesus and of His chosen angels, to maintain these principles without bias, doing nothing in a spirit of partiality" (1 Timothy 5:21).

4. Edifying communication

The Bible tells us:

> Let no unwholesome word proceed from your mouth, but only such a word as is good for edification according to the need of the moment, so that it will give grace to those who hear. Do not grieve the Holy Spirit of God, by whom you were sealed for the day of redemption. (Ephesians 4: 29–30)

There is power in the spoken word. When we talk to each other, we can damage, destroy, kill, or comfort, heal, and edify one another. Make no mistake: words have great power. Here is an example from the Old Testament. Jeremiah had a word of prophecy from the Lord. It was not pleasant for the men of Judah and the inhabitants of Jerusalem. They turned against the man of God and *killed him* not with the sword but with their tongues.

The Bible says:

> Then they said, "Come and let us devise plans against Jeremiah. Surely the law is not going to be lost to the priest, nor counsel to the sage, nor the divine word to the prophet! Come on and let us strike at him with our tongue, and let us give no heed to any of his words. (Jeremiah 18:18)

In this case, the prophet says that the human tongue can be used as a sword to strike at other people. We must be aware of these facts.

James warns us about the use of our tongue. We can bless, or we can curse other people with our mouths. He writes: "With it [the tongue] we bless our Lord and Father, and with it, we curse men, who have been made in the likeness of God" (James 3:9).

We are called to build each other up, not to tear down one another. We must use our words wisely. Paul writes: "Let your speech always be with grace, as though seasoned with salt, so that you will know how you should respond to each person" (Colossians 4: 6). We need wisdom and discernment in our conversations.

Before we open our mouths, let's ask ourselves: "Will I build up others with what I am going to say?" "Will my speech hurt, tear down, or damage someone?" The wise man Solomon writes: "Like apples of gold in settings of silver is a word spoken in right circumstances" (Proverbs 25:11). Wow! Well said, Solomon!

Remember that on Judgment Day, people will give an account for every word they speak. Matthew writes: "But I tell you that every careless word that people speak, they shall give an accounting for it in the Day of Judgment" (Matthew 12:36). This aspect should mean much more than just food for thought!

Moreover, whether we like it or not, what we cultivate in our hearts will spill out between our lips sooner or later. Dr. Luke writes: "The good man out of the good treasure of his heart brings forth what is good; and the evil man out of the evil treasure brings forth what is evil; for his mouth speaks from that which fills his heart" (Luke 6:45). We should ask ourselves every so often: "What do I have in abundance in my heart. What fills my heart?" I like very much what Dr. Neil T. Anderson writes in *Victory over Darkness*:

> If we said nothing to put others down and only to build up others as Ephesians 4:29 commands, we would be part of God's construction crew in the Church instead of members of Satan's wrecking crew.[97]

May God help us be builders, not demolishers.

5. Resolving all emotional problems related to the old man

Furthermore, Paul writes: Let all bitterness and wrath and anger and clamor and slander be put away from you, along with all malice. (Ephesians 4:31)

Emotions in themselves are amoral. But how we act or react under the influence of certain emotions can be wrong, immoral, or sinful. For example, if you feel depressed, it is not sinful in itself. But if someone kills herself because she is depressed, she commits a great sin. If someone in a particular situation feels anger building up inside him, acknowledges it, but limits himself to a responsible expression[98] of it, he does not sin. But if, under boiling anger, he says something offensive, hits someone or does anything wrong, this is a sin.

It does not matter where we came from. We all experienced some degree of hurt in our lives and accumulated some emotional baggage.

It does not matter where we came from—Europe, Asia, Africa, South America, or North America, raised by good parents or not so good. We all experienced some degree of hurt in our lives. All of us accumulated some emotional baggage. Some of us are extra-sensitive or prone to anger. Others are afraid of rejection or some hidden shame. We all have inherited specific ways of living from our ancestors: stubbornness, critical attitude, rivalry predisposition, or are given to anger.

Furthermore, we were all born with different personality types and characteristics that define our thoughts, feelings, and behavior.

The good thing is that we came to the saving faith. We accepted Jesus into our hearts. We were born again. Then, we were baptized in water. We started attending the local church. Later, we started preaching the Gospel. Then, we were asked to serve in various capacities, maybe even on a local church's Board of Elders. It does not matter. We got converted, but some emotional characteristics still need to be converted. They weigh us down; they give us problems.

We still get angry. Some of us may, from time to time, use our tongue to tear down our brother instead of building him up. We still raise our tone of voice, point the finger towards our sister, judge others, and put down this one or the other one, and so on. What is a disciple of Christ supposed to do? Should we leave these matters unattended and let these behaviors continue like this forever?

Should we continue to justify ourselves:

> Well, this is who I am. My father was the same way. I have spoken with this tone of voice for as long as I can remember. I get angry so quickly and often offend others. This is my way." No. God forbid. May it never be. In the abovementioned verse, Paul writes: "Let all bitterness and wrath and anger and clamor and slander be put away from you, along with all malice.

The Bible, God's grace, and the Holy Spirit call us to resolve all the emotional problems related to the old man. We cannot live like this forever! We cannot let those flesh patterns ruin our Christian testimony.

We must arrive at the point where we seriously tell God:

> Lord, I can't stand this in myself. I yield myself entirely

> into Your hand. I desire wholeheartedly that all issues (confess all of them one by one) be definitively done with and out of my life.

It is our responsibility to process these issues between us and God. We must also process many aspects between us and other family members and church members.

Most of the time, we can't process this just by ourselves. We must work with a skilled and experienced spiritual mentor, a good Christian counselor, or a spiritual life coach to process all this fleshly garbage. We can't just go on like this, year after year, being angry, heart-hardened, stubborn, judgmental, and tearing ourselves and others down. We must seek emotional healing, get transformation in all of those areas, and start building others up.

6. Forgiveness as lifestyle

Paul continues: "Be kind to one another, tender-hearted, forgiving each other, just as God in Christ also has forgiven you" (Ephesians 4:32). As believers, we are called to perpetual forgiveness. In other words, forgiveness must be our lifestyle.

Let us read slowly and meditatively the Lord's Prayer from Matthew 6:9–13:

> Pray, then, in this way: "Our Father who is in heaven, Hallowed be Your name. Your kingdom come. Your will be done, on earth as it is in heaven. Give us this day our daily bread. And forgive us our debts, as we also have forgiven our debtors. And do not lead us into temptation, but deliver us from evil. [For Yours is the kingdom and the power and the glory forever. Amen.]

Verse eleven points out that while living on this earth, we will accumulate debt and have people who are indebted to us. We need God's forgiveness, and we need to forgive others.

Dr. Tim Clinton, the President of the American Association of Christian Counselors (AACC), writes:

> Christ is, in effect, saying that our vertical relationship with God is much more related to our horizontal relationships with those around us than we would like to admit.[99]

To be sure that His disciples get the importance of forgiveness, Christ explains what He means:

> For if you forgive others for their transgressions, your heavenly Father will also forgive you. But if you do not forgive others, then your Father will not forgive your transgressions. (see Matthew 6:14–15)

We live in a culture infected by sin. We came from various subcultures, certain families, church backgrounds, and communities. Let's be honest. We are imperfect people living among imperfect people. It is impossible not to encounter stumbling blocks. Jesus told His disciples, "It is inevitable that stumbling blocks come, but woe to him through whom they come!" (Luke 18:1, see also Matthew 18:7). Despite all of these, our attitude must already be established: "I will not let myself be offended by this. I will forgive immediately. For me, practicing forgiveness is a lifestyle."

Often, it is much easier to bring sacrifices to the Lord rather than showing and practicing mercy. But God tells us: "I desire compassion, and not sacrifice" (Matthew 9:13). It seems so simple, but something inside causes us not to be compassionate. Maybe we consider it as a sign of weakness. But it is quite the opposite. Jesus came into our world because He had compassion for us. God loved us so much that He could not see us suffering in Hell. He sacrificed His only begotten Son for us to be free. Even the Old Testament states: "He has told you, O man, what is good; and what does the LORD require of you, but to do justice, to love kindness, and to walk humbly with your God?" (Micah 6:8).

As I mentioned before, we cannot play with the spirit of unforgiveness! Period. It is extremely dangerous! It leads to a deep root of bitterness. As believers, we must practice forgiveness as a lifestyle.

7. Walk in Love[3]

The Bible teaches us:

> Therefore, be imitators of God, as beloved children; and walk in love, just as Christ also loved you and gave Himself up for us, an offering and a sacrifice to God as a fragrant aroma. (Ephesians 5:1–2)

Paul writes: "But the goal of our instruction is love from a pure heart and a good conscience and a sincere faith" (1 Timothy 1:5). This means that amid a conflict we still have the same goal or target—***love.*** I know! This is extremely hard for us humans. But let us not forget that, as born-again believers, at the very core of our being we have the nature of God inside of us.

Because of the Zoe life and the agape love inside of us we can live—not based on our own resources but based on the Holy Spirit working in us and through us. Jesus said: "This is My commandment, that you love one another, just as I have loved you" John 15:12).

Please understand! The love that the Bible talks about in these passages does not refer to a velvet feeling which we feel towards another human being or an object. Not really! It refers to the agape love—the love with which God loves. God loves us not because we deserve to be loved. He loves us because that is His very nature—God is love (see 1 John 4:8).

Because of the Zoe life and the agape love inside of us we can live not based on our own resources but based on the Holy Spirit working in us and through us.

[3] AN: Since the subject of Love is inexhaustible, we are dedicating an entire chapter to this important topic.

Therefore, since we have experienced God's love, we can love others. "Beloved, if God so loved us, we also ought to love one another" (1 John 4:11). In fact, God does not ask us to do something without first empowering us by the Holy Spirit to do it. Otherwise, it would be an attempt of the flesh, which God detests. God poured out in us agape love through the Holy Spirit. Paul writes: "Because the love of God has been poured out within our hearts through the Holy Spirit who was given to us" (Romans 5:5).

Therefore, we can love like this. Walking in love means that we allow God's nature and character to manifest in us and through us. 93 Not walking in love means either disobedience and resistance towards the God of Love, or ongoing persistence in a spiritual and emotionally immature state. One way or the other, it is our responsibility to listen and obey, not to resist God anymore. It is our wake-up call to grow in Christ to mature in all aspects, emotionally and spiritually, into Him, who is the Head of the Body.

So, help us God.

Reflection Questions

Please reflect upon the following questions, briefly elaborate, and then share your thoughts with a friend or your small group.

1. What did the Holy Spirit whisper to your heart through this chapter? What did you like the most in this chapter?

2. What new concepts did you learn from this chapter? Which idea are you committed to implementing in your life?

3. From the seven areas the author discussed in this chapter which aspect resonated with more conviction in your own heart? Please elaborate.

4. After reading the section dealing with "Resolving all Emotional Problems related to the Old Man," what concepts stood out for you. Please elaborate.

5. List the best aha moments you had while reading this chapter.

Endnotes:

[92] Metanoia. Change of mind, repentance. Original Word: μετάνοια. Strong's Concordance number 3341. Short Definition: repentance, a change of mind, change in the inner man. www.biblehub.com. Accessed on October 12, 2016, http://biblehub.com/greek/3341.htm.

[93] Aristotle, "The Nicomachean Ethics." www.brainyquote.com. Accessed on October 13, 2016. http://www.brainyquote.com/quotes/authors/a/aristotle. html.

[94] Anger. www.merriam-webster.com. Accessed on October 12, 2016. http://www.merriam- webster.com/dictionary/anger.

[95] This statement appears in "The Gift of Anger." This article first appeared on January 1, 2004, issue of Christianity Today. Used by permission of Christianity Today, Carol Stream, IL 60188.

[96] Ed Chinn, "Changing an Angry spirit." www.focusonthefamily.com. Accessed on February 19, 2014. https://www.focusonthefamily. com/lifechallenges/emotional-health/changing-an-angry-spirit/changing-an-angry-spirit.

[97] Dr. Neil T. Anderson, *Victory over the Darkness,* (Ventura, CA: Regal Books, 2000), 69.

[98] Georgia Shaffer, *Taking Out Your Emotional Trash,* Harvest House Publishers, chapter 5. According to Shafer: "The first step in expressing your anger constructively is to recognize when you are angry and realize how you usually handle this emotion."

[99] Dr. Tim Clinton, "The Deep Oil of Forgiveness." www.aacc.net. Accessed on February 19, 2014. http://www.aacc.net/2014/02/18/ the-deep-oil-of-forgiveness-4/.

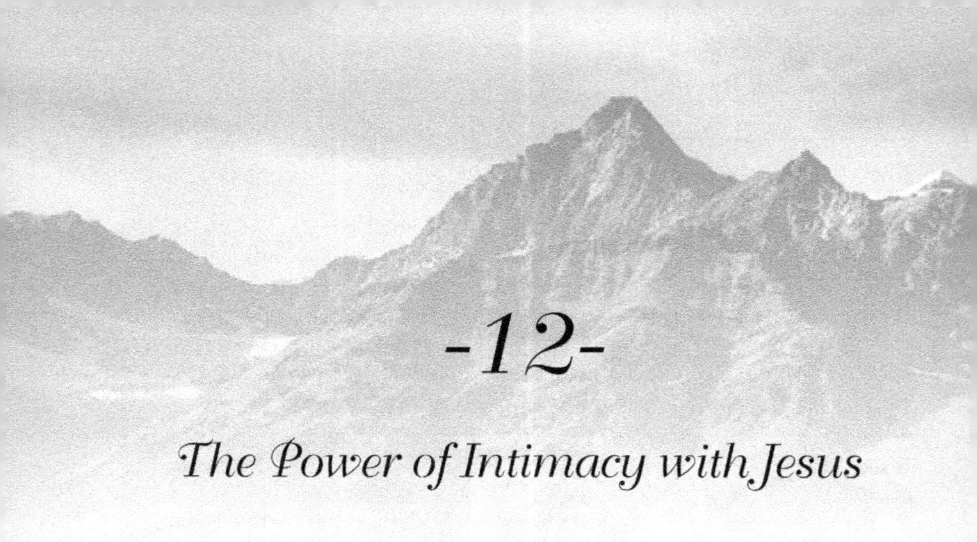

-12-

The Power of Intimacy with Jesus

When You said, "Seek My face," my heart said to You, "Your face, O LORD, I shall seek.
—Psalm 27:8

Draw near to God and He will draw near to you.
—James 4:8a

Becoming a mature disciple of Christ is the birthright of every believer. This process implies practicing personal spiritual disciplines. Let's listen to the teaching of Paul to his protégé Timothy: "Also if anyone competes as an athlete, he does not win the prize unless he competes according to the rules" (2 Timothy 2:5). Moreover, in his first letter to Corinthians Paul also writes: "Everyone who competes in the games exercises self-control in all things. They then do it to receive a perishable wreath, but we an imperishable" (1 Corinthians 9:24). Is Paul talking about legalism here? Of course not. He is just connecting genuine discipleship with spiritual disciplines. Christ's disciples are not practicing spiritual disciplines in order to be saved but because they are His disciples. Disciple and discipline come from the same root word. In other words, we cannot talk about discipleship and leave out spiritual disciplines.

Henry Nouwen explains the connection between discipleship and spiritual discipline:

> Discipline is the other side of discipleship. Discipleship without discipline is like waiting to run in the marathon without ever practicing. Discipline without discipleship is like always practicing for the marathon but never participating. It is important, however, to realize that discipline in the spiritual life is not the same as discipline in sports. Discipline in sports is the concentrated effort to master the body so that it can obey the mind. Discipline in the spiritual life is the concentrated effort to create the space and time where God can become our master and where we can respond freely to God's guidance.
>
> Thus, discipline is the creation of boundaries that keep time and space open for God. Solitude requires discipline; worship requires discipline, caring for others requires discipline. They all ask us to set apart a time and a place where God's gracious presence can be acknowledged and responded to.[100]

What is Spiritual Discipline? "Any practice that helps us draw near to God."[101] Lynne M. Baab explains that these practices can be: "Bible study, prayer, service, fasting, Sabbath keeping, and other disciplines have been practiced throughout the history of the Church." The Bible says: "Draw near to God and He will draw near to you" (James 4:8a). The key word is—draw near. Do you see this? God, who is omnipresent, places the responsibility of drawing near to Him on us.

I believe with all my heart that each disciple of Christ, in his or her spiritual formation journey, is called to practice spiritual disciplines.

I like the way Eugene Peterson renders Matthew 11:28–30 in *The Message*:

> Are you tired? Worn out? Burned out on religion? Come to Me. Get away with me and you'll recover your life. I'll show you how to take a real rest. Walk with Me

> and work with Me— watch how I do it. Learn the unforced rhythms of grace. I won't lay anything heavy or ill-fitting on you. Keep company with Me and you'll learn to live freely and lightly.

Isn't this a nice way to put it? Richard Foster, in his book Celebration of Discipline, presents twelve spiritual disciplines. He divides these disciplines in three groups. Group one refers to *The Inward Disciplines*. Among this group are: Meditation, Prayer, Fasting, and Study. The second group is *The Outward Disciplines*. This group contains: Simplicity, Solitude, Submission, and Service. And the last group talks about *The Corporate Disciplines*, which includes: Confession, Worship, Guidance; and Celebration.

It is not my intention here to expand on each of these spiritual disciplines. If you desire to learn more in this area, please read Foster's book. The point that I would like to stress here is that if you really desire to cultivate a genuine intimacy with Christ it is important to be intentional about creating the space for the Holy Spirit in your life.

I like the way John Ortberg explains the dynamic of discipleship and spiritual discipline.
He writes:

> Practices such as reading Scripture and praying are important—not because they prove how spiritual we are—but because God can use them to lead us into life.[102]

After attending church services, we are reading the Bible one more time, and memorizing ten more verses, then what? After reading all the Christian books we have on our list, listening to all recommended sermons, praying more pivotal prayers, going on missions, practicing the spiritual disciplines, and performing even better deeds, then what? What is the bottom line for our lives? What is God after? What does Jesus want with us and for us? What is Christ's Ultimate Intention with us? I am glad you asked!

The Ultimate Intention

> The *Ultimate Intention* of Christ for the Church is a mature disciple who knows God intimately and personally (John 17:3), who accepts the discipleship call and carries the cross daily (Luke 9:23, Galatians 2:20), whose mind and character are continuously renewed and transformed by the Spirit and the Word of God (Romans 12:2, 2 Corinthians 3:18, Galatians 5:22–23), who grows and matures into the fullness of Christ (Ephesians 4:11–16, Hebrews 5:11–14, 6:1–3), and who, ultimately, multiplies by making disciples according to Christ's and the apostles' discipleship model (Matthew 28:19–20, 2 Timothy 2:2).

I encourage each of you to take the time and read all these Bible verses from the paragraph above to gain a complete spiritual dimension of Christ's Ultimate Intention with us. How can we surrender to God to achieve this intention in our lives?

We must let the Spirit of God satisfy the inner thirst for God. We must develop genuine intimacy with Jesus by investing quality and quantity of time in our relationship with God.

We must accept the discipleship call. We must count the costs and overcome all the difficulties. We must understand that Christ is not looking just for converts who aim to be average Christians. God is looking for men and women who are entirely devoted to Him and His purposes. The grace of God already supplied all the resources we need for life and godliness.

The Apostle Peter writes with all confidence:

> Grace and peace be multiplied to you in the knowledge of God and of Jesus our Lord; seeing that His divine power has granted to us everything pertaining to life and godliness, through the true knowledge of Him who called us by His own glory and

> excellence. For by these He has granted to us His precious and magnificent promises, so that by them you may become partakers of the divine nature, having escaped the corruption that is in the world by lust. (2 Peter 1:2–4)

Thirst for God

Are you thirsty for the Word of God? Do you feel you have not grown spiritually for several years? Are you ready to pay the price and let the Holy Spirit mold you more and more into the likeness of Christ? Do you want to follow in the footsteps of those who followed Jesus? Do you desire to become all that God intends for you? Are you passionate about letting Christ make a difference in and around you? If your answer is "Yes!" to one or more of these questions, you are the perfect candidate, the ideal *mathetes*.[103]

If this is the case:

> We must drink from the spring to quench our thirst; sipping only makes us thirstier. Similarly, if we wish to think, write, and live like the prophets, the apostles, and the saints, we must abandon ourselves, like them, to God's purposes for us.[104]

Intimacy with Jesus requires Time

Intimacy with Jesus requires quality time and a reasonable quantity of time. One time, I was in a small group setting and wanted to stir up some interest in discipleship. So, I generated some dialogue with the members of my small group by asking some penetrating questions. Let me share some questions: "How much time did the first disciples spend with Jesus when He was on this earth?" The answer is simple: "Three years and a half." We figured out that if Jesus spent twelve waking hours a day with them for three and a half years, that was 15,120 hours. I agree with you that 15,120 sounds like a lot of hours. However, we cannot ignore the facts.

Now, let me ask you this: How many hours per week are invested by an average believer in their relationship with Jesus Christ? Let's assume they spend fifteen minutes each morning on personal devotion plus four minutes in prayer before meals. If we add an hour and a half on Sunday morning, and out of generosity, add another hour for the mid-week church service. How much time does this amount to? Approximately 300 minutes, or five hours, per week. At that rate, it would take an average believer 58 years to accumulate the same 15,120 hours of quality time spent with Jesus.

Intimacy with Jesus requires not only quality time but a reasonable quantity of time.

The Power of 10,000

When I did the exercise with my small group, I had yet to learn about the power of the 10,000. In the secular world, scientists and sociologists found that only practicing at least 10,000 hours could become a pro or an expert in a particular field. "You can't become a chess grandmaster unless you spend 10,000 hours on practice." ... "The tennis prodigy who starts playing at six is playing in Wimbledon at 16 or 17 [like] Boris Becker. The classical musician who starts playing the violin at four is debuting at Carnegie Hall at 15 or so."[105]

Interesting food for thought, at least!

> A new study by British scientists revealed that it takes 10,000 hours of practice to become an ace in a certain discipline. They say that top musicians, sportspeople, and chess players could become masters in their field by achieving the level where their practice time reached 10,000 hours.[106]

My point is simple, but please don't take this in a legalistic sense: To cultivate intimacy with Jesus, we need to sacrifice time. Years ago, we heard that what counts is quality time, not quantity. But I politely disagree with that statement. We cannot achieve quality without quantity.

I want to stress that I am not suggesting that we all quit our jobs, enroll full-time in Bible schools, get ordained, and then go into the mission field. That is not a bad idea if God calls you to do it, but I realize this would not be feasible for everybody.

I want to convey that discipleship, spiritual growth, and maturity must be intentional for each of us. If we are serious about surrendering ourselves to God to achieve the ultimate intention, we must make discipleship our highest priority. If not now, when? If not here, where? If not you, who? You decide for yourself.

Spiritual Disciplines

Interestingly, disciple and discipline derive from the same root word. Therefore, when we discuss discipleship, we must consider spiritual disciplines. Why do we practice reading the Scripture, studying the Bible, prayer and meditation, fasting and solitude, worship and service? Of course, we don't practice them to prove how spiritual we are; this would only lift us to the level of modern-day Pharisees. It will only make us arrogant and judgmental of others as the "hero" from the Gospel of Luke's story:

> The Pharisee stood and was praying this to himself: "God, I thank You that I am not like other people: swindlers, unjust, adulterers, or even like this tax collector. I fast twice a week; I pay tithes of all that I get." (Luke 18:11–12)

Some may argue that we live under grace, so why should we practice spiritual disciplines? We practice these disciplines regularly to intentionally create space for God and grow into a deeper intimacy with the Holy Spirit.

Intimacy

Webster Merriman Dictionary defines intimacy as "the state of being intimate." And intimate means (1) "to make known especially publicly or formally" and (2) "to communicate delicately." In other words, to deepen our intimacy with God, we need to know Him, by revelation.

To become intimate with the Holy Spirit, we must communicate with Him in prayer and meditation. Personally, I like the rendering of the word intimacy: *in–to–me–see.*

The Holy Spirit

The Holy Spirit is a Person. He is the third Person within the Trinity. The Holy Spirit is God. The Holy Spirit is the gentlest Person in the entire universe. The Holy Spirit is very jealous of us and desires intimacy with each one of God's children. James writes: "Or do you think that the Scripture speaks to no purpose, 'He jealously desires the Spirit which He has made to dwell in us'?" (James 4:5).

However, this gentle Person cannot force His will on us, and the Spirit of God cannot impose His desire for intimacy on us. The Spirit of Jesus agonizes on our behalf, so we will eventually spend quality time with God the Father, Son, and Holy Spirit.

The Apostle Paul captures this so beautifully in the book of Romans. He writes:

> In the same way the Spirit also helps our weakness; for we do not know how to pray as we should, but the Spirit Himself intercedes for us with groanings too deep for words; and He who searches the hearts knows what the mind of the Spirit is, because He intercedes for the saints according to the will of God. (Romans 8:26–27)

Quiet Time with the Holy Spirit

Think about the season you are in right now. How would you like to spend your days? Are you considering setting aside time to cultivate your intimacy with the Holy Spirit? How about scheduling at least 15–20 minutes every day with the best book in the world, the Bible, and spending some intentional quality time with the best Person in the universe—the Holy Spirit? I assure you that it would be excellent! Let's give it a try.

Ready, set, go. Please have your favorite Bible, a journal, and a pen available. Set aside at least 15–20 minutes for this spiritual discipline. Go to a quiet place, either in your home or somewhere outside. Going to a secluded and quiet place in a nearby park would be ideal. Please don't make this into a law. If practicing spiritual disciplines becomes legalism, it will not be helpful for your spiritual formation. Someone said spending fifteen minutes a day consistently is much better than having a one-hour guilt trip sporadically.

I hope that if we start small and keep increasing it to 30 minutes, then to one hour, or even more, we can begin experiencing more profound intimacy with God. Isn't this what we all, as disciples of Christ, really want?

Let's start:

1. Prepare your Mind to be in the Presence of God (1 minute)

Start with a minute of silence. Then, you may pray like this:

> Father God, I really desire to spend this time in Your Presence. I surrender all my thoughts to You right now. Dear God, please capture my attention with Your Presence. I pray in the name of Christ.

2. Read your selected Bible Passage (3–4 minutes)

For example, you could read the Prayer of Paul for the Ephesians from Ephesians 1:15–23. Read the passage slowly and meditatively, at least a couple of times.

If this is your everyday Bible, feel free to mark or highlight how the Holy Spirit impresses upon your heart.

3. Meditate on the Passage (3–5 minutes)

Suppose you are not familiar with Christian Meditation in the biblical sense. Meditation is the process of deliberately focusing on specific thoughts, such as a Bible passage, a phrase, or even a word, and reflecting on their meaning in the context of God's love. In other words, it means to muse or rehearse that particular verse, thought, or revelation in your mind.

For example, if I were to meditate on the passage from Ephesians 1:15–23, I would concentrate and meditate on the verse (18): "I pray that the eyes of your heart may be enlightened, so that you will know what is the hope of His calling, what are the riches of the glory of His inheritance in the saints." I would just rehearse that verse several times and just marvel at it.

4. Record Your Insights (3–5 minutes)

It is now time to pull out your journal and record in your own words the insights that the Holy Spirit has given to you. For example: "Wow! God has a calling for me. I am wondering what that calling is. Maybe it is ____."

5. Write your Prayer or Application (1–2 minutes)

Now, in your journal, write your prayer. Based on that passage, if I were you, I would write something like this:

Father God, please open my eyes to see Christ clearly, open my ears to hear the Holy Spirit accurately, open my mind to understand the Word precisely, open my heart to accept Your will with gladness, and give me the will to surrender totally to Your plan and calling in my life. In the name of Jesus, I pray. Amen.

6. Pray Passage Back to God (1–2 minutes)

At this point, you could personalize Paul's prayer and pray it back to God. Or you could just pray to God again, the prayer you wrote in step 5.

7. Pray about Other Things you Need (3–4 minutes)

It's not too difficult, is it? If we cultivate these quiet times and practice them regularly, it may develop into a good habit. The bottom line is this: spending time with God is what our inner being needs to grow and mature into the likeness of Christ.

I like the lyrics of one Christian song:

The more I seek You
The more I find you
The more I find You/
The more I love You.

Reflection Questions

Please reflect upon the following questions, briefly elaborate, and then share your thoughts with a friend or your small group.

1. What did the Holy Spirit whisper to your heart through this chapter? What did you like the most in this chapter?

2. What new concepts did you learn from this chapter? Which idea are you committed to implementing in your life?

3. What thoughts crossed your mind when you read *"The Ultimate Intention"* section and the verses included in it? What concepts stood out for you?

4. After reading the sections, *"Thirst for God"* and *"Intimacy with Jesus requires Time,"* what emotions you experienced, and what thoughts crossed your mind.

5. List the best aha moments you had while reading this chapter.

Endnoes:

100 Henri Nouwen, *Leadership,* Vol. 2, no. 3.
101 Lynne M. Baab, "I am Excited about Spiritual Disciplines," (published in Spanz: Presbyterian Church of Aotearoa, New Zealand, June 2008), 2. www.lynnebaab.com. Accessed on July 22, 2011, http://www.lynnebaab.com/articles/im-excited-about-spiritual-disciplines.
102 John Ortberg, *The Life You've Always Wanted,* (Zondervan, Grand Rapids, MI: 1997-2202), 39.
103 *Mathetes*: "means more than mere pupil or learner. It means an adherer who accepts the instruction given to him and makes it his rule of conduct." (Spiros Zodhiates, *The Complete Word Study Dictionary: New Testament,* AMG International, Chattanooga, TN, 37422, 1993.)
104 Jean-Pierre de Caussade, *The Sacrament of the Present Moment,* (New York: Harper One, 1989), 69.
105 Scott Myers, "What to think about our first scripts?", 2 December 2, 2009. www.medium.com. Accessed on July 22, 2011. https://gointothestory.blcklst.com/what-to-think-about-our-first-scripts-5b2d3d203c74.
106 "It takes 10,000 hours of practice to become-a-genius." www.infoniac.com. Accessed on January 22, 2011. http://www.infoniac.com/science/it-takes-10,000-hours-of-practice-to-become-a-genius.html.

-13-

A More Excellent Way

But earnestly desire the greater gifts. And I show you a still more excellent way.
—1 Corinthians 12:31

Some time ago I felt deep in my heart to re-read Paul's first epistle to Timothy. After the first few verses of introduction, I got to verse five: *"But the goal of our instruction is love from a pure heart and a good conscience and a sincere faith."* How many times have I read this letter? How many times have I read this verse? The reality is that many times I have preached from this epistle and from this specific verse. But this time I read this verse as if it was for the first time! What a wonderful experience!

Starting from this verse the Spirit of God led me through the Scriptures, both Old and New Testaments, and helped me see something I didn't notice before, at least not at this intensity. For a while, I felt the way the disciples on the road to Emmaus felt: *"Were not our hearts burning within us while He was speaking to us on the road, while He was explaining the Scriptures to us?"* (Luke 24:32). My heart started to pound faster as the Spirit expounded the Scriptures to me. This was one of those experiences when the light bulb came on.

In the following paragraphs, I would like to share with you something from that experience.

Let's read it again: *"the goal of our instruction is love."* Stop right there! The goal? What do you mean—the goal? Lord, I want to understand! According to the Merriam-Webster Dictionary, "goal" means the end toward which effort is directed. Synonyms are aim, ambition, aspiration, design, dream, end, ideal, intention, mark, meaning, objective, plan, purpose, target, and so on.

Here is the definition that I thought of when I studied these terms:

> The goal is everything that we aspire in life, every dream, ideal and intention, every plan we make, every effort we apply towards something, all our hard work and creativity, our entire propose and target in ministry as God's children. In other words, the goal is the ultimate intention in life for us as sons and daughters of God.

Let's go a step further. In verse five we read about instruction. Note that it is singular not plural. What? There is only one instruction. In other words, only one commandment. Yes, this is what is written—the goal of our instruction. We love the Word of God so much that we cannot ignore what is written in it (see 1 Corinthians 4:6). The conclusion is clear—*the Lord has only one commandment for us.* This motivated me to do a "on word" survey on the entire Bible. That word was—*commandment.*

Let's see what the Bible says about this. At the beginning of the Bible the Lord God gave man a single commandment:

> The LORD God commanded the man, saying, "From any tree of the garden you may eat freely; but from the tree of the knowledge of good and evil you shall not eat, for in the day that you eat from it you will surely die" (Genesis 2:16–17)

We know this story well. Adam and Eve violated the only one commandment the Creator gave them, and, consequently, they died, as the Lord said it would happen.

Since we all were in Adam, when he died spiritually, we died spiritually.

Fast forward to the Book of Exodus. After God Almighty powerfully delivered His chosen people from the Egyptian slavery, He gave them the Ten Commandments (see Exodus 20). The first of the Ten Commandments is: "You shall have no other gods before Me" (Exodus 20:3). However, Israel flagrantly violated God's commandments. The violation was directed towards God Himself, to the point that they made a golden calf and worshiped it. This was very displeasing to God. The chosen people defiantly disobeyed God by breaking the first and most important of the Ten Commandments. Their act of disobedience broke the heart of God. Unbelievable! His children, recently delivered from bondage, were worshipping a calf. And the person responsible to protect and defend the honor of God, Aaron—the high priest, declared: *"This is your god, O Israel, who brought you up from the land of Egypt!"* (Exodus 32:4). What a shame! How humiliating! It was like a sharp knife piercing the very heart of God. Their act angered even Moses, the gentlest and kindest person on earth.

As I was moving forward with my investigation regarding God's commandments, I discovered that Moses give them 613 more commandments and instructions designed to protect, bless, and keep the Israelites close to God. These instructions are written in the Torah—the first five Books of the Old Testament, or the Pentateuch. Of course, the Israelites could not keep these instructions. In fact, nobody can perfectly keep them, then or now.

After the Church was established, the leadership gathered together to discuss the Old Testament Law. After some debate they concluded: "Now therefore why do you put God to the test by placing upon the neck of the disciples a yoke which neither our fathers nor we have been able to bear?" (Acts 15:10). Please observe that they admitted that the Law was an unbearable yoke.

Let's continue our exploration through other books of the Old Testament. Let's make a short stop in the Book of

Proverbs, compiled by King Solomon, the wisest man the wisest man who ever lived on earth (except, of course, Lord Jesus.) This great king states that the Lord hates seven things.

Solomon writes:

> There are six things which the LORD hates, yes, seven which are an abomination to Him: Haughty eyes, a lying tongue, and hands that shed innocent blood, a heart that devises wicked plans, feet that run rapidly to evil, a false witness who utters lies, and one who spreads strife among brothers. (Proverbs 6:16–19)

I would like you to notice that none of these sins refer to violations of any activities related to the Tabernacle of Meeting or to the Temple of God. No! These violations are strictly related to the human heart. Amazing, isn't it? Later, the Lord Jesus confirmed that the problem of mankind is a heart problem.

Mark writes:

> Rightly did Isaiah prophesy of you hypocrites, as it is written: "These people honor me with their lips, but their heart is far away from me" ... And He said to them, "Are you so lacking in understanding also? Do you not understand that whatever goes into the man from outside cannot defile him, because it does not go into his heart, but into his stomach, and is eliminated?" (Thus, He declared all foods clean.) ... For from within, out of the heart of men, proceed the evil thoughts, fornications, thefts, murders, adulteries, deeds of coveting and wickedness, as well as deceit, sensuality, envy, slander, pride and foolishness. All these evil things proceed from within and defile the man. (Mark 7:6, 18–19, 21–23)

During the time of the Minor Prophets, the prophet Micah addressed something revolutionary for those days. God asks of people only three things: justice, mercy, and humility.

Micah writes: "He has told you, O man, what is good; and what does the LORD require of you but to do justice, to love kindness, and to walk humbly with your God?" (Micah 6:8).

Finally, we arrive at the New Testament period. During Jesus' time, the Pharisees, the Sadducees, the scribes, and the elders deliberately tried to catch the Lord Jesus making a mistake, so they could rightly accuse Him. But they couldn't. The Gospel of Mark relates an interesting conversation between one of the scribes and Jesus regarding the chief of all God's Commandments.

The Lord Jesus replied:

> The foremost is, "Hear, O Israel! The LORD our God is one LORD; and you shall love the LORD your God with all your heart, and with all your soul, and with all your mind, and with all your strength." The second is this, "You shall love your neighbor as yourself." There is no other commandment greater than these. (Mark 12:29–31)

This aspect is so important! Matthew, another evangelist, writes: *"On these two commandments depend the whole Law and the Prophets"* (Matthew 22:40). Phenomenal! With His answer, Christ shoot the mouths of the scholars. The Bible states: "After that, no one would venture to ask Him any more questions" (v.34). That point was the climax of their discussion. I am imagining that some mystic aroma was released filling the air. It wasn't smoke from the Altar of Incense or scent for the altar of the Burnt Offering; it was the sweet aroma of love—love for God and love for the neighbor.

In summary up to this point:

- From one commandment (cf. Genesis 2:16–17), to
- Ten Commandments (cf.in Exodus 20), to
- 613 Commandments in the Torah, to
- Seven things (cf. Proverbs 6:16–19), to
- Three aspects (cf. Micah 6:8), to
- Two commandments (cf. Mark 12:28–34).

Wow! What a great spiritual progression! But as I mentioned at the beginning of this chapter, in first Timothy 1:5, the Word tells us that: *"the goal of our instruction is love."* It talks about only one commandment. We made a full circle, from one restrictive commandment in Genesis to one everlasting commandment—***love;*** in the New Testament. We are talking not about just any kind of love, but agape—the very nature of God.

The Greek word agape— the highest dimension of love. This kind of love describes the goal of Christianity and spirituality.

Agape love is the highest and purest form of love, one that surpasses all other types of affection. It represents divine, unconditional, self-sacrificing, active, volitional, and thoughtful love.

In the Greek language there are more words which describe various dimensions of love. In 1 Timothy 1:5, Paul does not speak about *philos*—friendship, loyalty to friends, family, and community. Even though it requires virtue, equality, and familiarity, does not come even close to agape.

Paul did not use *storge*—affection, which refers to the natural affection, like that felt by parents for their children. The word for love in this passage is clearly not *eros*—passionate love, with sensual desire and longing. The Greek word, used by Paul here, is *agape*—the highest dimension of love. Christ gave His disciples only one commandment—to love. This kind of love describes the goal of Christianity and spirituality. Nothing more. Nothing less. Nothing else.

When I got to this point, my heart began to beat with even more intensity. I felt like an electric current traveled though my body. My eyes were moist. In absolute awe, I shed tears of joy! Wow! What a special moment!

Now let's survey the New Testament to validate the parameters and validity of our findings. I found out that, during the Upper Room Discourse before the crucifixion, Jesus gave His disciples *a new commandment.*

John writes:

> A new commandment I give to you, that you love one another, even as I have loved you, that you also love one another. By this all men will know that you are My disciples, if you have love for one another. (John 13:34–35)

Please observe that Jesus gave them one new commandment, not two, not three: just one commandment. He is very specific—*love one another*, even as I have loved you. What word is used here to describe love? It is agape. Christ loved us with agape love. He commands us to do the same—"you love one another, even as I have loved you." Amazing, isn't it?

The badge of discipleship is not the disciple's religion, or their theology; is not their church leadership position, the degree or level of education, or type of ministry. Absolutely not. The disciple's insignia is agape love—"By this all men will know that you are My disciples, if you have love for one another." This is it! This is a new commandment. Let's not complicate things anymore.

Let's continue our trek through the epistles to see how the early followers of Jesus were instructed. I found it amazing that all the New Testament writers, in one way or another, wrote about agape love.

Let me give you a list of my findings:

1. Love—Fulfillment of the Law

In Romans 13:9–10, Paul writes:

> For this, "You shall not commit adultery, you shall not murder, you shall not steal, you shall not covet," and if there is any other commandment, it is summed up in this saying, "You shall love your neighbor as yourself." Love does no wrong to a neighbor; therefore, love is the fulfillment of the law.

In his letter to Corinthians, Paul devotes a whole chapter

to agape love—1 Corinthians 13. We will return to this chapter later.

In Galatians 5:13–15 we read:

> For you were called to freedom, brethren; only do not turn your freedom into an opportunity for the flesh, but through love serve one another. For the whole Law is fulfilled in one word, in the statement: "You shall love your neighbor as yourself." But if you bite and devour one another, take care that you are not consumed by one another.

2. Only Through Love—Can we Reach the Fullness of God

If we carefully read Paul's epistle to Ephesians, it is impossible not to be awestruck by Paul's prayer right in the middle of it:

> For this reason, I bow my knees before the Father, from whom every family in heaven and on earth derives its name, that He would grant you, according to the riches of His glory, to be strengthened with power through His Spirit in the inner man, so that Christ may dwell in your hearts through faith; and that you, being rooted and grounded in love, may be able to comprehend with all the saints what is the breadth and length and height and depth, and to know the love of Christ which surpasses knowledge, that you may be filled up to all the fullness of God. (Ephesians 3:14–19)

Please observe that Paul is praying for the Church to gain an experiential knowledge of agape love. He asserts that only in this way can we reach the fullness of God.

3. The Humility of Agape Love

In Philippians 2:1–4 Paul writes:

> Therefore, if there is any encouragement in Christ, if there is any consolation of love, if there is any fellowship of the Spirit, if any affection and compassion, make my joy complete by being of the same mind, maintaining the same love, united in spirit, intent on one purpose. Do nothing from selfishness or empty conceit, but with humility of mind regard one another as more important than yourselves; do not merely look out for your own personal interests, but also for the interests of others.

Do you see what I see? Only those who truly love, with the agape love, may humble themselves before others and sincerely serve one another. There is no other way.

4. Agape Love—The Perfect Bond of Unity

In Colossians 3:14, we find: "Beyond all these things put on love, which is the perfect bond of unity." No wonder the enemy attacks us the most in this area. Why? Because if we stop loving each other, the process of spiritual formation is delayed, or even placed on hold. I found this theme in almost all New Testament writings.

Let's mention some of them:

- *1 Thessalonians 4:9*: "Now as to the love of the brethren, you have no need for anyone to write to you, for you yourselves are taught by God to love one another."
- *2 Thessalonians 3:5*: "May the Lord direct your hearts into the love of God and into the steadfastness of Christ."
- *1 Timothy 1:5*: "But the goal of our instruction is love from a pure heart and a good conscience and a sincere faith." (This is the verse that caused all of this survey.)
- *Titus 2:4*: "so that they may encourage the young women to love their husbands, to love their children."

What shall we say of the Epistle to Philemon? It is absolutely soaked in love!

Paul writes:

> I thank my God always, making mention of you in my prayers, because I hear of your love and of the faith which you have toward the Lord Jesus and toward all the saints. (Philemon 1:4–5)

5. Love Motivated Jesus to Suffer the Cross

Our investigation comes to the letter to Hebrews. In fact, the whole letter, if we think deeply, is dedicated to the love of God for us through Jesus Christ. The author of Hebrews exhorts us: "Fixing our eyes on Jesus, the author and perfecter of faith, who for the joy set before Him endured the cross, despising the shame, and has sat down at the right hand of the throne of God" (Hebrews 12:2). What motivated Jesus to endure the cross, to despise the shame and the scorn? Nothing but agape love (see also John 3:16).

6. A Fervent Love Covers a Multitude of Sins

The Apostle Peter in his simplicity, but with spiritual depth, says: "Above all, keep fervent in your love for one another, because love covers a multitude of sins" (1 Peter 4:8).

Then, in 2 Peter 1:5–7, he writes:

> Now for this very reason also, applying all diligence, in your faith supply moral excellence, and in your moral excellence, knowledge, and in your knowledge, self-control, and in your self-control, perseverance, and in your perseverance, godliness, and in your godliness, brotherly kindness, and in your brotherly kindness, love.

According to Peter, agape love is the highest level of our calling. There is no other goal to aim at than—*to love all people.*

We are called to exercise brotherly kindness and by doing so we eventually express our Father's nature—love for all people. Isn't it awesome?

We find similar instructions about agape love in other letters. For example, James asserts that agape love demonstrates genuine faith.

He writes:

> What use is it, my brethren, if someone says he has faith, but he has no works? Can that faith save him? If a brother or sister is without clothing and in need of daily food, and one of you says to them, "Go in peace, be warmed and be filled," and yet you do not give them what is necessary for their body, what use is that? (James 2:14–17)

James asserts that agape love demonstrates genuine faith.

We cannot be more practical than this, can we?

7. The Highest Level—God is Love

What shall we say when we get to the epistles of the Apostle John? After all, he is the Apostle of Love. In 1 John 4:8 we read: "The one who does not love does not know God, for God is love." As I said earlier, the badge of a genuine disciple of Jesus Christ is agape love. God is love. It means much more than the fact that God loves us. Agape love is the essence, the very nature, of God. I don't think that here on this earth we even have the right vocabulary to explain the entire meaning of agape love. To love is to express God's nature and character in and through you. That is why, remaining in love is the only proof that God lives in us.

Do you see? We have come to know—to experience-- God is love. Wonderful! In other words, God's love is the foundation for our brotherly kindness. I think John is among a handful of Scripture writers who comprehended the most essential aspect of Christianity—*agape love.*

Here's how he writes:

> We love, because He first loved us. If someone says, "I love God," and hates his brother, he is a liar; for the one who does not love his brother whom he has seen, cannot love God whom he has not seen. And this commandment we have from Him, that the one who loves God should love his brother also. (1 John 4:19–21)

To love is to express God's nature and character in and through you.

It is as simple as that. We can adore God on Sunday morning, and on Monday we ignore our neighbor. If that is the case, we are just a bunch of liars. This is the test! Keep in mind that John refers to only one commandment—*love one another*—he initially wrote about it in John 13:34. We also find the same teaching in 2 and 3 of John's letters.

Jude also writes:

> But you, beloved, building yourselves up on your most holy faith, praying in the Holy Spirit, keep yourselves in the love of God, waiting anxiously for the mercy of our Lord Jesus Christ to eternal life. (Jude 1:20–21)

In other words, when we pray in the Holy Spirit the most important aspect we are seeking is to abide more and more in God's love.

We arrived at the last book of the Bible—Revelation. Here we read what Jesus told the Church in Ephesus. This church was about to lose her lampstand, because she left her first love. This is monumental!

John writes:

> I know your deeds and your toil and perseverance, and that you cannot tolerate evil men, and you put to the test those who call themselves apostles, and they are not, and you found them to be false; and you have

> perseverance and have endured for My name's sake and have not grown weary. But I have this against you, that you have left your first love. Therefore, remember from where you have fallen, and repent and do the deeds you did at first; or else I am coming to you and will remove your lampstand out of its place—unless you repent. (Revelation 2:2–5)

So, the last book of the Bible speaks of agape love too. Isn't this amazing? I am praying and hoping that all of us will think more deeply about the agape love, and take our walk as disciples of Jesus very seriously.

Love vs. Lovers of Self

People who don't love are egoists. Elie Wiesel[107], Professor at Boston University, political activist, Nobel Laureate and Holocaust survivor, writes:

> The opposite of love is not hate, it's indifference. The opposite of beauty is not ugliness, it's indifference. The opposite of faith is not heresy, it's indifference. And the opposite of life is not death, but indifference between life and death.[108]

There is so much truth in that statement. What are some of the characteristics of lovers of self? What does it look like? Let's go to the Word of God to find out.

In 2 Timothy 3:1–5, Paul describes the landscape of lovers of self:

> But realize this, that in the last days difficult times will come. For men will be lovers of self, lovers of money, boastful, arrogant, revilers, disobedient to parents, ungrateful, unholy, unloving, irreconcilable, malicious gossips, without self-control, brutal, haters of good, treacherous, reckless, conceited, lovers of pleasure rather than lovers of God, holding to a form of

godliness, although they have denied its power; avoid such men as these.

Please notice that everything revolves around ***self***. Think about it. Lovers of self are in deep idolatry—worship of self. In other words, if we don't pay attention, we are in danger of worshiping a different kind of *trinity*, with small "*t*"—*Me, Myself, and I*. Ugly, isn't it? Let's be honest. The passage I quoted above describes with great fidelity the culture we live in today, doesn't it?

The 1 Corinthians 13 Test

Now, I would like to change gears a little bit and, as promised earlier, return to the Love Chapter. I am very impressed with the way Paul writes to the Corinthians.

First Corinthians chapter 12 is dedicated to spiritual gifts. Paul ends this chapter with a very interesting imperative: "*But earnestly desire the greater gifts. And I show you a still more excellent way*" (1 Corinthians 12:31). Breathtaking, isn't it? You guessed already that the "more excellent way" is love.

Then, Paul writes chapter 13. This is devoted exclusively to the nature and character of agape love. I believe this chapter is the description of our Lord Jesus Christ.

In first Corinthians chapter 12, Paul talks about the gift of the Holy Spirit. And in first Corinthians chapter 14, he talks about the administration of spiritual gifts. I found this detail amazing! Right in between those two chapters, under Holy's Spirit inspiration, Paul writes about agape love. In all practicality, in this chapter, Paul describes the nature and the character of God. With all these things fresh in our minds, let's take a test.

Paul clearly tells us: "Test yourselves to see if you are in the faith; examine yourselves! Or do you not recognize this about yourselves, that Jesus Christ is in you—unless indeed you fail the test?" (2 Corinthians 13:5).

I venture to challenge you: Test yourselves to see if you walk in love. The test is simple but at the same time it is deep.

I call it the "First Corinthian 13 Test." Socrates writes: "The unexamined life is not worth living" (Apology 38a).

Throughout church history, God's people practiced this discipline of personal examination. It is called "The Prayer of Examen."[109] It was developed by Ignatius of Loyola (1491–1556), founder of the Jesuits. The Prayer of Examen is spiritual meditation tool for sensing God's presence and asking for His guidance in daily life.

Let's pray first for wisdom, humility, and discernment. Then, read 1 Corinthians 13, slowly and meditatively, and as we do that replace the word love with your name. Where we find a mismatch, write it down in a journal. These aspects are the deficiencies we see as we allow the Spirit of God to zoom into our lives. These are the exact places where God desires to transform us, more and more, into the image of His Son, Jesus. We need to work with the Spirit of God and, in sincere repentance, surrender ourselves to the Potter's wheel.

As we present ourselves to God, we sincerely ask Him:

> *Here I am, O Lord, mold me and shape me according to Your plans and purposes. I truly desire to be an accurate expression of Your Nature and Your Character.*

This is a process. This kind of deep transformation doesn't happen overnight. We must press on. We must do it conscientiously and consistently.

Let's find a quiet and peaceful place and let's begin reading slowly and meditatively this amazing chapter. Let's be attentive to the Word of God and to the Spirit of God, as we read it:

> Love is patient, love is kind and is not jealous; love does not brag and [*love*] is not arrogant, [*love*] does not act unbecomingly; [*love*] does not seek its own, [love] is not provoked, [*love*] does not take into account a wrong suffered, [*love*] does not rejoice in unrighteousness, but [*love*] rejoices with the truth; [love] bears all things, [*love*] believes all things, [love]

hopes all things, [*love*] endures all things.

Let the testing start:

- Is Valy patient? Yes, or no? If not—why not? What are the specific issues causing Valy to lack patience? What is God's solution? (See James 1:2–4; Romans 5:3–4).
- Is Valy kind? Yes, or no? If not—why not? What are the concrete issues causing Valy not to be kind? What is God's solution? Perhaps it is as issue of unforgiveness? Maybe it is the root of bitterness? (See Ephesians 4:32; Colossians 3:13).
- Is Valy humble? Yes, or no? If not—why not? What are the specific issues causing Valy to boast? Maybe a deeper hurt, or childhood trauma? Feeling unappreciated? Feeling an inner turmoil, or insecurity? Or maybe he does not know his true spiritual identity in Christ? What is God's solution? (See Philippians 3:3; Romans 7:18; John 15:5).
- Does Valy endure all things? Yes, or no? If not—why not? What are the specific issues causing Valy to avoid suffering? Is it self-protection? Is it disbelief in God's protection? Is it seeking revenge? What is God's solution? (See 1 Peter 2:20–21, 3:17).

When we are ready to suffer all things—any injustice, any unfair or unethical treatment, any loss, even loss of life—then we come closer to the nature and character of God. In other words, we grow up, we mature. This is the real test of spiritual growth.

My dear brothers and sisters, we all have the nature of God— agape love—in us, but it is in a compressed form—as a seed. Therefore, it is absolutely necessary to abide in Christ (cf. John 15:5), to present ourselves to God (cf. Romans 12:1), and to ask His Holy Spirit to take that seed—which represents the DNA of our Father—and develop Christ's image in each of us (cf. 2 Corinthians 3:18). This way we truly grow and mature into the fullness of His Son (cf. Ephesians 4:13). Keep in mind that spiritual growth is nothing else but the manifestation of the nature and character of Christ in each of us individually.

I urge you, please do not forget: *"But the goal of our instruction is love from a pure heart and a good conscience and a sincere faith"* (1 Timothy 1:5). Love is God's nature. All born-again believers have the DNA of their Father.

Our calling is to express it so everybody will see and recognize the disciples of Christ (cf. John 15:31).

My dear brethren, have you noticed that from the Old Testament until now, things have simplified tremendously? We only have a single commandment—*to love one another as Jesus loved us*. There is no another goal that we need to strive to achieve. There is no other objective toward which to aim. The good news is that God *"has granted to us everything pertaining to life and godliness"* (cf. 2 Peter 1:3).

Moreover, God's very nature is planted deep inside of us. Paul writes: "And hope does not disappoint, because the love of God has been poured out within our hearts through the Holy Spirit who was given to us" (Romans 5:5).

The ultimate intention is agape love—*expressing God's nature and character in and through you*. This is the only way to the Fullness of Christ. Let's seal these thoughts with God's own pledge: "Faithful is He who calls you, and He also will bring it to pass" (1 Thessalonians 5:24).

Reflection Questions

Please reflect upon the following questions, briefly elaborate, and then share your thoughts with a friend or your small group.

1. What did the Holy Spirit whisper to your heart through this chapter? What did you like the most in this chapter?

2. What new concepts did you learn from this chapter? Which idea are you committed to implementing in your life?

3. What crossed your mind when you read about the progression: From *One Commandment* (Genesis 2:16–17), to *Ten Commandments* (Exodus 20), to *613 Commandments* (in Torah), to *Seven Things* (Proverbs 6:16–19), to *Three Aspects* (Micah 6:8), to *Two Commandments* (Mark 12:28–34), and ultimately to *One New Commandment* (John13:34)?

4. Thinking back on the seven dimensions of agape love. What dimension(s) spoke to your heart the most? Why? What emotions have you experienced, and what thoughts crossed your mind?

5. List the best aha moments you had while reading this chapter.

Endnotes:

[107] Elie Wiesel was born 30 September 1928.
[108] US News & World Report, 27 October 1986.
[109] "The Ignatian Examen." www.jesuits.org. Accessed on February 8, 2024. https://www.jesuits.org/spirituality/the-ignatian-examen/.
1. Place yourself in God's presence. Give thanks for God's great love for you.
2. Pray for the grace to understand how God is acting in your life.
3. Review your day — recall specific moments and your feelings at the time.
4. Reflect on what you did, said, or thought in those instances. Were you drawing closer to God, or further away?
5. Look toward tomorrow — think of how you might collaborate more effectively with God's plan. Be specific and conclude with the "Our Father.")

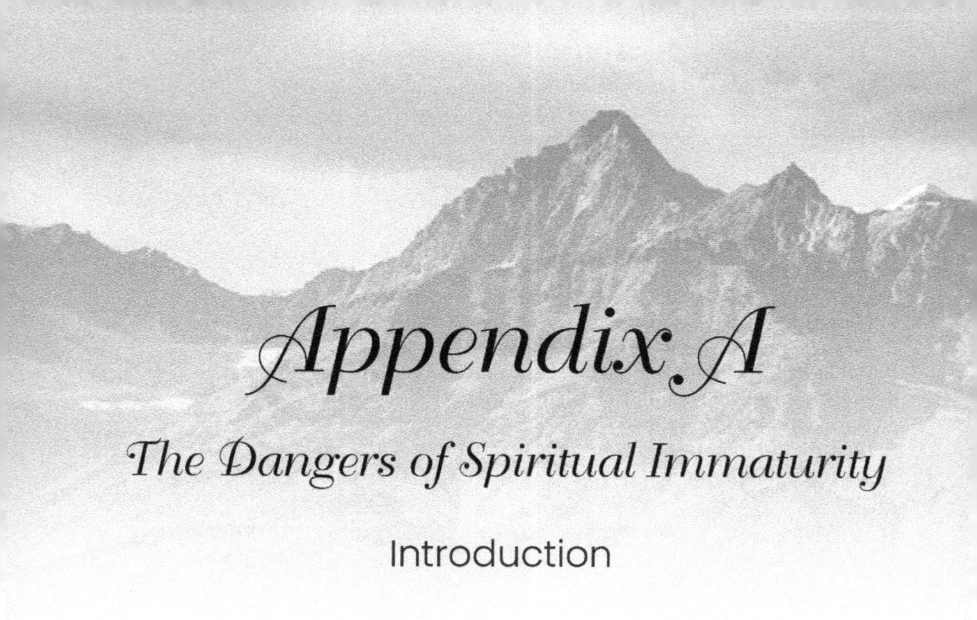

Appendix A

The Dangers of Spiritual Immaturity

Introduction

And I, brethren, could not speak to you as to spiritual men, but as to men of flesh, as to infants in Christ.
—1 Corinthians 3:1

Therefore, leaving the elementary teaching about the Christ, let us press on to maturity, not laying again a foundation of repentance from dead works and of faith toward God.
—Hebrews 6:1

In the mid-90s, I was drawn by the Holy Spirit into the field of spiritual growth and maturity. At that time, I had a tiny "office" in the basement of our home. After work and after completing necessary chores, I would crawl into that office. Many times, I spent hours at a time digging into the Scriptures to learn more about this marvelous field. So, the thoughts and ideas I will share next have been springing up from Ephesians 4:11–16, a passage that has become very important to me over the years. I usually use this portion of Scripture to explain the importance of spiritual growth and maturity. However, during a mission trip to India and Italy a few years ago, I felt strongly led to start teaching and writing about the dangers of spiritual immaturity.

While in those foreign lands, it was a brand-new message for me too. I had never preached from this passage in this manner before. The message came freely from the depths of my heart without prior preparation. Before reading this chapter, I suggest you pause and pray for a few minutes:

Father God, please open my eyes to see You, open my ears to hear the voice of the Spirit, open my heart and fill it with the love of Jesus, open my mind to comprehend the Scriptures, and empower me with the will to surrender my life one hundred percent to Your divine purposes. I pray in the wonderful name of Jesus Christ. Amen!

I have been praying for you, my readers, so I expect a deep understanding to come from above into your souls.

In Ephesians 4:11–16, Paul talks about the five-fold ministry of the church. I like to call it the "hand" of God. It contains the following "fingers":

- Apostles
- Prophets
- Evangelists
- Pastors
- Teachers

This unique hand is given for the overall edification of the Body of Christ. All these unique fingers are called for a specific three-prong objective:

- For the equipping of the saints,
- For the work of service,
- To the building up of the body of Christ.

This objective was not finished during the apostolic generation of the Church in the first century. It continues today. I firmly believe that this great objective must be accomplished before the return of Christ. In this passage, Paul is saying that in the process of accomplishing this great tri-fold objective, three significant aspects must be kept in focus:

- Attaining to the unity of the faith and of the knowledge of the Son of God,
- Reaching the stature of a mature man, and
- Attaining the fullness of Christ" (see Ephesians 4:13).

As I stated in the main book, my understanding is that attaining the fullness of Christ is God's ultimate intention for His Church.

> The *Ultimate Intention* of Christ for the Church is a mature disciple who knows God intimately and personally (John 17:3), who accepts the discipleship call and carries the cross daily (Luke 9:23, Galatians 2:20), whose mind and character are continuously renewed and transformed by the Spirit and the Word of God (Romans 12:2, 2 Corinthians 3:18, Galatians 5:22–23), who grows and matures into the fullness of Christ (Ephesians 4:11–16, Hebrews 5:11–14, 6:1–3), and who, ultimately, multiplies by making disciples according to Christ's and the apostles' discipleship model (Matthew 28:19–20, 2 Timothy 2:2).[110]

This was the case for the first-century Church, which is still in effect for the Church of the last days before His glorious return. That is why I am passionate about writing about the dangers of spiritual immaturity. I am firmly convinced that these aspects are extremely important and urgent! If believers continue to remain in a state of spiritual immaturity, they are in danger of forfeiting God's purpose for their lives. Luke writes: "But the Pharisees and the lawyers rejected God's purpose for themselves, not having been baptized by John" (Luke 7:30). In other words, we can say: "But some Christians rejected God's purpose by not taking heed to their spiritual growth and maturity; therefore, they forfeited the ultimate intention of God for them."

In this portion of Scripture (Ephesians 4:11–16), Paul is not talking about salvation. Expounding upon this passage, I am not talking about salvation either. I am talking about the great danger of not reaching the full potential our loving Father desires for each of us as His beloved children.

Sadly, many Christians today are content with the status quo. So many churchgoers falsely believe that spiritual maturity is done on some automatic pilot. They think that just going through the motions will eventually result in growth, spiritual development, and maturity. This is precisely what the enemy of our souls would like us to think. But that doesn't lead to maturity.

Jesus warned us in the parable of the Sower. "The seed which fell among the thorns, these are the ones who have heard, and as they go on their way they are choked with worries and riches and pleasures of this life, and bring no fruit to maturity" (Luke 8:14). Even though the fullness of Christ is what the Father desires for all of us, it will not happen automatically.

Belonging to a local church does not cut it either. Spiritual growth and maturity are the result of spiritual transformation led by the Holy Spirit. As a result, God displays the life and character of Christ through the believer. Discipleship is factored in by our intentions and decisions, and our faith in action translates it out. It will not happen by itself. I believe that this is precisely what the Holy Spirit is speaking to churches today:

> Believer, if you have an ear to hear, the will of the Father is to once again bring the cross of Christ to the forefront of the Church.

As the Holy Spirit impressed upon my heart, I perceived that there are five main dangers of spiritual immaturity. I invite you to investigate these dangers and decide accordingly.

May God bless you, my beloved!

Danger number one

Carnality

Carnality is a very great danger of immaturity. In his first epistle to the Corinthians, Paul writes:

> And I, brethren, could not speak to you as to spiritual men, but as to men of flesh, as to infants in Christ. I gave you milk to drink, not solid food; for you were not yet able to receive it. Indeed, even now, you are not yet able, for you are still fleshly. For since there is jealousy and strife among you, are you not fleshly, and are you not walking like mere men? (1 Corinthians 3:1–3)

In the endnotes section, please see various renderings of these verses from multiple Bible translations.[111] First Corinthians 3:1–3 is a fascinating passage of Scripture. Paul uses different words to contrast and describe the spiritually immature state of the believers in Corinth.

These words are:

- Spiritual men
- Men of flesh
- As to infants in Christ
- Milk to drink
- Solid food
- Fleshly
- Jealousy
- Strife
- Mere men

It is essential to have a clear understanding of what these

words really mean. The first expression used in this passage is spiritual men.

The term "spiritual," as used in the New Testament, indicates a person who has been regenerated, indwelt by Christ, enlightened by God, endued, and empowered by the Holy Spirit. They are conformed to the will of God, having the mind of Christ, and living a life led by the Spirit of God. The bottom line is that a spiritual person is a new creation born from above (cf. Romans 8:6; 1 Corinthians 2:15, 14:37; Colossians 1:9; 1 Peter 2:5). Spiritual men and women are committed followers of Jesus whom Christ indwells, and when a certain level of spiritual maturity is reached, these individuals display the Life and Character of Christ.

This type of person responded to the Gospel message (Romans 10:17) in faith (Ephesians 2:8–9) and with a repentant heart (Act 2:38), accepting Christ (Romans 10:9–10) as their personal Savior and Lord (Jude 1:25). Because of the redemption work (Romans 3:25) Jesus did on the Calvary cross (Colossians 1:20), through His blood (1 Peter 1:18–19), the Holy Spirit regenerated this person (John 3:3, 5–6) and brought them to spiritual life (Ephesians 2:4–5). This person was made a new creation in Christ (2 Corinthians 5:17), thus a spiritual person.

This marvelous work of grace is not for super-Christians. According to Galatians 3:28, it is for everybody, regardless of gender, race, social status, education, skin color, and so on. Please keep in mind that this is just the beginning. The work of grace does not stop at the spiritual birth event. The spiritual person continues in grace (2 Peter 3:18).

Spiritual men and women, at some point in their walk with Christ, accepted the call to discipleship (Matthew 16:24). By the Holy Spirit, they comprehended and experienced their co-crucifixion with Christ (Galatians 2:20). They understood their identity in the death (Romans 6:3), burial (Romans 6:4a), resurrection (Ephesians 2:6a), and ascension (Ephesians 2:6b) with Christ. Now, because of these active truths working in their lives, they gladly carry their cross daily (Luke 9:23) and willingly present their lives on God's altar as a genuine act of worship (Romans 12:1). They don't do these things to earn or keep their salvation.

Salvation is God's gift (2 Timothy 1:9). God is the only one who can preserve them. Since they are in Christ, nobody can snatch them from Christ's hand (John 10:28–29). Spiritual men and women do these things for the Kingdom's sake (Mathew 6:33), motivated by God's love (John 14:15), and out of reverence for Christ (Hebrew 12:28).

Spiritual men and women are actively part of spiritual growth (2 Peter 1:5–7), and God's work (Ephesians 2:10), for the benefit of others (2 Corinthians 12:15).

Please let me get a bit technical here and provide some definitions of the word "spiritual."

According to *Vine's Complete Expository Dictionary of the Old and New Testament Words,* the Greek word used in 1 Corinthians 3:1–3 is πνευματικός—*pneumatikos.* It corresponds to Strong's #4152. Pneumatikos: "always connotes the ideas of invisibility and of power." It does not occur in the Septuagint nor the Gospels. It is, in fact, an after-Pentecost word.

According to *Thayer's Greek Lexicon, Strong's New Testament* (Strong's #4152) πνευματικός—*pneumatikos*—has these meanings:

1. Relating to the human spirit, or rational soul, as the part of man which is akin to God and serves as his instrument or organ.
2. Belonging to a spirit, or a being higher than man but inferior to God, i.e., wicked spirits, Ephesians 6:12.
3. Belonging to the Divine Spirit;

a. in reference to things; emanating from the Divine Spirit, or exhibiting its effects and so its character.
b. in reference to persons; one who is filled with and governed by the Spirit of God (1 Corinthians 2:15). According to Galatians 5:16, 25, a spiritual man is one who walks by the Spirit and manifests the fruit of the Spirit in his own ways.[112]

Moreover:

> According to the Scriptures, the spiritual state of the soul is normal for the believer, but to this state, all believers do not attain, nor when it is attained is it always maintained. Thus, the Apostle, in 1 Corinthians 3:1–3, suggests a contrast between this spiritual state and that of the babe in Christ, i.e., of the man who, because of immaturity and inexperience, has not yet reached spirituality, and that of the man who by permitting jealousy, and the strife to which jealousy always leads, has lost it. The spiritual state is reached by diligence in the Word of God and in prayer; it is maintained by obedience and self-judgment.[113]

The second phrase used here is men of flesh. Simply put, men of the flesh mean people controlled by their fleshly desires instead of by the Holy Spirit. According to Vine's Complete Expository Dictionary of the Old and New Testament Words, the Greek word used here is σαρκικός—sarkikos. It corresponds to Strong's #4559. It derives from sarx, which means flesh.

Sarkikos signifies:

> (a) "Having the nature of flesh," having its seat in the animal nature, or excited by it, as in 1 Peter 2:11. "Fleshly" or as the equivalent of "human," with the added idea of weakness. It also communicates the idea of un-spirituality, of human wisdom, "fleshly," as in 2 Corinthians 1:12.
> (b) "pertaining to the flesh" (i.e., the body), as in Romans 15:27 and 1 Corinthians 9:11.[114]

Furthermore, the Greek word σάρκινος—sarkinos—fleshly corresponds to Strong's #4560.

Sarkinos denotes:

> "Of the flesh, fleshly" as in 2 Corinthians 3:3 KJV: "but in fleshy tables of the heart." "The adjectives "fleshly," and "carnal" are contrasted with spiritual qualities in Romans 7:14; 1 Corinthians 3:1,3,4; 2 Corinthians 1:12; Colossians 2:18. Speaking broadly, the carnal denotes the sinful element in man's nature by reason of descent from Adam. On the other hand, the spiritual is that which comes by the regenerating operation of the Holy Spirit.[115]

> The word carnal here σαρκ ι νο ι ς—sarkinois, is not the same word which is in 1 Corinthians 2:14, which is translated as "natural" ψυχ ι κός— psuchikos. "That" refers to one who is un-renewed and who is wholly under the influence of his sensual or animal nature, and is nowhere applied to Christians.[116]

"The carnal state is a state of continual sinning and failure."[117] "Carnal Christians are persons under the influence of fleshly appetites, coveting and living for the things of this life."[118] Unfortunately, most believers in Corinth were in a carnal state.

According to Gill's Exposition of the Entire Bible:

> The carnal state Christians are not as unregenerate men are; but had carnal conceptions of things, were in carnal frames of soul, and walked in ... a carnal conversation with each other; though they were not in the flesh, in a state of nature, yet the flesh was in them, and not only lusted against the Spirit, but was very predominant in them, and carried them captive so that they are denominated from it.[119]

Andrew Murray, in *The Master's Indwelling,* writes: "In these carnal Corinthians, there was a little of God's Spirit, but the flesh predominated; the Spirit had not the rule of their whole life."[120]

Pastor J. B. Hall, in the "Carnal Christian" sermon, posted

on sermoncentral.com, explains:

> The carnal Christian then, much like the lost person, serves to oppose the work of God in a church. He has his own agenda and is completely insensitive and unresponsive to the spiritual work God is trying to accomplish in His church.[121]

During my online research, when I typed the question, "What is a carnal Christian?" I got this answer:

> The key thing to understand is that while a Christian can be, for a time, carnal, a true Christian will not remain carnal for a lifetime.[122]

I like Andrew Murray's perspective on this subject:

> We shall say to Him, "It must be changed. Have mercy upon us." But, ah! that prayer and that change cannot come until we have begun to see that there is a carnal root ruling in believers; they are living more after the flesh than the Spirit; they are yet carnal Christians.[123]

This angle is even more interesting! According to Andrew Murray, it is impossible for Christians to grow from the carnal state into the spiritual state. He considers it deception.
He writes:

> There are Christians who think that they must grow out of the carnal state into the spiritual state. You never can.[124]

Then what is the solution? He continues:

> What could help those carnal Corinthians? To give them milk could not help them, for milk was a proof they were in the wrong state. To give them meat would

> not help them, for they were unfit to eat it. What they needed was the knife of the surgeon. Paul says that the carnal life must be cut out. "They that are Christ's have crucified the flesh" (Gal. 5:24). When a man understands what that means and accepts it in the faith of what Christ can do, then one step can bring him from carnal to spiritual. One simple act of faith in the power of Christ's death, one act of surrender to the fellowship of Christ's death as the Holy Spirit can make it ours, will make it ours, will bring deliverance from the power of your efforts.[125]

Furthermore, Andrew Murray writes:

> So, in the spiritual life, you may go to teacher after teacher, and say, "Tell me about the spiritual life, the baptism of the Spirit, and holiness," and yet you may remain just where you were. Many of us would love to have sin taken away. Who loves to have a hasty temper? Who loves to have a proud disposition? Who loves to have a worldly heart? No one. We go to Christ to take it away, and He does not do it; and we ask, "Why will He not do it? I have prayed very earnestly." It is because you wanted Him to take away the ugly fruits while the poisonous root was to stay in you. You did not ask Him that the flesh should be nailed to His cross and that you should henceforth give up self entirely to the power of His Spirit. The key is in trusting and surrendering it to God.
>
> It is the Holy Spirit alone who, by His indwelling, can make a spiritual man. Come then and cast yourself at God's feet with this one thought, "Lord, I give myself an empty vessel to be filled with Thy Spirit."[126]

The good news is that prayers like this receive a quick answer from the Father.

O, dear Father, I come before You with my empty vessel

cleansed by the Blood of the Holy Lamb. "My God will fulfill His promise! I claim from Him the filling of the Holy Spirit to make me, instead of a carnal, a spiritual Christian.[127]

All these things sound so good on paper, don't they? But when the rubber meets the road, things appear to be different. The question is: Is there a genuinely spiritual life? Is such a thing possible for ordinary people like you and me? If it is: How can you and I enter such a life? Well, I am glad you have asked! Let me see if I can explain it in plain terms.

First, God is asking for it, and He promises this type of life. The Bible teaches: "Therefore you are to be perfect, as your heavenly Father is perfect" (Matthew 5:48). Jesus is telling us: "I came that they may have life, and have it abundantly" (John 10:10b).

Second, based on these two passages, it is clear that living this kind of life is impossible when believers try to live independently of God. Only Christ, through the Holy Spirit, operating in us, can live that kind of life. After all, it is His life.

So, what must we do? A few things are of vital importance:

- We must be filled with the Spirit (Ephesians 5:18),
- We must be led by the Spirit (Romans 8:14),
- We must walk by the Spirit (Galatians 5:25).

If we don't see these aspects clearly, we must repent. In other words, we must change our minds about carnality of any kind and see it as—incompatibility with God's nature of which we are partakers (2 Peter 1:4). It must be settled once and for all that for a genuine believer in Christ, these outbreaks of carnality should be an exception, not the rule.

Third, the believer must be convicted of the bankruptcy of their flesh. We must see something terribly wrong with our carnal state as believers and agonize before God to deliver us from it. Paul writes: "Wretched man that I am! Who will set me free from the body of this death?" (Romans 7:24). Without this deep conviction, we can never become truly spiritual men. Transitioning from the carnal to the spiritual state is one step away. At this point, we see Galatians 2:20 with a different set of eyes. We declare: "it is no longer I who live, but Christ lives in me." There must be a legal breakup with the flesh. And rest assured that the cross has done that (past tense). This is the place where Christ desires His brothers and sisters to live and operate, by Him and through Him. And this requires total surrender (Romans 12:1)—not just a one-time deal, but daily surrender, picking up and carrying the cross.

Spiritual and abundant life is a daily walk. It is a vibrant life, not a static one. Only in the position of total surrender can the Word of God renew the believer's mind. Only with the renewal of the mind (cf. Romans 12:2) and transformation of character (cf. 2 Corinthians 3:18) can the believer increasingly display the life and character of Christ, and thus be less and less carnal. As others may explain, this process is known as progressive sanctification.

If the Holy Spirit has convicted you about your own spiritual state, I highly encourage you to declare before God three positive things:

- Father God, I desire to eat solid food. Please help me to grow.
- Dear Lord, I am so disappointed in how carnal I am because I am still clinging to the flesh. I realize now "that nothing good dwells in me, that is, in my flesh" (Romans 7:18). Take Your "knife" and cut it off.
- Dear Holy Spirit, assist me and guide me in the process of spiritual growth and maturity.

Now that you have made these powerful declarations let's pray to seal them at the heart level.

I am suggesting this prayer:

Oh, Abba Father, I know that You love me. I present before You my empty vessel cleansed by the pure Blood of Your Son,

Jesus. I know that whoever comes to You will not be ashamed. I claim the filling of the Holy Spirit to make me a spiritual Christian instead of a carnal one. I pray in the wonderful name of Christ.

Danger number two

Instability

One of the most visible dangers of spiritual immaturity is instability. Paul writes: "As a result, we are no longer to be children, tossed here and there by waves and carried about by every wind of doctrine, by the trickery of men, by craftiness in deceitful scheming" (Ephesians 4:14). According to Merriam Webster Dictionary, "to toss," means to "to throw (something) with a quick, light motion, to move or lift quickly or suddenly, to move (something) back and forth or up and down."[128]

Paul uses four words to warn believers about the danger of spiritual immaturity:

- Trickery
- Craftiness
- Deceitful
- Scheming

The word trickery in this verse refers to the opposite of being honest, truthful, frank, and open. According to Merriam-Webster Dictionary, the word craftiness is "the skill in achieving one's ends through indirect, subtle, or underhanded means."[129]

Deceitful means to do something based on or using dishonest methods to acquire something of value.

The fourth word used by Paul is scheming, which means being clever at attaining one's ends by indirect and often deceptive means.

Paul is not using this combination of words to impress the believers in Ephesus with his elevated Greek vocabulary. Under the inspiration of the Holy Spirit, Paul wanted to emphasize the danger of instability when believers remain in a childlike state. In other words, if we don't want to be carried about by every wind of doctrine, we must grow up in the knowledge and grace of Christ.

Immature believers do not have a stable theological stand. If a preacher says something, they are moved in that direction. If a different teacher comes in and preaches something else, they are thrown in that direction. Without spiritual maturity, believers are in danger of being carried away by the trickery of men. Deceitful men win over people who are carried about with ease. These men have some false charisma to gain the sympathy of their audience. The bottom line is that immaturity, a childlike state, is dangerous because of instability.

If this describes you, then please acknowledge this danger in your life. I am asking you to declare three positive things:

- God, I need stability.
- Lord Jesus, I have decided to grow.
- Holy Spirit, please make me stable and consistent in my faith and walk with You.

After making these necessary declarations, I encourage you to kneel before God and pray this prayer:

Father God, I want to be stable. I have decided to embrace the process of spiritual growth and maturity. Dear Lord Jesus, I realize that growing and maturing in Your knowledge and grace is the only way I can be stable. Precious Holy Spirit, please work in me, transform me, and develop me according to God's plans and purposes. My only desire is to display the Life and the Character of Christ. I pray in the name of Jesus. Amen.

Danger number three

Repulsion towards Solid Food

Spiritually speaking, *milk* stands for the "elementary teaching about Christ." According to Hebrews 6:1-2, the *milk diet* includes teachings about "repentance from dead works," teachings about "faith towards God," teachings about Church Sacraments, "resurrection of the dead and eternal judgment."

Milk is good! No question about it. But milk is the primary food for babies, not for adults. As any good parent, our Father does not want His children to continue indefinitely on the milk diet. God desires us to "grow in respect to salvation," as Peter puts it so well in 1 Peter 2:1–3. For this to happen, we must "press on to maturity" (Hebrews 6:1), which requires a willful decision. Pressing on is not an easy task; it implies overcoming resistance; it requires stick-to-it-ness.

Moreover, pressing on requires advancing, heading toward, making headway, and progressing. As you can see, all these words suggest something dynamic, not static.

Solid food stands for advanced teaching regarding the righteousness of God and spiritual discernment.

According to 2 Peter 3:18, solid food refers to mature teaching about the grace and knowledge of Christ.

According to Paul's prayers in Ephesians 1:15–23 and 3:14–21, solid food means an enlightened understanding of our identity in Christ and a deep comprehension of agape love and its spiritual dimensions.

Based on Paul's teaching in Romans 8:14 and Galatians 5:16–26, solid food represents a correct understanding of what it really means to be led by the Holy Spirit.

Moreover, solid food implies a deep knowledge of what it means to be transformed into Christlikeness (2 Corinthians 3:18; 1 Corinthians 5:2–3).

Immature believers have a natural tendency to dislike solid food. Repulsion is a feeling of intense dislike or disgust towards something.

D. A. Carson writes:

> But there are Christians who are international-class projectile vomiters, spiritually speaking, after years and years of life. They simply cannot digest what Paul calls "solid food." You must give them milk, for they are not ready for anything more. And if you try to give them anything other than milk, they upchuck and make a mess of everyone and everything around them. At some point, the number of years they have been Christians leads you to expect some mature behavior from them, but they prove disappointing. They are infants still and display their wretched immaturity even the way that they complain if you give them more than milk. Not for them solid knowledge of Scripture, not for them mature theological reflection; not for them growing and perceptive Christian thought.
> They want nothing more than another round of choruses and a "simple message"—something that won't challenge them to think, to examine their lives, to make choices, and to grow in their knowledge and adoration of the living God. So, the Corinthians, then, are wretchedly immature believers.[130]

In my travels around the world teaching about spiritual growth and maturity, I heard so many excuses (even from Christian leaders) regarding spiritual growth. Let me share just a few of them:

- It is so hard! Even the Bible in Ecclesiastes 12:12 tells us that too much teaching is weary to the body.
- I do not want to acquire too much knowledge because God will expect much from me. (See Luke 12:48).

- I don't have to study the Bible before I preach or make myself a plan or a sermon sketch because the Holy Spirit will give me the exact words I must speak. (See Mark 13:11).
- It is written not to have too many teachers. (See James 3:1).

If you look at the Bible references, I provided, all these Scriptures are taken out of context, proving further the danger of spiritual immaturity.

Obviously, a biological baby cannot be transitioned overnight from milk to solid food. It would be foolish to have such unrealistic expectations. It is a gradual process. They must be weaned first.

The taste buds of a baby must be cultivated to like solid food. In the same way, our spiritual "taste buds" must be cultivated to desire solid food over some time. But by no means should the weaning period take forty years; perhaps three or four, but not more than that.

Charles R. Swindoll writes:

> You see, in order for a Christian to handle solid food, he has to have a grown, mature digestive system. He needs teeth. He needs to have an appetite that is cultivated over a period of time for deep things, for the solid things of God. Spiritual babies must grow up. Some of the most difficult people to live with in the church of Jesus Christ are those who have grown old in the Lord but haven't grown up in Him.[131]

The more we delay our exposure to solid food, the longer it takes to like it. It requires a willful decision to move from milk to solid food; otherwise, we will remain "dull of hearing."

The author of Hebrews puts it this way: "But solid food is for the mature, who because of practice have their senses trained to discern good and evil" (Hebrews 5:14).

You probably noticed this already, but assessing spiritual maturity is difficult. Many believers erroneously assume that they will automatically mature spiritually as time passes.

Unlike physical maturity, which is primarily a function of time, spiritual maturity is not. The time factor is obvious when it comes to physical maturity. We can easily differentiate between a three-year-old boy and a thirty-year-old man.

In the spiritual realm, growth and maturity are not a function of time but rather a function of our spiritual diet. For example, some Christians out there could have been attending the local church for thirty years and still be at the level of a toddler, acting like a three-year-old Christian. With proper discipleship, it is possible for a Christian who received Christ three years ago to be spiritually mature, displaying the life and character of Christ. (See Galatians 5:22–23; John 15:8).

Spiritual immaturity affects our speech, thinking, and decision-making. Paul writes: "When I was a child, I used to speak like a child, think like a child, reason like a child" (1 Corinthians 13:11a). Therefore, it is imperative to engage in the process of spiritual growth and maturity immediately so we can do away with childish things. Paul continues: "when I became a man, I did away with childish things" (1 Corinthians 13:11b).

The opposite of immaturity, of course, is spiritual maturity. Maturity is the high calling of every child of God, and one's priorities primarily evidence it. Do we continue to pursue the things and success of this world or seek the goal of God set before us—Christ?

Paul writes: "I press on toward the goal for the prize of the upward call of God in Christ Jesus" (Philippians 3:14). If the great apostle Paul felt the need to "press on," how much more you and I must do it?

Paul admonishes Christians engaged in the process of perfection with these words: "Let us, therefore, as many as are perfect, have this attitude; and if in anything you have a different attitude, God will reveal that also to you" (Philippians 3:15).

Christian maturity does not mean sinless perfection. It does not mean that mature people are of a higher class than individuals who cannot humble themselves to live in unity with others. By no means!

The Greek word perfection (Gr. τέλειος, *teleios*) used by Paul in Philippians 3:15 means:

> Full age, adulthood, full-grown, of persons, meaning full-grown in mind and understanding (cf. 1 Corinthians 14:20); in the knowledge of the truth (cf. 1 Corinthians 2:6; Philippians 3:15, Hebrews 5:14); in Christian faith and virtue (cf. Ephesians 4:13).[132]

Paul explains: "However, let us keep living by that same standard to which we have attained" (Philippians 3:16). As Meldenius Rupertus a German Protestant theologian of the 17th century (aka Peter Meiderlin) once said: "In essential unity, in non-essential liberty, in all things charity."[133]

Spiritual maturity is not a competition between who can recite more theological facts. Instead, spiritual maturity is evidenced by love—agape love.

The Bible teaches us: "But the goal of our instruction is love from a pure heart and a good conscience and a sincere faith" (1 Timothy 1:5). In other words, genuine spiritual maturity is characterized by displaying a genuine and mature agape love, which is the very nature of God.

Believe me, it was not pleasant to write this section, and I am sure it was not pleasant for you to read it, either. Please, do yourself a great favor, and declare before God three positive things:

- God, I am hungry for solid food.
- Holy Spirit, I desire to eat like a mature Christian.
- Dear Lord Jesus, I am in pursuit of spiritual growth.

My deep desire is to be a mature Christian. I invite You to display the life and character of Christ in me.

Now that you have declared these critical statements, please seal them in a prayer like this:

Dear God, please plant a deep desire for Your Word in me. Please develop my taste buds for solid food. O, Lord Jesus, please carry me in Your arms and take me to green pastures so I can grow more and more into Your grace and knowledge. So, help me, God. Amen!

Danger number four

Spiritual Identity Ignorance

What a tragedy to be a child of God and yet still be ignorant about your spiritual identity. If Christians only see themselves as *sinners saved by grace*, they have a view that is highly detrimental to their core identity. Immature believers cannot comprehend who they are in Christ. They don't understand that they are already righteous in God's sight. As God's children, we have access to all that God has. Due to immaturity, practically speaking, we cannot possess His riches yet.

Let me illustrate this point. While slaves in Egypt, God promised the Jews a country flowing with milk and honey—the Promised Land.

God told Moses:

> So, I have come down to deliver them from the power of the Egyptians, and to bring them up from that land to a good and spacious land, to a land flowing with milk and honey, to the place of the Canaanite and the Hittite and the Amorite and the Perizzite and the Hivite and the Jebusite. (Exodus 3:8)

At least 600,000 adult-male Jews received this promise from God. This was a glorious offer. As we all know, God cannot lie (cf. Hebrews 6:18). Still, because of their unbelief, which, according to Hebrew 3:17–19, leads to disobedience, only two of them entered the "land flowing with milk and honey." This represents only 0.00033% of the Jews who received the promise. I think that this is heartbreaking for the heavenly Father. Spiritual immaturity is dangerous and costly. Paul writes: "Now I say, as long as the heir is a child (Gr. νήπιος, népios[134]), he does not differ at all from a slave[135] although he is the owner of everything. (Galatians 4:1)

The person who lacks maturity cannot speak spiritual thoughts using spiritual words because they are unlearned and unenlightened (1 Corinthians 2:13–14). Therefore, they cannot handle the spiritual inheritance of God. As a result, the Father cannot entrust them with anything of importance.

As God's children, we have been seated with "Him in the heavenly places in Christ Jesus" (Ephesians 2:6). By spiritual birth, this is our rightful position. However, without developing "wings" through spiritual maturity, we cannot fly like eagles; instead, we keep gobbling the same words as turkeys going around and around the same old barn.

To receive and handle spiritual responsibilities, God's children are required to grow and mature in "the grace and knowledge of Christ" (2 Peter 3:18). For us to leave the spiritual poverty of the old "barn," we need to grow wings like eagles and fly higher in the sky.

The author of Hebrew writes so boldly about this: "For everyone who partakes only of milk is not accustomed to the word of righteousness, for he is an infant" (Hebrews 5:13). Therefore, when it comes to spiritual identity, the doctrine of the believer's righteousness is crucial.

Righteousness is the state of moral perfection required by God to enter heaven. Dikaiosuné,[136] which means righteousness: "is the thus conformity to the claims of higher authority and stands in opposition to anomia (Strong Number 458), lawlessness.[137]"

According to Merriam-Webster Dictionary, to be righteous means: "Acting in accord with divine or moral law: free from guilt or sin."[138] Fairness, goodness, honor, justness, rectitude, respectability, uprightness, and virtue are synonyms for righteousness.[139]

The entire Old Testament Law, including the Ten Commandments plus the "moral" Law which, according to some Old Testament experts, amounts to approximately 613 laws, represents the moral character of God. The "Law is holy, and the commandment is holy and righteous and good" (Romans 7:12). But when it comes to conferring us His righteousness, because of the flesh, the Law is impotent (Romans 8:4). The New Testament teaching is clear that "by the works of the Law no flesh will be justified" (Galatians 2:16).

To make sure I am not taking it out of context, I would like to say a few things about the Law.

- First, the role of the Law was to show how horrible sin is. Paul explains "that through the commandment (Law) sin would become utterly sinful" (Romans 7:13).
- Second, the Law was just a tutor for us, to direct us to Christ. The Bible says, "Therefore the Law has become our tutor to lead us to Christ, so that we may be justified by faith" (Galatians 3:24).

The Scripture makes it clear that when Christ came, there was no longer a need to remain under this "tutor." "But now that faith has come, we are no longer under a tutor" (Galatians 3:25).

When it comes to the theme of righteousness, Paul sets the record straight. He teaches that we "may be found in Him, not having a righteousness of my own derived from the Law, but that which is through faith in Christ, the righteousness which comes from God on the basis of faith" (Philippians 3:9).

According to the New Testament, the foundation for our righteousness as New Covenant believers is solely based on the finished work of Christ on Calvary's Cross—His death, resurrection, and His ascension.

A New Testament believer is considered righteous by faith in Jesus Christ (see Romans 4 and 5). More profoundly, righteousness is more than being right with God. The Bible teaches that our righteousness is Christ Jesus Himself who dwells in our hearts (see Philippians 1:20–21, Romans 8:10, 1 Corinthians 1:30, Galatians 2:20, Ephesians 3:17, Colossians 3:4).

Moreover, in his prophetic writings, Jeremiah speaks about Messiah as "a righteous Branch" (Jeremiah 23:5) and that He will be called "The LORD our righteousness" (Jeremiah 23:6). This was prophesied several hundred years before the crucifixion of Christ! No wonder Paul writes so confidently that Jesus Christ is our righteousness: "But by His doing you are in Christ Jesus, who became to us wisdom from God, and righteousness and sanctification, and redemption" (1 Corinthians 1:30).

Regarding righteousness, 1 Corinthians 1:30 is one of my all-time favorite verses. Also, 2 Corinthians 5:21 spells it out very clearly: "He (God) made Him who knew no sin to be sin on our behalf so that we might become the righteousness of God in Him." According to this verse, as God's children, we have righteousness as valuable and precious as Christ's righteousness. Why? Because He is our righteousness.

The basis of our salvation and the only hope for righteousness stands firm on:

(a) Christ's blood on Calvary (see Romans 4:25, 5:9, 8:3–4, 1 Corinthians 15:3, Galatians 2:20, Ephesians 1:7, Hebrews 9:14, 1, Peter 1:18–19, 1 John 4:10), and
(b) His resurrected life in our hearts (see: Romans 4:25, 5:9-10; 8:10–11, Galatians 2:20, Colossians 3:1–3).

Paul is the expert in the doctrine of righteousness. He argues and demonstrates this vital topic from multiple angles.

The first part of Romans is dedicated to receiving righteousness by faith. He writes: "For in it (the Gospel) the righteousness of God is revealed from faith to faith; as it is written: "But the righteous man shall live by faith" (Romans 1:17).

Then in Romans 3:21–22, we read:

> But now apart from the Law the righteousness of God has been manifested, being witnessed by the Law and the Prophets, even the righteousness of God through faith in Jesus Christ for all those who believe; for there is no distinction.

Secondly, Paul does not say anywhere in the New Testament that righteousness is obtained by observing the Old Testament Law. He writes: "Because by the works of the Law no flesh will be justified in His sight" (Romans 3:20). Even the righteousness Abraham received, he received by faith.

Paul writes:

> For what does the Scripture say? Abraham believed in God, and it was credited to him as righteousness... But to the one who does not work, but believes in Him who justifies the ungodly, his faith is credited as righteousness. (Romans 4:3, 5)

Otherwise, it would be based on merit, and the promise would be invalidated, as Paul explains: "For if those who are of the Law are heirs, faith is made void, and the promise is nullified. (Romans 4:14)

Some may ask: *"Brother Valy, are you suggesting that since we have Christ's righteousness, it does not matter how we conduct our lives?"* May it never be! This is a big misunderstanding. Paul was misunderstood as well.

Remember how Paul responded to this kind of question: "What shall we say then? Are we to continue in sin so that grace may increase?" (Romans 6:1). He answered his own rhetorical question: "May it never be! How shall we who died to sin still live in it?" (Romans 6:2).

To be righteous at the inner core of our beings and continue in sin is incompatible. It is like going against our very nature.

Let me try to illustrate it for you. A lion is a carnivore. It is in his nature to eat meat. A cow is an herbivore. It is in her nature to eat grass. For a lion to eat grass would be against his very nature. For a cow to eat meat would be against her very nature. For a Christian to continue in sin would be incompatible with their very nature—a saint and partaker of God's nature.

Does all this mean that God is not interested in moral

behavior or in character development just because we have Christ's righteousness? Of course not. This is a deception coming from the pit of hell. God is very interested in our behavior, but He does not grant us His righteousness based on our changed behavior. This would mean re-instituting the Old Testament Law.

So how did God get around this? In Christ, God crucified us also and then resurrected us in Him, thus making us as righteous as Christ. God placed us in Christ, and when Christ died on the cross, we died with Him (cf. Romans 6:3–4); when He was raised from the dead, we were raised with Him (Colossians 2:12); when He ascended to the right hand of the Father we were (past tense) also seated with Him at the right hand of the Father in Christ (Ephesians 1:12, 2:6). Pretty awesome!

Now, because of our position in Christ and since He is in us (Colossians 1:27), sin no longer has dominion over us, so we can freely live for God. It appears simple, but it is not simplistic. The Bible teaches us: "Present yourselves to God as those alive from the dead, and your members as instruments of righteousness to God" (Romans 6:13).

Since we are not under the Law, but under grace (cf. Romans 6:14), we continue to be saved by Christ's life. Paul writes: "For if while we were enemies we were reconciled to God through the death of His Son, much more, having been reconciled, we shall be saved by His life" (Romans 5:10).

The secret of living a victorious and fulfilled life is Christ's life. Because Christ indwells us, we can present ourselves and all our members to God in obedience, and, as a result, we enjoy practical righteousness. The Bible tells us: "Do you not know that when you present yourselves to someone as slaves for obedience, you are slaves of the one whom you obey, either of sin resulting in death, or of obedience resulting in righteousness?" (Romans 6:16). Now, because of our special position in Christ, we became slaves of righteousness (cf. Romans 6:18).

Is God interested in holiness? Of course, He is. His standards of holiness have not changed, not even by one micron.[140] More than that, God is looking for genuine holiness. How can Christians attain it? Only in one way—by presenting ourselves and our members as slaves to righteousness. This will result in sanctification.

Please make a note and keep it handy: *This is the only way Christians arrive at genuine holiness.* Yes, (cf. Matthew 22:11–12) Christians are required to be holy people. But make sure this is read in the context of Revelation 19:7–8.

Does this mean that salvation is by faith and sanctification by works? Of course not! This is the enemy's trap to cause us to act independently from God. This is living and walking after the flesh. Paul strongly rebukes this way of thinking and acting. He writes: "Are you so foolish? Having begun by the Spirit, are you now being perfected by the flesh?" (Galatians 3:3).

"Brother Valy, I am confused!" some may exclaim. *"Do you mean I cross my arms over my chest and do nothing? Am I being perfected by some automatic pilot?"* No. Not at all! The Bible teaches us that we have an active role in the process of progressive sanctification. Paul explains: "So then, my beloved, just as you have always obeyed, not as in my presence only, but now much more in my absence, work out your salvation with fear and trembling" (Philippians 2:12).

Some may say: *"Well… that sounds like "work" to me."* It may sound like that, but it isn't. In God's economy, the power source and motivation make all the difference. Paul is saying to work out our salvation, not to work for our salvation. The following verse explains it: "For it is God who is at work in you, both to will and to work for His good pleasure" (Philippians 2:13). In the end, what counts is Christ's life being manifested in and through us.

Furthermore, Paul writes: "When Christ, who is our life, is revealed, then you also will be revealed with Him in glory" (Colossians 3:4). That is why knowing who we are in Christ is an essential key to spiritual victory. Therefore, when it comes to the theme of our spiritual identity, we must be honest with ourselves; otherwise, it will cost us dearly.

With a much fuller understanding now, let's declare before

God three positive things:

- God, I am so ignorant of who I really am.
- Dear Lord Jesus, I want to grow into my rightful position as a mature son (*huios*[4]) and thrive in God's household.
- Holy Spirit, please reveal to me my spiritual identity.

Now let's bow before God in prayer with these words:

Father God, I thank you for placing me in Christ, so I died with Him when He died on the cross. I believe with all my heart that when You raised Jesus from the dead, You also justified me and made me righteous in Him. I have no words to thank You for the glorious position of being seated with Christ at Your right hand in heaven. This is my identity, my destiny; this is my new life now. I am the righteousness of God in Christ. I pray in the wonderful name of Jesus, Who is my life, my everything. Amen.

[4] AN: See endnote # 9 for more.

Danger number five

Inability to Make a Meaningful Contribution to the Spiritual Body of Christ

Paul writes:

> But speaking the truth in love; we are to grow up in all aspects into Him who is the head, even Christ, from whom the whole body, being fitted and held together by what every joint supplies, according to the proper working of each individual part, causes the growth of the body for the building up of itself in love" (Ephesians 4:15–16).

It is vitally important to understand that God is looking at both the spiritual growth and maturity of the individual member and the growth of the entire body.

- First: "We are to grow up in all aspects into Him."
- Second: "The whole body... according to the proper working of each individual part, causes the growth of the body."

Do you see this spiritual dynamic? I hope you do! The conclusion is clear. Immaturity in individual members of the Church causes stagnation of the spiritual growth of the entire body. And this is the greatest danger of spiritual immaturity.

I believe that five essential aspects derive from Ephesians 4:16. They are:

1. The whole body, being fitted together
2. The whole body, being held together
3. By what every joint supply

4. Every individual part must contribute to the work of spiritual growth and maturity of the entire body,
5. The body—the Church—is to be built on love.

Allow me to say a few things about each of these five aspects.

1. The whole body, being fitted together

This sounds good on paper, but the question is: what can accomplish the fitting together of the Body of Christ?

I think you'll agree that love binds the Body together. In his letter to the Colossians, Paul indicates that compassion, kindness, humility, gentleness, patience, and forgiveness are all important for the local church's overall spiritual and emotional health. Then he writes: "Beyond all these things put on love, which is the perfect bond of unity" (Colossians 3:14). You see? Love is the perfect bond of unity.

We can only arrive at this profound point of understanding through a personal experience of the death and resurrection of Christ. The Bible teaches us:

> For the love of Christ controls and urges and impels us, because we are of the opinion and conviction that [if] One died for all, then all died; and He died for all, so that all those who live might live no longer to and for themselves, but to and for Him who died and was raised again for their sake. (2 Corinthians 5:14–15 AMP)

Only when we understand our identification in Christ's death and resurrection can we live for Him, not ourselves. There is no other cure for our self-centeredness than the cross of Christ. If we are to "grow up in all aspects into Him," we must practice speaking the truth in love. In other words, in our fellowship with one another, we must exercise enough transparency and acceptance to speak the truth, not in hurtful ways, but in love. John writes so tenderly: "Little children, let us not love with word or with tongue, but in deed and truth" (1 John 3:18). At the opening of his second letter, John writes: "Grace, mercy, and peace will be with us, from God the Father and from Jesus Christ, the Son of the Father, in truth and love" (2 John 1:3). Similarly, in the third letter, John writes: "The elder to the beloved Gaius, whom I love in truth" (3 John 3:1). Agape love cannot exist without truth; and truth cannot exist without agape love. These two go hand in hand and contribute to our spiritual growth.

2. The whole body, being held together

This speaks of profound organic unity! But the question is: what keeps (or holds) the Body of Christ together?

The only thing that can accomplish this is truth. Truth is the only force that keeps the Christian Church together. Only the Person of Truth—Christ Himself—holds us together. Here is a powerful Scripture: "He is before all things, and in Him all things hold together" (Colossians 1:17). Christ, in a sense, is the belt of truth that wraps around us. Paul writes: "stand, therefore, having your loins girded about with truth, and having on the breastplate of righteousness" (Ephesians 6:14). "Having your loins girded about with truth," means "to encircle with a belt or band" and "to prepare (oneself) for action."

In the Old Testament, it is written:

> These words, which I am commanding you today, shall be in your heart. You shall teach them diligently to your sons and shall talk of them when you sit in your house and when you walk by the way and when you lie down and when you rise up. You shall bind them as a sign on your hand, and they shall be as frontals on your forehead. (Deuteronomy 6:6–8)

Commenting on this verse, John Wesley writes:

> Thou shalt bind them—Thou shalt give all diligence,

> and use all means to keep them in thy remembrance, as men often bind something upon their hands, or put it before their eyes to prevent forgetfulness of a thing which they much desire to remember.[141]

In other words, we should behold the Lord Jesus and be constantly mindful of His words. The wise king of the Old Testament writes: "Bind them on your fingers; Write them on the tablet of your heart" (Proverbs 7:3).

3. By what every joint supply

We all agree that Christ has only one Church. He is coming for a single Bride, not for 41,000[142] little brides. The Body of Christ is not a member by itself but many members in unity! Still, practically speaking, God's people live in much disunity. Paul understood the principle of organic unity very well. He writes: "For the body is not one member, but many" (1 Corinthians 12:14).

I challenge you to keep in mind the following principle: "What makes the physical body powerful is not the individual members separated from each other but rather the joints coming together in unity." The same is true in the spiritual arena. When believers are tightly bound with God and each other by obeying His commands, they can fight to advance His kingdom instead of quarreling with each other. The Bible promises: "How could one chase a thousand, and two put ten thousand to flight" (Deuteronomy 32:30a).

Allow me to illustrate. Let us look at the shoulder. The human shoulder is made up of three bones: the clavicle (collarbone), the scapula (shoulder blade), and the humerus (upper arm bone), as well as associated muscles, ligaments, and tendons. If any of these three bones were separated from each other, they could do nothing. What makes the shoulder powerful is that all these parts between the shoulder bones come together to make up the shoulder joints.

Let me give you another example: the elbow. The human elbow joint is the synovial hinge between the upper arm's humerus and the radius and ulna in the forearm, which allows the hand to be moved towards and away from the body. Obviously, these components (the humerus, the upper arm, and the radius and ulna) by themselves cannot perform (if separated from each other) what the elbow (as a joint) can do. Should I go further? Should I explain how the hip operates?

The hip joint, scientifically referred to as the acetabulofemoral joint, is the joint between the femur and acetabulum of the pelvis. Its primary function is to support the body's weight in static (standing) and dynamic (walking or running) postures. The hip joints are the most critical part of retaining balance. The pelvic inclination angle, the single most important element of human body posture, is adjusted at the hips. The coming together of the femur and acetabulum forms this important joint. These elements alone can do nothing, but together the hip joint helps the whole body when standing or running. Isn't this amazing? We could go on with these examples from the human body.

If these are true for the human body, it is the same for the spiritual Body—the Church. Paul writes: "For even as the body is one and yet has many members, and all the members of the body, though they are many, are one body, so also is Christ" (1 Corinthians 12:12). Think about a body that is decapitated! Can that body perform anything? Of course not! It does not function. It is dead.

In the same way, the spiritual body, the Church, cannot function. The Church is dead without her perfect union with Christ. That is why the Lord Jesus clearly tells his disciples, "Abide in Me, and I in you. As the branch cannot bear fruit of itself unless it abides in the vine, so neither can you unless you abide in Me" (John 15:5). I hope we get this sooner rather than later.

3. Every individual part must contribute to the work of spiritual growth and maturity of the entire body

Now we reached the point where the rubber meets the road. In the same way that the three bones, the clavicle, the scapula, and the humerus, come together to form the joint of the shoulders, so it must be done in the body of Christ. The prophet Isaiah foretold about the coming of the Child who will be given to us. He stated, "the government will rest on His shoulders" (Isaiah 9:6). I don't think it would be stretch to say that Christ's "shoulders" on this earth are us—the Church, coming in unity to serve God's purposes. I like this connection! I hope you do too!

The Pareto principle, the law of the vital few, also known as the 20/80 Rule, states that: "for many events, roughly 80% of effects come from 20% of the causes."[143] This principle seems to affect churches as well. If we are sincere, we must attest to these facts:

- 20% of Christians complete 80% of the ministries of the local Church.
- 80% of financial contributions are donated by 20% of supporters.

Interesting, isn't it?

Moreover:

> According to researchers Scott Thumma and Warren Bird, most churches—mega-sized and small, black and white—are run by 20 percent of the congregation. The other 80 percent, they say, tend to act like spectators: they are minimally involved and attend infrequently or not at all.[144]

This is staggering! However, God does not want the 20/80 Rule to be in effect in His Church. God wants the 100/100 Rule to be in effect inside Christ's Body. The Bible tells us: "From whom the whole body, being fitted and held together by what every joint supplies, according to the proper working of each individual part, causes the growth of the body for the building up of itself in love" (Ephesians 4:16). In other words, there should be no idleness in the body of Christ.

No individual member should be "unemployed," but all should be involved in something good for God and others. Paul writes: "Now you are Christ's body, and individually members of it" (1 Corinthians 12:27). This has been written to discourage any forms of divisions inside the Body of Christ "so that there may be no division in the body, but that the members may have the same care for one another" (1 Corinthians 12:25).

4. The Body—the Church—is to be built on love

This, in a sense, is a climax in Paul's writings. He writes:

> In whom the whole building, being fitted together, is growing into a holy temple in the Lord, in whom you also are being built together into a dwelling of God in the Spirit" (Ephesians 2:21–22).

Paul continues this idea in chapter 4: "According to the proper working of each individual part, causes the growth of the body for the building up of itself in love" (Ephesian 4:16b). I believe with all my heart that if every Christian were conscientious of this principle—the body of Christ is built on love—it would bring a tremendous revival. This would be a love revolution with every church member declaring: Not me but Him. Not us but the Kingdom of God!

No matter what, God will be consistent with His nature (agape love) and all His principles.

Paul warns us:

> Now if any man builds on the foundation with gold, silver, precious stones, wood, hay, straw, each man's work will become evident; for the day will show it because it is to be revealed with fire, and the fire itself will test the quality of each man's work. (1 Corinthians 3:12–13)

The more I investigate the vast theme of spiritual growth

and maturity, the more I am convinced that as the individual members of any local church experience spiritual growth, spiritual joints are being formed by the Holy Spirit within the Universal Body. The Body of Christ reaches the point of "being fitted and held together." This is done by formation of joints. It is clear that the formation of the joints depends on "the proper working of each individual part." Do you see the chain of events? If Satan could keep most individual members of a local church disinterested in spiritual maturity, in a sense, he can prevent spiritual maturity in the entire local body. I have a suspicion that this is precisely the strategy the enemy uses.

That is why the Scripture is filled with the expressions "one another" and "each other." Before His crucifixion, in the most intimate setting (Holy Communion), Christ said:

> A new commandment I give to you, that you love one another, even as I have loved you, that you also love one another. By this all men will know that you are My disciples, if you have love for one another. (John 13:34-35)

As believers, we are called to:

- Be devoted to one another in love (Romans 12:10)
- Be of the same mind toward one another (Romans 12:16)
- Do not judge one another (Romans 14:13)
- Build up one another (Romans 14:19, 1 Thessalonians 5:11)
- Accept one another (Romans 15:7)
- Admonish one another (Romans 15:14; Colossians 3:16)
- Greet one another with a sincere love (Rom. 16:16, 1 Peter 5:14)
- Display the same care for one another (1 Corinthians 12:25)
- Be kind to one another (Ephesians 4:32)

- Be tender-hearted, forgiving each other (Ephesians 4:32)
- Speak life to one another (Ephesians 5:19)
- Be subject to one another (Ephesians 5:21)
- Serve one another in love (Galatians 5:13)
- Bear one another's burdens (Galatians 6:2; Colossians 3:13)
- Display sincere understanding for one another (Ephesians 4:2)
- Regard one another as more important than yourselves (Philippians 2:3)
- Abound in love for one another and love each other (1 Thessalonians 3:12, 4:9; 2 Thessalonians 1:3, 1 Peter. 1:22, 4:8; 1 John 3:11, 4:7, 4:11, 4:12; 2 John 1:5)
- Comfort one another (1 Thessalonians 4:18)
- Encourage one another (1 Thessalonians 5:11; Hebrew 3:13, 10:25)
- Live in peace with one another (1 Thessalonians 5:13)
- Seek good for one another (1 Thessalonians 5:15; Hebrews 10:24)
- Do not speak against one another (James 4:11)
- Do not complain against one another (James 5:9; 1 Peter 4:9)
- Confess your sins to one another (James 5:16)
- Pray for one another (James 5:16)
- Be hospitable to one another (1 Peter 4:9)
- Serve one another (1 Peter 4:10)
- Display genuine humility toward one another (1 Peter 5:5)

These are just a few references based only on the New Testament epistles. Imagine how long the list would be if we included the entire Bible.

Now is the best time to declare before God three positive things:

- God, I realized that up until now, I have just been a consumer in the Body of Christ.
- Dear Lord Jesus, please make me and mold me in such a way that I may fulfill my role and destiny in Your Spiritual Body.
- Holy Spirit, please reveal to me the place, the function, and the gift I have and, most importantly, where I belong in the Body of Christ. Make me part of that special joint that only I was created to fulfill.

Let's pray this prayer:

Father God, thank you for the gift I have in Christ. Now I am part of Your Eternal Family. I desire to be productive in the place you ordered me to be. My heart longs to be effective in the function You have given me. Lord Jesus, I want to be organically connected with you to produce much fruit for God's glory. Holy Spirit, please form and mold me into the spiritual joint I have been designed to be. My chief desire is that, together with the rest of the members of the Church, we may work in unity for one cause only. That is the Body of Christ, to shine so the whole universe will see Your great work. I pray in the wonderful name of Jesus. Amen!

Reflection Questions

Please reflect upon the following questions, briefly elaborate, and then share your thoughts with a friend or your small group.

1. What did the Holy Spirit whisper to your heart through this chapter? What did you like the most in chapters 1-5?

2. What new concepts did you learn from chapters 1-5? Which idea are you committed to implementing in your life?

3. From the five dangers the author discussed in the book, which danger do you consider the deadliest?

4. After carefully studying the five dangers, please write short summaries of each. If necessary, use a separate piece of paper.
Danger 1

Danger 2:

Danger 3

Danger 4.

Dangers 5:

4.1. *Carnality.* Which aspects resonated in your own heart? In what areas did you sense the conviction of the Holy Spirit?

4.2. *Instability.* Which aspects resonated in your own heart? In what areas did you sense the conviction of the Holy Spirit?

4.3. *Repulsion towards Solid Food.* Which aspects resonated in your own heart? In what areas did you sense the conviction of the Holy Spirit?

4.4. *Spiritual Identity Ignorance.* Which aspects resonated in your own heart? In what areas did you sense the conviction of the Holy Spirit?

4.5. *Inability to Make a Meaningful Contribution to the Spiritual Body of Christ.* Which aspects resonated in your own heart? In what areas did you sense the conviction of the Holy Spirit?

5. List the best aha moments you had while reading this book.

Endnotes:

Introduction:

110 Valy Vaduva, *Advanced Discipleship Training* (ADT)—Registration Manual, (Novi, MI, Upper Room Fellowship Ministry, 2010), 7.

1. Carnality:

111 Parallel Verses from various Bible Translations:

- *New International Version:* Brothers and sisters, I could not address you as people who live by the Spirit but as people who are still worldly--mere infants in Christ.
- *New Living Translation:* Dear brothers and sisters, when I was with you I couldn't talk to you as I would to spiritual people. I had to talk as though you belonged to this world or as though you were infants in the Christian life.
- *English Standard Version:* But I, brothers, could not address you as spiritual people, but as people of the flesh, as infants in Christ. *New American Standard Bible:* And I, brethren, could not speak to you as to spiritual men, but as to men of flesh, as to infants in Christ.
- *King James Bible:* And I, brethren, could not speak unto you as unto spiritual, but as unto carnal, even as unto babes in Christ.
- *Holman Christian Standard Bible:* Brothers, I was not able to speak to you as spiritual people but as people of the flesh, as babies in Christ.
- *International Standard Version:* Brothers, I couldn't talk to you as spiritual people but as worldly people, as mere infants in the Messiah.
- *NET Bible:* So, brothers and sisters, I could not speak to you as spiritual people, but instead as people of the flesh, as infants in Christ.
- *Aramaic Bible in Plain English:* And I, my brethren, have not been able to speak with you as with spiritual ones but as with the carnal and as to babies in The Messiah.
- *GOD's WORD® Translation:* Brothers and sisters, I couldn't talk to you as spiritual people but as people still influenced by your corrupt nature. You were infants in your faith in Christ.
- *Jubilee Bible 2000:* And I, brothers, could not speak unto you as unto spiritual, but as unto carnal, even as unto babes in Christ.
- *King James 2000 Bible:* And I, brethren, could not speak unto you as unto spiritual, but as unto carnal, even as unto babes in Christ.
- *American King James Version:* And I, brothers, could not speak to you as to spiritual, but as to carnal, even as to babes in Christ.

- *American Standard Version:* And I, brethren, could not speak unto you as unto spiritual, but as unto carnal, as unto babes in Christ.
- *Douay-Rheims Bible:* And I, brethren, could not speak to you as unto spiritual, but as unto carnal. As unto little ones in Christ.
- *Darby Bible Translation:* And I, brethren, have not been able to speak to you as to spiritual, but as to fleshly; as to babes in Christ.
- *English Revised Version:* And I, brethren, could not speak unto you as unto spiritual, but as unto carnal, as unto babes in Christ.
- *Webster's Bible Translation:* And I, brethren, could not speak to you as to spiritual, but as to carnal, even as to babes in Christ.
- *Weymouth New Testament*: And as for myself, brethren, I found it impossible to speak to you as spiritual men. It had to be as to worldlings—mere babes in Christ.
- *World English Bible:* Brothers, I couldn't speak to you as to spiritual, but as to fleshly, as to babies in Christ.
- *Young's Literal Translation:* And I, brethren, was not able to speak to you as to spiritual, but as to fleshly—as to babes in Christ.

[112]Pneumatikos. www.biblehub.com. accessed on May 1, 2018. http://biblehub.com/greek/4152.htm.

[113] W.E. Vine, Merrill F. Unger, William Whote, Jr., *Vine's Complete Expository Dictionary of the Old and New Testament Words,* (Nashville, TN: Tomas Nelson Publishers, 1996), 594-95.

[114] Sarkikos. www.studylight.org. Accessed on June 10, 2014. http://www.studylight.org/ dictionary/ved/view.cgi?n=411.

[115] W.E. Vine, Merrill F. Unger, William Whote, Jr., *Vine's Complete Expository Dictionary of the Old and New Testament Words,* (Nashville, TN: Tomas Nelson Publishers, 1996), 243.

[116] Sarkinois. www.studylight.org. Accessed on May 30, 2014. http://www.studylight.org/commentaries/bnb/view.cgi?bk=45&ch=3.

[117] 1Andrew Murray, *The Master's Indwelling,* 4. www.ccel.org/. Accessed on June 12, 2014. http://www.ccel.org/ccel/murray/indwelling.html.

[118] "Carnal Christians," *Adam Clarke Commentary on 1 Corinthians 3:1-3.* www.studylight.org. Accessed on May 30, 2014. http://www.studylight.org/commentaries/acc/view.cgi?book= 1co&chapter=003.

[119] "Carnal state Christians," *Gill's Exposition of the Entire Bible.* www.biblestudytools.com. Accessed on May 30, 2014. http://www.biblestudytools.com/ commentaries/gills-exposition-of-the-bible/1-corinthians-3-1. html.

[120] Murray, *Indwelling,* 5. www.ccel. Org. Accessed on June 12, 2014. http://www.ccel. org/ccel/murray/indwelling.html

[121] J B Hall, Carnal Christian, 5, May 30, 2008. www.sermoncentral.com. Accessed on June 10,
2014. http://www.sermoncentral.com/sermons/carnal-christian- j-b-hall-

sermon-on-growth-in-christ-120681.asp?Page=1.
[122] "What is a carnal Christian?" www.gotquestions.org. Accessed on May 30, 2014. http://www.gotquestions.org/carnal-Christian.html.
[123] Murray, *Indwelling*, 6.
[124] Ibid, 8.
[125] Ibid, 9.
[126] Ibid, 10.
[127] Ibid, 10.

2. Instability:

[128] To toss. www.merriam- webster.com. Accessed on April 23, 2014. http://www.merriam- webster.com/dictionary/tossed.
[129] 1Craftiness. www.merriam- webster.com. Accessed on May 29, 2014, http://www.merriam- webster.com/thesaurus/craftiness.

3. Repulsion towards Solid Food

[130] D. A. Carson, *The Cross and Christian Ministry,* (Grand Rapids, MI: Baker Books, 2004), 72.
[131] Charles R. Swindoll, *The Tale of the Tardy Oxcart,* (Nashville, TN: Word Publishing, 1998, 80.
[132] τ έλε ι ος, (*teleios*): Short Definition: perfect, full-grown, perfect, (a) complete in all its parts, (b) full grown, of full age, (c) specially of the completeness of Christian character. www.biblehub.com. Accessed on August 11, 2014. http://biblehub.com/greek/5046.htm.
[133]Mark Ross, "In Essentials Unity, In Non-Essentials Liberty, In All Things Charity." www.ligonier.org. Accessed on February 13, 2024. https://www.ligonier.org/learn/articles/essentials-unity-non-essentials-liberty-all-things.

4. Spiritual Identity Ignorance

[134] Spiros Zodiathes, *The Complete Word Study Dictionary: New Testament,* (AMG International, Chattanooga, TN, 37422), 1993 νήπ ι ος, népios – Strong number 3516: One who cannot speak, hence, an infant, child, baby without any definite limitation of age. By implication, a minor, one not yet of age (as in Gal. 4:1) Generally, in the Septuagint, used of a child playing in the streets (as in Jer. 6:11; 9:21); asking for bread (as in Lam. 4:4). Metaphorically a babe, one unlearned, unenlightened, simple, innocent (as in Matt. 11:25, Luke 10:21, Rom. 2:20). Implying censure (as 1 Cor. 3:1; Gal. 4:3; Eph. 4:14; Heb. 5:13). Synonyms: *teknon*—Strong number 5043: child, newborn child, infant. Antonyms: *huios*: Strong number 5207: a mature son or daughter.

[135] δοῦλος, doúlos – Strong number 1401: someone who belongs to another; a bond-slave, without any ownership rights of their own. www.biblehub.com. Accessed on August 11, 2014. http://biblehub.com/greek/1401. htm.
[136] δικαιοσύνη, dikaiosuné – Strong number 1343: righteousness: "divine approval," "God's judicial approval." "deemed right by the Lord (after His examination)," "what is approved in His eyes." www.biblehub.com. Accessed on May 1, 2018. http://biblehub.com/greek/1343.htm.
[137] Lawlessnes. Spiros Zodiathes, *The Complete Word Study Dictionary: New Testament*, (AMG International, Chattanooga, TN: 37422), 1993.
[138] Righteous. www.merriam- webster.com. Accessed on January 24, 2013. http://www.merriam-webster.com/dictionary/righteous.
[139] Synonyms of righteous. www.thesaurus. Com. Accessed on January 24, 2013, http://thesaurus. com/browse/righteousness.
[140] One micron is one-millionth of a meter. There are 25400 microns in one inch. The eye can see particles to about 40 microns. www.engineeringtoolbox.com. Accessed on August 12, 2014. http://www.engineeringtoolbox.com/particle-sizes-d_934.html.

5. Inability to Make a Meaningful Contribution to the Spiritual Body of Christ

[141] *John Wesley's Explanatory Notes,* Deuteronomy 6:6-8. www.christianity.com. Accessed on May 1, 2018. https://www.christianity.com/bible/commentary. php?com=wes&b=5&c=6.
[142] Mary Fairchild, "How Many Christians Are In the World Today?" Updated on April 16, 2020. www.learnreligions.com. "According to the Center for the Study of Global Christianity (CSGC) at Gordon-Conwell Theological Seminary, there are approximately 41,000 Christian denominations and organizations in the world today." Accessed on February 14, 2024. https://www.learnreligions.com/christianity-statistics-700533.
[143] Olivia Guy-Evans, MSc, "The Pareto principle." Updated on September 21, 2023. www.simplypsychology.org. https://www.simplypsychology.org/pareto-principle.html.
[144] Stephanie Samuel, "Churches' Dilemma: 80 Percent of Flock Is Inactive." Posted on Jun 26, 2011. www.christianpost.com. https://www.christianpost.com/news/authors-pastors-must-goafter-lost-sheep-to-increase-church-participation-51581/.

Upper Room Fellowship Ministry

In 1996, in response to God's calling and by the guidance of the Holy Spirit, *Upper Room Fellowship Ministry* (URFM) was formed in order to serve the body of Christ. It is a non-profit and non-denominational Christian organization.

UPPER ROOM
FELLOWSHIP MINISTRY

Vision

Fully alive through mind renewal and spiritual transformation for God's glory.

Mission

Our desire is to assist believers to experience healing for the wounded heart, restoration for the soul, and spiritual growth in Christ. Our prayer and deep desire are that through the Holy Spirit you will experience Jesus Christ as your very source of life.

Through individual or small group meetings and retreats, our ministry is committed to creating an environment where healing, restoration, and spiritual freedom can be experienced. Under the guidance of the Holy Spirit, URFM is making disciples and equipping them for the Kingdom of God. This organization ministers for the spiritual growth of all believers.

The goal is that every member of Christ's Body would attain the Ultimate Intention—*the fullness of Christ.*

Most Christians have been taught that Jesus Christ died for their sins. Some embraced Christ as their Lord. Only a few have been taught the truth that they died with Him and experience Christ as their Life. Consequently, even fewer find victory in their lives. Although they have been set free from their sins, they have not been set free from themselves.

Our desire and fervent prayer for all of Jesus' disciples are that they all will become everything that God intends for them to become, in other words—*the fullness of Christ.*

Meet the Author

Valy Vaduva was born in Romania, a beautiful country in Eastern Europe. Romania was, at that time, a communist country. The government was against the Bible and biblical Christianity. His parents were Christian Orthodox, but they were not born-again believers, so he did not grow up going to Sunday school, and Bible stories were not read to him during his childhood. When he was twelve, his stepbrother took Valy to his apartment in Bucharest for a couple of weeks during his summer vacation. One of the neighbors was a believer and gave him the most amazing gift ever: a New Testament. Since he had plenty of time left in his vacation, he read this exciting book at least three times during that summer. This was Valy's first contact with the Word of God. He recalls it as an incredible experience!

A few years passed, and he started high school. Little did he know that God orchestrates all things in great detail. God placed a Christian student in his class. Valy sensed that this boy was different from the other teenagers. He took a risk and witnessed to Valy about the Lord and invited him to attend his church. It was in the fall of 1976. At the first opportunity, Valy went to church and enjoyed the preaching and teaching from the Bible. After a while, he gave his heart to Jesus and got baptized in water. His born-again (regeneration) experience was a very powerful one! It was February 1977, just several days before the powerful earthquake devastated downtown Bucharest. After the water baptism, he felt like he was flying for several weeks. He did not feel like he was touching the ground when walking. He had never been that happy and fulfilled in his entire life!

Valy's friend from high school gave him a Bible. He was so excited! In a short time, he ventured into this marvelous and unique book, reading it from Genesis to Revelation. He fell deeply in love with the Word of God. He started witnessing to his friends and relatives, including his parents. As a result, he endured a lot of persecution from the high school faculty and personnel and his classmates. However, God delivered him and gave him strength during these times of testing. In fact, those were great experiences with God. Valy always sensed Jesus alive in his life and being there for him amid persecutions.

After a while, Valy's pastor asked him to teach Youth Sunday School. He responded with great delight. Soon, he realized he loved teaching and preaching the Word of God. Valy wished to go to a Bible College, but his father strongly suggested that he would be better off going into a technical field. That is why he attended the Polytechnic University of Bucharest and became a mechanical engineer. However, his passion for the Word of God remained in his heart throughout the years.

A couple of years after his born-again experience, he met his future wife, Elena, at a prayer meeting. It was in the late 1970s. There was a group of people who prayed fervently. He also wanted that kind of prayer life for himself, so he attended more and more meetings. He fasted for several days. His strong desire was to get closer to the Lord. While praying with a close group of friends, one of those days, he sensed the Lord's presence because He touched him significantly. He recalls this infilling with the Holy Spirit as a great and very powerful experience.

After Valy got married, he and his wife started a small group Bible study in their apartment. This lasted almost a decade. Despite several encounters with the secret police and some persecutions, he greatly enjoyed these times! Seeing these people's lives transformed by the Word of God was enriching!

In 1989, a popular revolution in Romania ended the 45-year communist regime. At that time, it was clear to Valy that it was the opportune moment to immigrate with his family to the USA. In the States, he attended a Romanian Christian Church. Very soon, he noticed the great need for Bible study, discipleship, and counseling among Christians, especially among the youth and young families. He felt strongly that religious services alone were not sufficient for spiritual growth. Something was missing.

In 1995, Valy and his wife heard a commercial on a Christian radio station about advanced discipleship and Christian counseling training. Immediately, he and his wife enrolled and attended those classes. The Exchanged Life[5][1] teaching they received during that intensive training was marvelous! They learned about brokenness and the need to come to the end of the self-life so that Christ's Life will be manifested in us and through us. How the co-crucifixion concept from Galatians 2:20 was explained to them was unique! That was a spiritual revolution for Valy. He understood that he did not have to perform religious activities, start another Bible study, or anything like that. What he needed the most was the Life of Christ[6]1F[2] to be manifested in his life. But there was a problem. He needed to surrender his own life to have His Life to the fullest, and by God's grace, he did it! The exchanged life experience was the chief of all experiences up until that time. He testifies that this experience revolutionized his life, ministry, view of God, himself, and others.

In 1996, the Holy Spirit guided Valy and Elena to establish Upper Room Fellowship Ministry (URFM), a non-profit and non-denominational Christian organization dedicated to Christian discipleship, spiritual maturity, and growth ministries. However, he continued working as an engineer to support his family. But the more time that went by, the more miserable and spiritually unfulfilled he felt. This situation culminated in an unforgettable experience that took place in 2002. A series of circumstances resulted in a very stressful condition that led to a devastating stroke. However, God is always in control! He bestowed His mercy upon Valy and rescued him from this trial with minimal intervention from the medical team. God completely rehabilitated him without side effects! More than 75 percent of his speech was restored in less than 6 hours. Marvelous! No doubt, that was miraculous!

---

5 For a detailed explanation, see "The Greatest Exchange Ever" section of the *Fullness of Christ*. To get it click on the link https://amzn.to/3mTcDBp.

6 For more about the Life of Christ or Indwelled by Christ, see the "Definitions for Deeper Spiritual Realities" section of the *Fullness of Christ*.

Even though the healing was significant, the focus is not on that experience alone. Something else must be brought into the spotlight. A few hours after Valy was admitted to the hospital, the neurologist came to his bedside and asked: "What is your occupation?" Despite his speech difficulties, Valy replied quite proudly: "I am a preacher." Please note that he did not reply, "I am an engineer," even though this statement was true. After that, he added: "I am going to get well from this condition with no side effects because God called me to preach the gospel." Indeed, this was precisely what happened.

After a few more hours, his medical condition improved. This was visible to the entire medical team responsible for his care. They were surprised by Valy's swift recovery. His wife and entire family glorify God for His miraculous intervention. They appreciate the friends, the church, and the hundreds of believers everywhere who prayed insistently on his behalf. Glory be to God for His divine healing in Valy's life!

After a recovery period, he returned to his full-time job as an engineer, but his life was not the same. He no longer found joy in his career. The rest of the year, and into 2003, was a living nightmare. He was severely depressed. His doctor's efforts to treat him were unsuccessful. He felt that an internal spiritual battle tore his life apart: on one side, his engineering responsibilities and his role as the provider for his family; on the other side, his passion and deep desire to preach the Gospel of Jesus. However, not even during these circumstances did Valy find the strength to quit his job and start the full-time ministry God called him to from his youth.

This complex and painful battle lasted until mid-2004. At the beginning of July 2004, his boss entered his office and closed the door behind him. He said: "Valy, our department will taper down and close. All the engineers working in this department will be let go. Even I will have to find something else to do. The sad news is that you are the first to be let go. Starting tomorrow, your job is eliminated."

Even though he expected something like this to happen, hearing "starting tomorrow, you no longer have a job" roared like a thunder in his soul. After a few minutes, he pulled himself together and went outside to call his wife. "Hey, I am calling to let you know I am a free man!" "What do you mean?" she asked Valy. "Don't tell me that you are laid off." "Well, it's true," he replied, "but I am taking it from the hand of God. He freed me up to work for Him and His Kingdom."

Finally, Valy understood it! In July 2004, he dedicated himself, spirit, soul, and body to the ministry's work. Gradually, God healed the depression that lasted for over two years. After almost twenty years of intensively working for the Kingdom of God, he is joyful and fulfilled. This is a sacred joy that does not come from the world, not from finances, earthly rewards, or comfort, but rather from walking in the central will of God.

As many of you know, working in full-time ministry requires much time, effort, and the strength to fight spiritual battles. It also relies heavily on financial resources and a team of dedicated and talented people. However, once we decide to do God's will, the joy from the Lord is incomprehensible and does not compare with anything this world may offer us. The devil is relentless in fighting against us, and, unfortunately, he sometimes succeeds in deceiving us. We may be fooled into finding happiness and fulfillment in the things of this world instead of walking in obedience to the Holy Spirit.

Since consecrating himself to the ministry, Valy has been actively involved in mission trips in the United States and worldwide. He offers personalized spiritual life coaching sessions, mind renewal classes, and transformation prayer ministry and teaches Advanced Discipleship Training locally and over the Internet in English and Romanian.

Valy, his wife, Elena, their four grown children, and ten grandchildren live in southern Michigan.

www.ingramcontent.com/pod-product-compliance
Lightning Source LLC
Chambersburg PA
CBHW021136090426
42740CB00008B/814
9781930529342